This edition is published by Hermes House,
an imprint of Anness Publishing Ltd, 108 Great Russell Street,
London WC1B 3NA; info@anness.com

www.hermeshouse.com; www.annesspublishing.com

If you like the images in this book and would like to investigate using
them for publishing, promotions or advertising, please visit our website
www.practicalpictures.com for more information.

© Anness Publishing Ltd 2014

All rights reserved. No part of this publication may be reproduced, stored
in a retrieval system, or transmitted in any way or by any means,
electronic, mechanical, photocopying, recording or otherwise, without the
prior written permission of the copyright holder.

A CIP catalogue record for this book is available from the British Library.

PUBLISHER: Joanna Lorenz
EXECUTIVE EDITOR: Linda Fraser
EDITORS: Margaret Malone
Finny Fox-Davies
DESIGNER: Luise Roberts
PHOTOGRAPHY: Gus Filgate (recipes),
Craig Robertson (equipment and
techniques, steps and still lifes)
FOOD FOR PHOTOGRAPHY: Joanna Farrow (recipes),
Annabel Ford (equipment and
techniques, and steps)
STYLING: Penny Markham
COPY EDITOR: Jenni Fleetwood

## NOTES

Bracketed terms are intended for American readers.
For all recipes, quantities are given in both metric and imperial measures and, where
appropriate, in standard cups and spoons. Follow one set of measures, but not a
mixture, because they are not interchangeable.
Standard spoon and cup measures are level.
1 tsp = 5ml, 1 tbsp = 15ml, 1 cup = 250ml/8fl oz.
Australian standard tablespoons are 20ml. Australian readers should
use 3 tsp in place of 1 tbsp for measuring small quantities.
American pints are 16fl oz/2 cups. American readers should use 20fl oz/
2.5 cups in place of 1 pint when measuring liquids.

Medium (US large) eggs are used unless otherwise stated.

## PUBLISHER'S NOTE

Although the advice and information in this book are believed to
be accurate and true at the time of going to press, neither the
authors nor the publisher can accept any legal responsibility
or liability for any errors or omissions that may have been
made nor for any inaccuracies nor for any loss, harm or
injury that comes about from following instructions
or advice in this book.

# the ice cream book

Over 150 irresistible
ice cream treats
from classic vanilla
to elegant bombes
& terrines

Joanna Farrow
and Sara Lewis

Photography by Gus Filgate

HH
HERMES
HOUSE

T0168784

# the ice cream book

**ABOVE:** *Ice cream factory in Holstich, Germany 1895.*

In a column box:

### MAKING ICE CREAM AT HOME

With the increased availability of affordable ingredients and improvements to ice cream makers, middle class housewives sought the advice of highly skilled cooks, such as Mrs Agnes B. Marshall and Mrs Beeton. In 1885 Agnes Marshall published her first book, in which she included detailed advice on making a range of ice creams, such as "cheap", "ordinary" and "common" ice cream. Her "cheap ice cream" was made using 1 pint [600ml|2½ cups] of cream, 8 egg yolks and ¼lb [115g|4oz|½ cup] of sugar. Next came her "ordinary ice cream", in which the cream was replaced with milk. Her "common ice cream" was made with the same quantity of milk and sugar, but only two whisked eggs, while the "ordinary ice cream" dispensed with eggs altogether, and thickened the sweetened milk with arrowroot (15g|½ oz|2 tbsp).

**ABOVE:** *An ice cream mould.*

**RIGHT:** *An early hand-cranked ice cream machine.*

**RIGHT:** *Illustration from* Süsse Speisen und Eisbomben, *published in Germany in 1907, showing a variety of iced confections.*

In Russia, the first ice cream factory was built in the 1920s by Anastas Mikoyan, and the people of the former Soviet Union enjoyed ice cream at any opportunity. To Western tastes, it may seem rather odd to eat ice cream in extreme winter temperatures, but this was one of the few permitted luxuries and as such greatly enjoyed whatever the weather.

By the 1920s England was also producing ice cream on a large scale, first by the famous Wall's company and a year later by the Lyons group best known for its triple flavoured Neapolitan ice cream and the Lyons Corner Houses in London. Originally known for his meat pies, Thomas Wall first introduced ice cream manufacture into the business as a way of improving summer profits. At first ice cream production was small and made with sophisticated American production techniques. The ice cream was shaped and frozen in small brickettes, each one hand-wrapped in paper and sold by street sellers riding tricycles featuring a "stop me and buy one" sign. As popularity and production grew, so the company expanded from just one ice cream factory in Acton with seven street sellers in the 1920s to 136 depots and 8,500 tricycles by 1939.

With the outbreak of the Second World War, Wall's ice cream production stopped as food rationing was introduced. Many European factories also closed and soon the American armed forces became the biggest manufacturers of ice cream in the world.

Americans still have perhaps the greatest love of ice cream of all countries and consume 21 litres|37 pints per person per year, compared to just 8 litres|14 pints per person in England.

### ELECTRIC DEEP FREEZERS

Early mechanical refrigerators didn't appear until the beginning of the 20th century and followed the development of the steam driven motor and later the electric motor. The very first electric refrigerator was a Domelre, made in America in 1913. A later version, the Kelvinator model, made in Detroit in 1914, soon came on the market, but both were noisy and extremely expensive. Not surprisingly most Americans preferred the cheaper wooden insulated cabinets or chests which they cooled with regular ice supplies.

In 1922 Baltzar von Platen and Carl Munters, two young engineering students in Stockholm, developed a cooling machine which could convert heat to cold by absorption. It could be driven by electricity, gas or kerosene. Initially called the D fridge, it was marketed by Electrolux in 1925. As technology advanced so prices came down, and by 1935 the early air-cooled refrigerators were within the reach of many households. Although gaining in popularity and availability in America, the British were more cautious. Frigidaire first tried marketing refrigerators in Britain in 1924 but they remained a luxury item for the very rich until after the Second World War. It must also be remembered that supplies of electricity were unreliable and expensive and usually only available in the homes of the wealthy; working people had to rely on gas.

The chilled and frozen food industry originated in America when Clarence Birdseye revolutionized shopping and the preparation of food for the American and British housewives by going into partnership with the English ice cream manufacturer, Thomas Wall. By 1960, half the population of England had access to a domestic refrigerator, and by the 1970s, many homes owned a deep freezer, making the storage of bought and home-made ice cream possible.

# A surfeit of choice

*Ice cream has come a long way since the first ice cream parlour opened in 1776. Swirled, layered and mixed, in almost every conceivable flavour, ices are now available to suit every occasion, taste and preference, from low-fat sorbets to rich dairy premium ice cream, and sold in any quantity from a single cone to a half-gallon tub.*

### THE ICE CREAM CONE

It was a young Italian immigrant to America, Italo Marchiony, who first came up with the idea of an edible container for ice cream. When he started selling his ice creams and sorbets on Wall Street in New York, he spooned them into glasses. These were cumbersome and wasteful, so he started making shaped cups from waffle mixture. The cups proved very popular and he patented them in 1902. Two years later, he patented an ice cream cone, although the credit for this innovation is often given to a Syrian, Ernest A. Hamwi. According to the story, Mr Hamwi was selling waffles at the World's Trade Fair in St Louis in 1904 when a nearby ice cream seller sold out of dishes. He persuaded Mr Hamwi to roll one of his waffles to a cone, let it cool and filled it with his ice cream.

Made with a mixture of flour, milk and sugar, the ice cream cone quickly became popular. To help prevent breakages and spillages, a ring of non-crushable biscuit was also shaped to the top of the cone, making it ideal for small children as it caught any drips of melting ice cream.

The British traders of the 1920s were reluctant to sell these large imported cones as they were more costly and needed a greater quantity of ice cream to fill them. They preferred to sell ice cream brickettes sandwiched between much cheaper rectangular wafer biscuits. In the 1930s a box of 1200 wafers were very cheap to produce, making it possible to sell ice creams for 1 penny. However, by 1935 waffles for ice cream were introduced to supersede wafers; with the rather unusual advertising line of "Have a waffle in the cinema". Sales of wafers continued until the 1950s, until soft ice cream and the famous "99" ice cream was introduced, complete with its much loved chocolate flake bar.

**ABOVE:** *With the rise in the number of street sellers, ice cream was now becoming a more available treat for all. No longer sold in unhygienic glass dishes, but in small hand-wrapped brickettes, they were sold in Britain from the famous "stop me and buy one" Wall's tricycle.*

### THE ICE CREAM SUNDAE

In late 19th century America, druggists (chemists) made and sold soda water in drug stores throughout the country. Flavoured with fruit syrups and whipped cream, these drinks were popular with young and old. In 1874 Robert Green of Philadelphia ran out of cream when making sodas for the 50th anniversary of the Franklin Institute. He substituted ice cream, much to the delight of the guests.

The ice cream soda soon became very popular, but you couldn't buy one on a Sunday. This was because many people believed soda water to be alcoholic, even though it was nothing of the kind, and drinking it was regarded as improper, particularly on Sundays. An ingenious drugstore concessionaire got around the ban by serving the ice cream and syrup without the soda water. He called it Ice Cream Sunday. The name was later changed to Sundae, which was judged more seemly.

**LEFT:** *Ice cream cornets, now called cones, are given free to children in London, UK, to celebrate Coronation Day in 1937.*

## ICE CREAM PARLOURS

The first ice cream parlour is reputed to have been opened in New York City in 1776, but the business really boomed during the prohibition years. Bar owners had always served ice cream in the summer months, and when prohibition came in 1920, the more enterprising among them saw that swapping ice cream for hard liquor was one way of staying in business. By 1930, ice cream parlours were very much a part of the American scene. To stay competitive, manufacturers developed new flavours and shapes of ice cream. Eskimo pie and popsicles – or ice lollies, as they are now known – became popular.

## MODERN DEVELOPMENTS

The majority of homes in America and Europe now have a refrigerator and a deep freeze, and many of us add a tub of ice cream to our weekly shopping trolley as a regular item. Not only is ice cream available in a wide range of flavours, with prices varying from the budget family-sized tub of strawberry, up to the most expensive and decadent chocolate combinations, but it is also easier now than ever before to make ice cream at home with electrical labour-saving gadgets that make tasks such as beating frozen ice cream quite effortless.

**ABOVE:** *An ice cream parlour, popular in the US since the prohibition when enterprising brewers converted their liquor bars to milk bars and served chilled ice cream sodas and thick creamy milk shakes instead.*

**ABOVE:** *The 1 penny wafer of the 1930s, and later the larger American ice cream cones, quickly grew in popularity for the young and the "young at heart".*

**LEFT:** *Lolly sticks at a factory in Lyon, France, 1963.*

Ice cream is loved the world over, and although it will always remain a seaside treat, it is now also seen as an everyday luxury. Probably consumed in the greatest quantities by the Americans, it is also enjoyed across Europe and India; even in the Russian winter they enjoy ice cream bought from street kiosks when there is snow on the ground!

Ways of serving ice cream have also changed dramatically over the centuries. While there is still a place for refreshing and fruity sorbets and water ices, rich creamy dairy ice creams still remain top of all opinion polls. Meanwhile, food trends have moved away from the multi-coloured, pile it high, knickerbocker glory style ice cream sundae of the 1950s or the 60s' banana split, and contemporary tastes now favour simpler, softly scooped ice creams with more imaginative but subtle flavours.

From such elitist beginnings it would have been hard to imagine that by the beginning of the 21st century there would be 500 commercially prepared ice creams available, ranging from the classic vanilla, chocolate and fruit flavours to the more exotic and eccentric such as peanut butter, lobster or tomato soup.

Dedicated ice cream cafes, parlours and franchized scoop shops now flourish in all the world's major cities. Ice cream is swirled, rippled, layered and mixed; you can buy low-fat ice cream, kosher ice cream, yogurt ice cream and a huge range of sorbets in every shape and size, from tiny individual pots and on sticks, to half-gallon tubs.

Efficient ice cream makers are now affordable, so more and more people are discovering the delights of making their own ice cream at home. This book aims to teach you to do just that, and also offers suggestions for incorporating both home-made and bought ice cream into a wide range of exciting and delicious desserts.

Ice cream, however simple or elaborate, should be full of natural taste and body. If you make it with the very best of ingredients, you will always enjoy the most delicious home-made ice cream.

# making
# ice cream

Making ice cream at home is surprisingly simple, needs little equipment and is enormously satisfying to prepare as well as to eat. Covering every aspect of making ices in all their variety, as well as sauces, cones, baskets and decorations, this chapter provides all the skills and techniques for even the most ambitious and elaborate iced desserts.

# Essential equipment

*You will probably already have most of the equipment you need to make successful ice creams and water ices.*
*Ices made by hand can simply be frozen in a plastic tub or box in the freezer, although very keen ice cream*
*enthusiasts may want to invest in a free-standing electric machine.*

## BASIC EQUIPMENT FOR MAKING ICES

Making ices by hand is the simplest method of all, and is known as "still freezing". All that you need are glass bowls and a fork, a manual or electric hand-held whisk for beating and a freezerproof container with a lid. You will also need a heavy pan for making the custard, sugar syrups and cooking fruits, plus a sieve (strainer) for puréeing and a lemon squeezer and fine grater for citrus fruits.

A food processor is a useful aid for breaking down the ice crystals, although it can be wasteful of ingredients; however, this time saving method does produce a similar texture to that made in an electric ice cream maker.

## For storage

You will need a selection of freezerproof containers in varying sizes, with tight fitting lids to eliminate the transfer of strong smells and prevent the surface of the ice cream from drying out. Use containers a little larger than the quantity of ice cream, to allow for beating during freezing and increased volume when frozen. A headspace of 2cm/¾in is adequate. Granita is the exception to this, as it requires as shallow a container as possible to reduce freezing time. Only use stainless steel or aluminium while making ice cream or sorbet as other metals can impart a metallic taste.

## The freezer

An upright or chest domestic freezer is the essential item of equipment. For making ice cream the temperature should be -18°C/-66°F. A freezer thermometer is a very useful tool. The colder the freezer the more quickly the ice will freeze, making smaller ice crystals and smoother ice cream. If the freezer is badly packed the motor will have to work harder to maintain temperature.

## Adding volume

**1** Using a fork requires more effort, but is an effective way of increasing volume by introducing air into sorbet and granitas.

**2** For making large quantities of ice cream, a hand-held electric whisk saves time and adds even more volume to the mixture.

## For making parfait

You will need all the items for making ices, plus a good sugar thermometer; they can be expensive but do ensure perfect results. Choose one with a clip to hold it in place on the pan.

## For making moulded iced desserts

Specialist equipment is available, but you can usually improvise with bowls and basins from your kitchen.

## ICE CREAM MAKERS

These time-saving electric machines vary greatly in price. The two basic types are those with a built-in freezing unit and those with a detachable double-skinned bowl which has to be pre-frozen before use. There are also ice cream machines that can be run inside a standard freezer. These have very poor motors and similar, if not better, results can be obtained by making ice cream by hand.

The most efficient – and most expensive – models are those with an integral freezing unit. Motors vary, depending on the make of the machine. If you are investing in an ice cream maker, choose the one with the most powerful motor and if possible see it in operation, as

noise levels vary considerably. As this type of ice cream maker tends to be larger than a food processor, working and storage space are prime considerations. These machines come with two bowls, a stainless-steel bowl built into the unit and a separate aluminium bucket that can be slotted into the larger fixed bowl. Most machines of this type have a see-through lid for easy viewing, plus a vent for pouring in additional ingredients. This plastic top simply slides off for easy washing.

*RIGHT: Ice cream maker with integral motor and freezing unit.*

### Pre-freezing ice cream maker

For a slightly cheaper option, look out for a model with a detachable double-skinned bowl filled with freezing liquid. This type of machine will need to be frozen for at least 18 hours before use. When you are ready to use the ice cream maker, you simply fit the motor and paddle to the frozen bowl, switch on the power, and fill the bowl with the ice cream or sorbet mixture. It usually takes 25–40 minutes for the ice cream to churn.

If the freezer is large enough, the bowl can be stored there, giving the option to make home-made ice cream at any time. For larger quantities, it is very useful to have a second detachable bowl on standby and make two batches of ice cream.

When possible, eat the ice cream soon after it is made to fully enjoy the wonderful texture of machine-made ice cream.

**ABOVE:** *Simple ice cream maker with motorized paddles.*

---

#### FOR THE BEST RESULTS

- Pre-cool the machine or double-skinned bowl following the instructions given in the manufacturer's handbook.

- Chill all ice cream or water ice mixtures thoroughly before freezing; never add them to the machine while still warm.

- Do not overfill the ice cream maker.

- Allow plenty of room for ventilation while the machine is running.

---

# Useful extras

### Scoops

There are plenty of ice cream scoops on the market. Choose from half-moon-shaped stainless-steel scoops with sleek steel handles, simple spoon-shaped scoops with metal handles, easy-grip shaped plastic handles or brightly coloured plastic scoops with quick release levers. To be really impressive use silver scoops.

**ABOVE:** *Ice cream scoops are available in many different shapes, materials and colours.*

### Cone moulds

For a really professional finish use wooden moulds. These are available only by mail order but you can improvise by making your own cone moulds from foil-covered cardboard.

**ABOVE:** *This wooden cone mould is a very simple but useful tool for making professional-looking cones.*

### Melon ballers

Ice cream looks very attractive when scooped with a melon baller. Available from good cookshops in varying sizes, from pea to grape size, the larger size is best for ice cream. To make a ball, press the upturned cup into slightly softened ice cream, then rotate it. Arrange in a glass dish or on a plate, with fresh fruits.

**ABOVE:** *Use melon ballers to make miniature scoops of ice cream and sorbet, and pile them up on a plate.*

### Kulfi moulds

Freeze Indian-style ice creams in these traditional kulfi moulds available from some large Indian supermarkets. You can also use lolly moulds, dariole moulds or plastic cups.

**ABOVE:** *Unmoulding kulfi is easy with a specially designed all-in-one kulfi mould.*

# Basic ingredients

*Nothing beats the cool, creamy smoothness of the ultimate indulgence, home-made ice cream. The choice of flavours and flavour combinations is limited only by your own imagination, so begin with our basic formulae and adapt or develop them to incorporate all the tastes you love. You will rapidly build a repertoire of wonderful iced desserts, all completely additive-free and made with only the ingredients that you choose to be there.*

## Ice cream

### Cream

You just couldn't make true ice cream without lashings of cream. Surprisingly, whipping cream, with its natural creamy taste, makes the best ice cream, especially when mixed with strong rich ingredients such as coffee, toffee or chocolate. Double (heavy) cream is, however, a must for vanilla or brown bread ice cream. Clotted cream and crème fraîche, the thick, rich lightly soured French-style cream, make delicious additions to fruit, honey and spice ice creams. Do be careful when using double or clotted cream as their high butter-fat content can give the ice cream a buttery flavour and texture. Avoid UHT creams as the flavour is so obvious and strong.

### Milk

There is a wide choice of milks in most supermarkets, from skimmed, semi-skimmed (low-fat), full-fat (whole) and breakfast milk to the now more readily available goat's milk and soya milk. Skimmed milk is best avoided when making ice cream at home, due to its low fat content and "thin" taste, but it is difficult to distinguish between semi-skimmed or full-fat milk, especially when they are mixed with cream. Full fat, semi-skimmed and goat's milk all make delicious ice cream.

### Yogurt

The choice of yogurt is highly personal: it seems people either love ice cream which contains yogurt, or absolutely hate it! If you are not sure how your family will react, start with the mild bio-style natural (plain) yogurt, with its creamy smoothness, and, if that is successful, work up to the stronger, sharper sheep's and goat's milk yogurts.

**ABOVE:** *New-laid eggs and double (heavy) or whipping cream gives home-made ice cream its luxury flavour.*

### Cheeses

Light, virtually fat-free fromage frais or crème fraîche can be added to fruit or vanilla ice creams and is ideal for those who adore ice cream but have to watch their fat intake. Ricotta, an Italian whey cheese, has a white, creamy, soft texture. It is rather like a cross between cottage and cream cheese and can be used successfully in certain ice creams. For the richest results of all, try mascarpone, another Italian cheese. It has a deep-buttery yellow colour and a texture similar to that of cream cheese. For the best of both worlds, mix mascarpone with fromage frais for a rich tasting, fat reduced dessert.

### Non-dairy products

Look out for soya milk, either unsweetened or sweetened, in longlife cartons, and canned coconut milk – both ideal for vegans or those on a milk-free diet. Coconut milk is also a great standby for a dinner party ice cream when mixed with lime or lemon.

### Eggs

Where possible use new-laid, organic eggs for the best colour and flavour. They cost very little more than ordinary eggs but do make such a difference to the finished result of home-made ice cream.

**ABOVE:** *Muscovado (molasses) sugar can be a delicious sweetener.*

## Sweeteners

Caster (superfine) sugar has been used in the majority of the recipes, as its fine crystals dissolve quickly in the custard, maintaining a smooth, silky texture. Granulated (white) sugar is used for making praline, a delicious ingredient in some of the speciality ices. Light brown and dark brown muscovado (molasses) sugar can also be used as a sweetener in some recipes, where the darker colour and stronger flavour is used to great effect. Honey and maple syrup also make delicious additions, either on their own or mixed with caster sugar. They are good in ice cream flavoured with nuts.

## Cornflour (cornstarch)

Many purists will throw their hands up in horror at the idea of cornflour being used in the custard for an ice cream. They might well argue that it is far better to make the custard in a double boiler or a large heatproof bowl set over simmering water. It is certainly true that cornflour is not a standard ingredient in a classic custard, but it does help to stabilize the custard and reduces the risk of curdling. Custard which contains a little cornflour is easier to handle, so can be gently cooked in a heavy pan. It will thicken in 4–5 minutes as against 15 minutes or more in a double boiler, greatly reducing the cooking time.

**COOK'S TIP** *Put leftover egg whites in a small plastic box. Cover with a tight-fitting lid and label the box clearly. Freeze up to 6 months and thaw at room temperature for 4 hours. Use to make pavlovas, meringues and meringue-based ice creams.*

# Water ices

## Sugar syrup

A simple sugar syrup is made by heating a mixture of caster (superfine) sugar and water in a medium pan, stirring until the sugar has dissolved. It is no longer thought essential to boil the syrup, just to heat it for long enough to dissolve the sugar. Caster sugar has been used for syrups in the recipe section of this book because it dissolves very rapidly, but granulated (white) sugar can also be used, as can light brown sugar or honey. Once made and cooled, the syrup can be stored in the refrigerator for several days.

## Flavouring

Choose from a wide range of fresh fruit purées such as strawberry, raspberry, peach or pineapple, or mix with some of the more exotic fruits such as passion fruit, mango and lime. Dried fruits are sometimes steeped in apple or grape juice or in water and brandy or a liqueur mixture before being puréed. Citrus rinds (orange, lemon or lime) can be infused in the hot syrup for extra flavour and then fresh juice added to heighten and strengthen the flavour. Spice infusions or mixtures of spices and fruits also work very well and create unusual ices that are particularly successful with those that prefer a light dessert that is not too sweet.

**ABOVE:** *Honey can be used on its own or with sugar.*

## Egg white

The purpose of adding egg white to a semi-frozen sorbet is twofold. Firstly, it helps to stabilize the mixture, which is important for those sorbets that melt quickly, and secondly, it can be used to lighten very dense or fibrous sorbets such as those made from blackcurrants or blackberries. The egg white requires only the minimum beating with a fork to loosen it and need not be beaten until frothy or standing in peaks as used to be suggested.

### HOW TO SEPARATE AN EGG

Crack the egg on the side of a bowl. Gently ease the halves apart, keeping the yolk in one half and letting the white fall into the bowl below. Separate any remaining egg white from the yolk by swapping the yolk from one shell half to the other. Do this several times if necessary, until all the egg white has fallen into the bowl and what remains is the pure egg yolk. If you do drop any egg yolk into the bowl below, scoop it out with one of the eggshell halves; the jagged edges will trap the yolk and prevent it from sliding back into the bowl.

# Making ice cream

*Many classic ice creams are based on a custard made from eggs and milk. It is not difficult to make, but as it is used so frequently, it is worth perfecting by following these very simple guidelines.*

## How to make a classic ice cream

**Making the custard-base**

**INGREDIENTS**

FLAVOURING to INFUSE (optional)

300ml | ½ pint | 1¼ cups
SEMI-SKIMMED (LOW-FAT) MILK

4 medium EGG YOLKS

75g | 3oz | 6 tbsp CASTER (SUPERFINE) SUGAR

5ml | 1 tsp CORNFLOUR (CORNSTARCH)

---

**BATCH COOKING**

If you are planning to make ice cream for a party, make double quantities of custard to save time. It is not advisable, however, to increase the quantities any more than this or it would be difficult to heat the custard evenly. It is quicker and easier to make up two double quantity batches in separate pans and a lot safer than running the risk of curdling one pan of custard made with a dozen eggs!

---

**1** Prepare any flavourings. Split vanilla pods (beans) with a sharp knife; crack coffee beans with a mallet. Cinnamon sticks, whole cloves, fresh rosemary and lavender sprigs or bay leaves can be used as they are.

**2** Pour the milk into a pan. Bring it to the boil, then remove the pan from the heat, add the chosen flavouring and leave to infuse for 30 minutes or until cool.

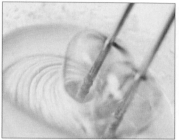

**3** If you have used a vanilla pod, lift it out of the pan, and scrape the seeds back into the milk to enrich the flavour. Whisk the egg yolks, caster sugar and cornflour in a bowl until thick and foamy. Bring the plain or infused milk to the boil, then gradually whisk it into the yolk mixture. Pour the combined mixture back into the pan.

**4** Cook the mixture over low heat, stirring it continuously until it approaches boiling point and thickens to the point where the custard will coat the back of a wooden spoon. Do not let the custard overheat or it may curdle. Take the pan off the heat and continue stirring, making sure to take the spoon right around the bottom edges of the pan.

**5** Pour the custard into a bowl and cover the surface with clear film (plastic wrap) to prevent the formation of a skin, or cover the surface with a light sprinkling of caster sugar. Leave to cool, then chill in the refrigerator until required. If you are making the ice cream in a machine, ensure the custard is chilled before starting.

**COOK'S TIP** *Reduce the temperature of custard by pouring it into a cool bowl. Stand this in a larger bowl of cold or iced water and change the water as it warms.*

---

**RESCUING CURDLED CUSTARD**

Quickly take the pan off the heat and plunge it into a sink or a roasting pan, half filled with cold water. Stir the custard frequently, taking the spoon right into the bottom edges of the pan. Keep stirring for 4–5 minutes until the temperature of the custard has dropped and the custard has stabilized. You may also find it helpful to whisk the mixture. If all else fails, strain it.

## Using flavourings

If you haven't infused the milk, you may wish to flavour the custard. To make chocolate custard, break white, dark (bittersweet) or milk chocolate into pieces and stir these into the hot custard in the pan, off the heat. Stir occasionally for 5 minutes until the chocolate has melted completely, then pour the flavoured custard into a bowl, cover and cool. Chill in the refrigerator.

Other flavourings that can be added include strong coffee (either filter or instant dissolved in boiling water), flower waters such as orange flower water or rose water and sweeteners that also add flavour, such as maple syrup or honey. Vanilla, peppermint or almond extract are popular flavourings. These should be added to the custard after it has cooled.

### FRUIT AND CREAM COMBINATIONS

Although you can make delicious fruit ice creams with a custard base, the combination of custard, cream and fruit purée can sometimes be too rich a combination and dull the fresh fruit flavour, robbing it of its intensity. Many cooks prefer to omit the custard and simply use strained fresh berry fruit, simple purées or lightly poached and puréed orchard fruits stirred into whipped cream.

If you are making a fruit ice cream in an ice cream maker, you can speed up the churning time by partially freezing the purée before stirring in the cream.

### THE TASTE TEST

If you like to be imaginative and invent your own flavour combinations for ice cream, taste the mixture before freezing. Aim for a taste that is a little stronger or sweeter than you would like the finished dessert to be as the formation of ice crystals in the ice cream will slightly dilute the flavour of the finished ice cream. There is no limit to the combinations that can be tried, and ice cream making is a perfect expression for the creative cook. Flavour combinations that work well with other dishes will often adapt to ice creams but always remember to taste the result.

## Adding cream

If you are making ice cream in an ice cream maker, follow the preliminary instructions for your specific machine, pre-cooling the machine or chilling the bowl in the freezer. Stir whipping cream, whipped double (heavy) cream or any soft cream cheeses into the chilled plain or flavoured custard and churn until firm.

Creams with a high fat proportion – double (heavy) cream, clotted cream or crème fraîche – should only be added to ice creams that are partially frozen, as they have a tendency to become buttery if churned for too long. Double cream is sometimes added at the start, but only for small quantities and minimal churning times.

Make the ice cream by hand in a freezerproof container, by folding soft whipped cream into the chilled plain or flavoured custard and pouring the mixture into the tub. Allow enough space for beating the ice cream during freezing. Crème fraîche, clotted cream and cream cheeses can also be added at this stage.

# Parfaits

### Making a basic parfait

Made correctly, a parfait is a light, cream-based confection with a softer, smoother texture than ice cream. Unlike ice cream, it does not need beating during freezing, so is ideal for anyone who does not have an electric ice cream maker.

Parfaits are traditionally set in moulds, tall glasses, china dishes or, more recently, in edible chocolate cups. The secret of a good parfait lies in the sugar syrup. Dissolve the sugar gently without stirring so that it does not crystallize, then boil it rapidly until it registers 115°C | 239°F on a sugar thermometer, which is known as the soft ball stage.

Quickly whisk the syrup into the whisked eggs. Cook over hot water until very thick. Cool, then mix with flavourings, alcohol and whipped cream. Freeze until solid and serve straight from the freezer.

**SERVES FOUR**

**INGREDIENTS**

115g | 4oz | generous ½ cup CASTER (SUPERFINE) SUGAR

120ml | 4fl oz | ½ cup WATER

4 medium EGG YOLKS

FLAVOURINGS

300ml | ½ pint | 1¼ cups DOUBLE (HEAVY) CREAM

**1** Mix the sugar and water in a pan. Heat the mixture gently, without stirring, until the sugar has dissolved completely. Meanwhile, half fill a medium pan with water and bring it to simmering point.

**2** Bring the sugar syrup to the boil and boil it rapidly for 4–5 minutes until it starts to thicken. It will be ready to use when it registers 115°C | 239°F on a sugar thermometer, or will form a soft ball when dropped into water.

**3** Put the eggs in a heatproof bowl and whisk until frothy. Place over the simmering water and gradually whisk in the hot sugar syrup. Whisk steadily until creamy. Take off the heat and continue whisking until cool and the whisk leaves a trail across the surface when lifted.

**4** Fold in the chosen flavourings, such as melted chocolate and brandy, ground cinnamon and coffee, whisky and chopped ginger, kirsch and raspberry purée or kir and strawberry purée. In a separate bowl, whip the cream lightly until it just holds its shape. Fold it into the mixture.

> **FLAVOURINGS**
>
> Traditionally flavoured with coffee or chocolate and a dash of brandy or whisky, parfaits are also delicious made with ground spices such as cinnamon with apple or ginger with banana. Double (heavy) cream adds just the right degree of richness, although crème fraîche or whipping cream can also be used with very good results. Another traditional combination is fruit purées mixed with liqueurs such as kirsch, Cointreau or Grand Marnier; these make a sophisticated iced dessert at a dinner party.

**5** Pour the parfait mixture into moulds, dishes or chocolate-lined cases. Freeze for at least 4 hours or until firm. Decorate, if liked, with whipped cream, spoonfuls of crème fraîche, caramel shapes or chocolate-dipped fruits. Serve immediately.

**COOK'S TIP** *Double (heavy) cream adds just the right degree of richness to parfaits, although crème fraîche or whipping cream can also be used with good results.*

## Boiling sugar successfully

**1** If you don't have a sugar thermometer, check whether the boiling sugar syrup has cooked to the right consistency, the soft ball stage, by lowering a spoon into it and then lifting it up. If the syrup falls steadily from the spoon it is not yet ready to use and if you were to add it to the eggs at this stage, the frozen parfait would set hard. Cook it for a little longer and check again with the spoon.

**2** The syrup is ready to test for the soft ball stage when it looks tacky, and forms pliable strands when two spoons are dipped in it, back to back, and then pulled apart.

Take the pan off the heat and then test the boiling syrup by dropping a little of it into a bowl of iced water. The syrup should form a ball. Wait a few seconds until it cools, then lift the ball of solidified syrup out. You should be able to mould it with your fingertips.

**3** Once the syrup has reached soft ball stage prevent it overcooking by plunging the base of the pan into cold water, either in a sink or in a shallow container. If the syrup is allowed to overcook it will crystallize in the pan and form brittle glass-like strands that snap. Adding over-cooked syrup to the eggs, will cause the mixture to solidify into a rock-solid mass that would be impossible to mix.

# Freezing ice cream

### Beating or churning

Freezing is obviously a crucial stage in the making of a home-made ice cream, and there are two basic methods. Freezing without a machine is also known as "still freezing", while the action in an ice cream maker is "stir freezing". We are so used to electrical machines that it is hard to envisage how time-intensive it must have been for the cooks of one hundred

or more years ago beating ice cream by hand in churns stood in packed ice hewn from frozen rivers. Making ice cream by hand today requires freezing it in a tub or similar container and beating it several times during the freezing process. It is this beating or churning process that is done automatically in an ice cream maker.

The secret of a really good ice cream is the formation of minute ice crystals. The finished

ice cream should be light and taste cold, not icy. If the ice crystals are large, the ice cream will have a grainy, coarse texture, which will detract from the creamy, smooth taste you are aiming to achieve. Beating the ice cream, either by hand or with an ice cream maker, breaks down the crystals. The more it is beaten while it is freezing, the finer and silkier the finished texture will be.

### Freezing with an ice cream maker

**1** Having prepared your ice cream maker according to the manufacturer's instructions, pour the chilled custard and whipping cream into the bowl, fit the paddle, fix on the lid and begin churning.

**2** After 10–15 minutes of churning, the ice cream will have begun to freeze. The mixture will thicken and will start to look slushy. Continue to churn the mixture in the same way.

**3** After 20–25 minutes, the ice cream will be considerably thicker. It will still be too soft to scoop, but this is the ideal stage to mix in your chosen additional flavourings, such as praline or browned breadcrumbs.

# Making water ices

*Sorbets, like water ices, are made with a light sugar syrup flavoured with fruit juice, fruit purée, wine, liqueur, tea or herbs. They should not contain milk or cream, and are best made in an ice cream maker, as the constant churning ensures that the ice crystals are as tiny as possible.*

## Sorbet

### Making a basic sorbet

**SERVES SIX**

**INGREDIENTS**

150–200g | 5–7oz | ¾–1cup CASTER (SUPERFINE) SUGAR

200–300ml | 7–10fl oz | ¾–1¼ cups WATER

FLAVOURING

1 EGG WHITE

**FRUIT PURÉES**

As an approximate guide, 500g | 1¼lb | 5 cups of berry fruits will produce about 450ml | ¾ pint | scant 2 cups purée. Mix this with 115g–150g | 4–5oz | generous ½–¾ cup caster sugar (depending on the natural acidity of the fruit), which has been dissolved in 300ml | ½ pint | 1¼ cups boiling water and then made up to 1 litre | 1¾ pints | 4 cups with extra cold water, lemon or lime juice.

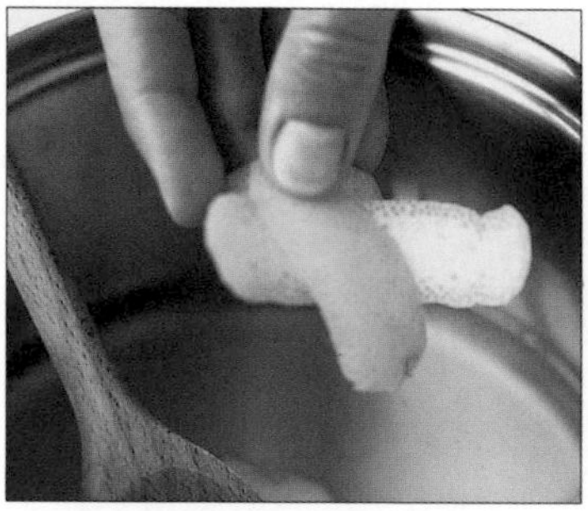

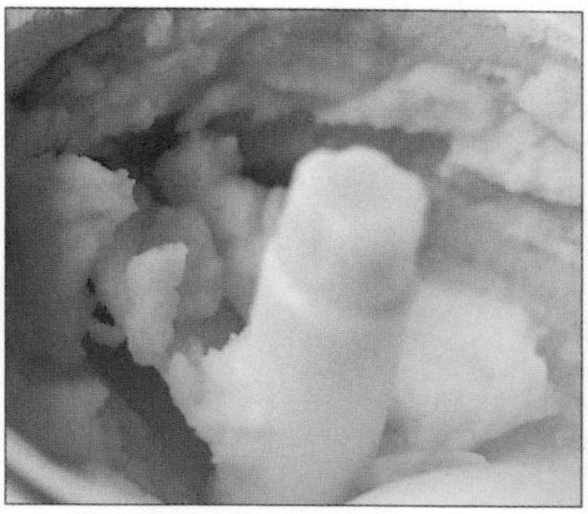

**1** Put the sugar and water in a medium pan and heat the mixture, stirring, until the sugar has just dissolved.

**2** Add pared citrus rinds, herbs or spices, depending on your chosen flavouring. Leave to infuse. Strain and cool, then chill well in the refrigerator. Mix with additional flavourings such as fruit juices, sieved puréed fruits, herbs or tea.

**3 USING AN ICE CREAM MAKER:** Pour the syrup mixture into the machine and churn until it is thick but still too soft to scoop.

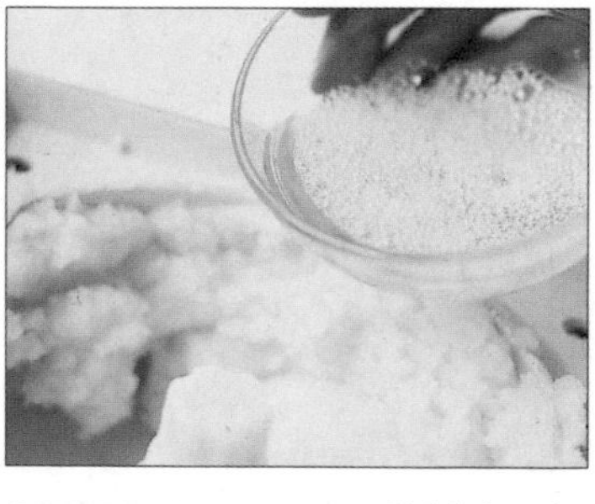

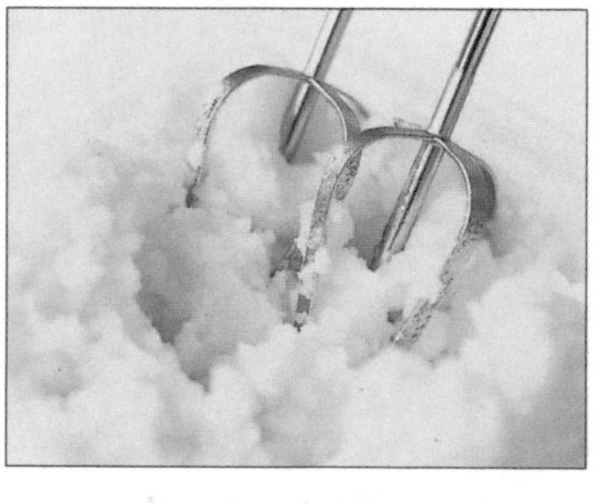

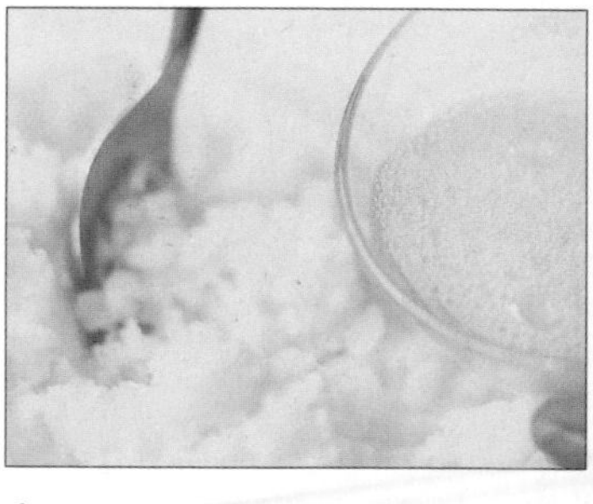

**4 USING AN ICE CREAM MAKER:** Lightly beat the egg white with a fork and pour it into the ice cream maker, either adding it through the top vent or removing the lid and stirring it in, depending on the method recommended by the manufacturer of your machine. Continue churning the sorbet until it is firm enough to scoop with a spoon.

**5 BY HAND:** Pour the mixture into a plastic tub or similar freezerproof container. It should not be more than 4cm | 1½in deep. Cover and freeze in the coldest part of the freezer for 4 hours or until it has partially frozen and ice crystals have begun to form. Beat until smooth with a fork, or hand-held electric whisk. Alternatively, process in a food processor until smooth.

**6 BY HAND:** Lightly beat the egg white and stir it into the sorbet. Freeze for a further 4 hours or until firm enough to scoop.

**COOK'S TIP** *If making by hand, ensure that the freezer temperature is as low as possible to speed up the freezing process, and beat at regular intervals.*

# Granitas

### Making a citrus granita

This wonderfully refreshing, simple Italian-style water ice has the fine texture of snow and is most often served piled into pretty glass dishes. You don't need fancy or expensive equipment, just a medium pan, a sieve (strainer) or blender for puréeing the fruit, a fork and room in the freezer for a large plastic container.

### INGREDIENTS

There are no hard-and-fast rules when it comes to the proportions of sugar to water, nor is there a standard amount of flavouring which must be added. Unlike sorbets, granitas consist largely of water, with just enough sugar to sweeten them and prevent them from freezing too hard. A total of 1 litre | 1¾ pints | 4 cups of flavoured sugar syrup will provide six generous portions of granita.

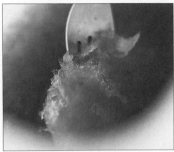

**1** Squeeze the juice from six lemons, oranges or four ruby grapefruit. Add 115–200g | 4–7oz | generous ½–1 cup caster (superfine) sugar, the precise amount will depend on the natural acidity of the fruit. Dissolve the sugar in 300ml | ½ pint | 1¼ cups boiling water, then mix it with the citrus juice and rind. Top up to 1 litre | 1¾ pints | 4 cups with extra water or water and alcohol. Add enough alcohol to taste but don't be over generous or the granita will not freeze.

**2** Pour the chilled mixture into a large plastic tub or similar freezerproof container. It should not be more than 2–2.5cm | ¾–1in deep. Freeze it in the coldest part of the freezer for 2 hours until it is mushy around the edges.

Take the container out of the freezer and beat the granita well with a fork to break up the ice crystals. Return the granita to the freezer. Beat it at 30 minute intervals for the next 2 hours until it has the texture of snow.

### Making a hot infusion

Some of the most delicious granitas are based on hot mixtures. Coffee is just one example. Pour hot, strong filtered coffee into a bowl or pan and stir in sugar to taste. For a ginger granita, infuse finely chopped root ginger in boiling water, then sweeten it. Chocolate granita is made by mixing unsweetened cocoa powder to a smooth paste with a little boiling water and sweetening to taste. All hot infusions must be left to cool, then chilled in the refrigerator before being frozen.

### Making a fruit-flavoured granita

To make a fruit-flavoured granita, purée berry fruits such as raspberries or strawberries, then strain the purée to remove the seeds. Alternatively, purée ripe peaches, then strain to remove the skins. To make a melon granita, scoop the seeds out of orange- or green-fleshed melons, then purée the flesh. Peeled and seeded watermelon can be puréed in the same way, or the flesh can be puréed along with the seeds and then strained afterwards.

---

### SERVING AND STORING GRANITAS

Coffee granita is classically served in a tumbler with a spoonful of whipped cream on top. Other types of granita look pretty spooned into tall glasses and decorated with fresh fruits or herb leaves and flowers. Because of its soft, snow-like texture, a granita is best served as soon as it is made. If this is not possible, you can leave it for a couple of hours in the freezer, beating it once or twice more if convenient. If you must freeze a granita overnight or for even longer, let it thaw slightly and beat it really well with a fork before serving. The ice crystals will become smaller but the taste will be the same. As a granita does not contain dairy products there are fewer concerns with food contamination or deterioration.

**COOK'S TIP** *Before you make the granita, make sure that the container you choose will fit in your freezer. A new stainless steel roasting pan can be used to freeze the granita mixture. As this metal is such a good conductor the granita will freeze very much faster than it would in a plastic container. Do not use aluminium as the metal could react with the fruit acids to give a metallic taste to the finished granita.*

# Serving ice creams and sorbets

*Impress your friends at your next supper or dinner party by trying one of the following serving suggestions. They are not difficult to achieve, but look stunningly professional.*

## Oval shapes

These quenelle shapes are very easy to make and look attractive especially when three different flavours of ice cream or sorbet are used. Arrange them on a plate flooded with chocolate sauce or Melba sauce and complete the picture with a sprig of redcurrants, a few whole fruits, a mint leaf or a few pieces of chocolate caraque.

**1** You need two large dessertspoons. Take a scoop of ice cream with one spoon. Slide the second spoon underneath the ice cream, transferring the oval, then repeat the process.

**2** Gently ease the ice cream oval on to a plate, then draw the edge of the spoon along the top of the ice cream to create a decorative line.

## Shavings

Pare off long shavings of ice cream or sorbet by pressing a large dessertspoon into the surface and dragging it at an angle of 45°. Mixtures that are soft-set, can be scooped straight from the freezer, but in most cases ice cream or sorbet should be allowed to soften slightly before being scooped.

## Using a melon baller

**1** Press a medium or large melon baller into the frozen sorbet, rotate it, then put the ball in a dessert glass or serving dish.

**2** Add more balls in the same way, piling them up attractively. Decorate with wafer biscuits or mint leaves dusted with icing (confectioners') sugar.

**3** Another very effective presentation is to arrange balls of grape juice or apple sorbet on a flat plate to look like a bunch of grapes, adding a grape, strawberry or mint leaf to the top.

**4** Balls of raspberry sorbet arranged in a circle on a plate flooded with apricot sauce look wonderful, especially when the middle is filled with fresh raspberries.

### Using an ice cream scoop

Dip the scoop into warm water, press it into the ice cream and run the scoop along the surface, pressing it against the side of the ice cream container until a well rounded scoop has been formed. Put this on a serving dish. Rinse the ice cream scoop and continue.

### Piping shapes

Whirls of sorbet can be piped straight on to serving plates or into fruit cases or chocolate moulds from a large piping (pastry) bag fitted with a cream nozzle. The ice cream or sorbet must be soft enough to pipe, so choose a variety that will not melt too quickly. If you are using sorbet, you may need to set it slightly with a little gelatine before piping and freezing it.

### Creating a bed of ice

On very hot summer days, keep ice cream and sorbets cold by scooping them into dishes set over a plate or shallow dish filled with crushed ice. To crush the ice, wrap ice cubes in a clean dish towel and break them up by hitting them with a rolling pin. Keep the chunks of ice fairly large so that they will not melt too quickly.

### Using citrus shells

**1** Fresh fruit shells look very pretty filled with sorbet. Cut the top off a lemon, lime or orange, loosen the edges of the flesh with a small, sharp knife then scoop out all the flesh with a teaspoon, taking care to keep the shell intact. Having prepared more shells in the same way, rinse them all with cold water and drain them well. Use the flesh in another dessert.

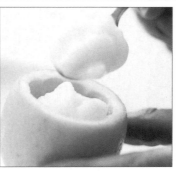

**2** Pipe or spoon the prepared sorbet into the hollowed fruit shells, wrap them in clear film (plastic wrap) and freeze them until they are needed. Serve each sorbet garnished with a tiny sprig of fresh mint. Freeze with the "lids" replaced, if you like.

**3** If you have a cannelle knife (zester), you can cut decorative grooves in the skin of the fruit before cutting a slice off the top, hollowing out the middles and filling them with sorbet.

**COOK'S TIP** *Do not be tempted to repeatedly thaw ice cream until it is soft enough to scoop and then refreeze the leftovers. The rich dairy content and fluctuating temperature will make this the perfect breeding ground for bacteria.*

---

#### SERVING TEMPERATURE

We have all been faced at some time with a tub of ice cream that is just too hard to serve. The majority of home-made ice creams will freeze very hard, so it is worth taking the ice cream out of the freezer and transferring it to the refrigerator for 20 minutes or so before serving, or while you eat your main course. This allows the ice cream to soften slightly and also to "ripen", so that the full flavour of the ice cream can be enjoyed. Alternatively, it can be thawed slightly in a microwave for 2–3 minutes on the defrost setting or for 1 minute on full power and then left at room temperature for 10 minutes. If you forget, serve the ice cream by dipping the scoop into a jug (pitcher) of hot water each time you form a ball of ice cream.

# Flavourings for ices

*Visit a modern ice cream parlour and you'll be dazzled by the number of flavours available. Yet this has no comparison to the endless possibilities you can create at home. Spices, herbs, fruits of every kind, flower waters, chocolate, coffee and nuts can all be used – singly or in combination. Experiment to find the tastes you and your family like best, remembering that freezing dulls some flavours, so you can often afford to be bold.*

## Herbs and flowers

### Edible flowers
A sprinkling of just a few petals or tiny flower heads from the garden can turn even a few simple scoops of home-made strawberry or vanilla ice cream into a dinner party dessert. A few vibrant pansies or tiny violas mixed with primrose petals or even a few dainty violets would be perfect for a springtime party, while pastel rose petals, borage flowers or sprigs of lavender would make a fine decoration in summer, as would a misty haze of elderflowers or sweet cicely flowers. For something bolder, use yellow or orange marigold petals (but not French marigolds) or nasturtiums. If selecting other flowers, please be aware that not all flowers are edible. Avoid plants which grow from a bulb or which would not be found in a herb garden.

### Flower waters
Orange flower or orange blossom water and rose water add a delicate fragrance to ground almond or summer berry ice creams and sorbets. Add a few drops and seal the bottle well to prevent evaporation.

### Herbs
Rosemary, bay, mint and lavender make wonderful additions to creamy ice creams, sherbets or sorbets. For best results infuse a few sprigs of rosemary or lavender, two to three whole bay leaves or a small bunch of fresh mint in cream or sugar syrup which has just come to the boil. Leave in the liquid until cool, then sieve. You can also add a little fresh chopped mint or other extra herbs to the finished ice cream or sorbet.

**RIGHT:** *Sprigs of flowers or flower water give a delicate flavour to ice creams and sorbets.*

## Spices

### Ginger
**TYPES/FORMS:** The rhizome of an elegant tropical plant, ginger appears in many guises. The root is widely available fresh and is also preserved in sugar syrup as stem ginger. Chopped candied ginger and crystallized ginger are other forms of this delicious spice.
**USES:** Ginger makes a wonderful ice cream ingredient just on its own but it gives a glorious lift to fruit ices, especially with fruit such as rhubarb or pears and it is a natural partner for tropical fruit. Preserved ginger, ginger syrup and ginger wine make delicious ice cream sauces.
**PREPARATION:** Peel root ginger, then slice or chop it thinly. Alternatively, grate it with the fine-tooth surface of a grater. Slice or chop preserved stem ginger; finely chop candied or crystallized ginger if pieces are large.

### Using ginger

**1** Peel away the skin on the ginger root, using a swivel-blade vegetable peeler or a small, sharp knife. Take care when peeling to remove only the thin outer skin.

**2** Grate the ginger on the fine section of a regular grater or a nutmeg grater. This is easiest to do if the ginger is frozen. It will thaw instantly on being grated.

## Vanilla

**TYPES/FORMS:** Seed pods (beans) of the climbing vanilla orchid plant are sold singly or in pairs. The spice is also finely ground, mixed with sugar and sold in sachets labelled vanilla sugar. It is best known, however, as vanilla extract.

The pods are picked while still unripe. On drying, their yellow colour deepens to a dark brown and they acquire a natural coating of vanillin crystals, which are the source of the characteristic spicy aroma. The word "vanilla" comes from the Spanish "*vainilla*", meaning "little sheath". Although always associated with sweet dishes, the vanilla pod is not itself sweet.

Beware of cheap vanilla flavourings as their harsh, almost bitter, flavour can be overpowering and could spoil the delicate flavour of some ice creams. The better quality vanilla extract is always labelled "natural vanilla extract".

**USES:** Vanilla is delicious in ice cream, whipped cream and custard and is used extensively when making patissiere cream and confectionery.

**PREPARATION:** Slit the whole vanilla pod, add it to cream or milk that has just come to the boil, then leave to cool and infuse. Lift up the pod, and holding it over the liquid, scrape the tiny black seeds with a knife so that they fall into the liquid. The flavoured cream or milk makes good ice cream. Don't throw pods away after use. Rinse under cold water, pat dry with kitchen paper and store two or three in a jar of caster (superfine) sugar to make your own vanilla sugar. Vanilla extract is highly concentrated and you only need 2.5–5ml | ½–1 tsp for ice cream.

## Cinnamon

**TYPES/FORMS:** Cinnamon is obtained from the bark of the cinnamon tree, which is native to India. The bark is rolled into sticks or quills and dried. Cinnamon is also sold finely ground. The ground spice is seldom used in ice creams, except as a decoration, although it is widely used in baking. Cassia is a related spice. It resembles cinnamon in terms of aroma and flavour but is coarser and more pungent. Cassia is usually cheaper than cinnamon.

**USES:** Ice cream may not be the obvious use for cinnamon, a spice better known as an ingredient in cakes, biscuits (cookies) and savoury dishes, but it adds a delicious flavour, especially with fruits such as peaches or nectarines.

**PREPARATION:** Infuse halved cinnamon sticks in milk or cream that has just come to the boil. When it has imparted its flavour, strain the milk or cream and use it to make custard as the basis for ice cream. Cinnamon sticks can also be used to flavour fruit purées or compotes by infusing in the liquid in the same way.

### Using vanilla

Using a sharp knife, slit a whole vanilla pod (bean). Add it to milk or cream that has just come to the boil. For maximum flavour, scrape out the tiny black seeds from the pod and let them fall into the milk or cream.

## Nutmeg

**TYPES/FORMS:** Sold whole, nutmegs are the dried seeds of the fruit of the nutmeg tree, which is native to the tropics. Blades of mace, the pretty orange outer coating, are also sold separately, and both are sold ground.

**USES:** Nutmeg's wonderfully aromatic and slightly bitter flavour complements both sweet and savoury dishes. It is delicious in milk-based desserts such as ice cream.

**PREPARATION:** For the best flavour, grate a little off a whole nutmeg as and when you need it, using a fine-toothed surface of a grater or, better still, a small nutmeg grater. Ready ground nutmeg rapidly loses its pungency when stored.

## Star anise

These pretty star-shaped pods are a favourite of Chinese cooks, but are becoming popular in the West. Use them whole for sauces and compotes or infuse them in sugar syrups or custards for ices with a lovely aniseed flavour.

### Using cardamom

Traditionally used in Indian, Arabian and North African cooking, cardamom also adds a wonderful delicate aromatic fragrance to sorbets, ice creams and fruit compotes. If the recipe calls for cardamom seeds, crush the pods with the back of a cook's knife until they split. If necessary, use the tip of the knife to remove any remaining seeds from the pods. Use both the pod and the seeds for maximum flavour.

## Cloves

**TYPES/FORMS:** The unopened flower buds of a tree related to the myrtle, cloves look like tiny nails. They are available whole and ground.

**USES:** Although cloves are most commonly used in savoury dishes, they are also widely used in desserts, particularly with apples and other fruits. Their pungent flavour means that they are a somewhat unlikely ingredient in ice cream, but if used sparingly, they add an intriguing flavour.

**PREPARATION:** Infuse whole cloves in milk or cream. This is especially appropriate when making a custard to form the basis of a fruit ice cream. Don't overdo this flavouring – the taste should be subtle and not strident.

## Lemon grass

Mainly known for the delicate lemon fragrance it contributes to Thai and Vietnamese cookery, lemon grass is now widely available. Most supermarkets stock the fresh stems, which are pale green and tipped with white; it is also available as dried whole stems or ground lemon grass and sold in jars. To extract the delicate flavour the dried stems must be soaked in warm water for at least two hours before use. Fresh lemon grass can be finely sliced or crushed and infused in the milk to be used for custard-based ice cream or infused in the sugar syrup for a granita or sorbet.

# Chocolate

## CHOOSING THE BEST

A chocolate with a good, strong flavour is vital when making ice creams as the flavour of the chocolate is dulled when it is mixed with custard and cream. For the best and strongest flavour choose a good quality dark (bittersweet) or bitter chocolate with a high proportion of cocoa solids. Confectioners and good food shops will have a selection of superior chocolates but many of the larger supermarkets now stock several different types of good quality cooking chocolate. Choose one with "luxury" or "Belgian" on the label as it will almost certainly have at least 75% cocoa solids and good flavour and taste will be guaranteed.

Chocolate Menier can also be used. It has a stronger flavour and is less sweet than some other types of chocolate, but is well suited to ice cream making. Plain (semisweet) dessert chocolate contains between 30 and 60% cocoa solids. Check the side of the pack for details – the higher the cocoa solids, the stronger the chocolate flavour will be, so avoid using any chocolate with less than 45% cocoa solids.

In general, chocolate cake coverings should be avoided, as these have a mild, less chocolatey taste. With their added vegetable fat, they are more suited to making chocolate curls or caraque. What you can do, however, is to mix cake covering with an equal quantity of luxury dark chocolate. This way, you get the easy melting and moulding qualities of the former, coupled with the superior taste of the latter.

## How to melt chocolate

## Couverture

This pure chocolate contains no fats other than cocoa butter. It is used mainly by professionals and is only available from specialist suppliers. It generally requires "tempering" before use to distribute the cocoa fat evenly. This is quite a lengthy process that involves warming and working the chocolate until it reaches 32°C | 90°F. Couverture is usually used for moulding or decorating because of its glossy finish. It is available as white, milk and dark (bittersweet) chocolate drops or as a block.

## White chocolate

As when buying chocolate, choose "luxury" white chocolate or "Swiss" white chocolate for the best flavour. White chocolate is made from cocoa butter extracted during the production of cocoa solids. Although it includes about 2% cocoa solids many purists would argue that this is not nearly enough to make it a true chocolate, especially as the cocoa butter is then mixed with milk solids, sugar and flavourings.

As a result of these additional ingredients, white chocolate does require extra care when being melted: it quickly hardens if overheated. Do check the pack before buying, and choose a brand with a minimum of 25% cocoa butter, as any chocolate with less than this will be difficult to melt. The more cocoa butter there is the creamier and softer the chocolate will be. Some brands may even include vegetable fat or oils, so always check the ingredients list.

## Melting chocolate in a microwave

Break dark (bittersweet) or milk chocolate into squares, and place them in a bowl that can be safely used in a microwave. Heat it on Full Power allowing 2 minutes for 115g | 4oz chocolate; 3 minutes for 200g | 7oz. The chocolate will retain its shape until you stir it. Don't be tempted to heat if for longer or you may spoil the chocolate. White chocolate melts easily and is best microwaved on Medium Power or in a bowl placed over a pan of "just boiled" water.

**1** Pour water into a pan until it is about one third full. Bring to the boil, turn the heat off, then fit a heatproof bowl over the pan, making sure that the water does not touch the base of the bowl. Break the chocolate into pieces and put it in the bowl.

**2** Leave the chocolate pieces for 4–5 minutes, without stirring, until the chocolate has melted, the chocolate pieces will hold their shape. Stir the chocolate briefly before folding it into ice cream, or using it as the basis of a sauce.

## Cocoa

This rich, strong, dark powder is made by
extracting some of the cocoa butter during
chocolate production. What remains is a block
containing around 20% cocoa butter, but this
varies with each manufacturer. The cocoa is
then ground and mixed with sugar and starch.
The addition of starch means that cocoa needs
to be cooked briefly to remove the raw, floury
taste. This can be done by mixing it to a paste
with a little boiling water, which is the usual
technique when flavouring ice cream. If the
cocoa is to be used in a sauce, it will probably
be mixed with hot milk.

The very best cocoa is produced in Holland.
It is alkalized, a process that removes the
acidity and produces a cocoa with a mellow,
well-rounded flavour. The technique was
devised by the manufacturer, Van Houten, some
150 years ago and this is still the very best
cocoa available. Although it is more expensive
than some other brands, it is definitely worth
using for ice cream and chocolate sauces.

## Milk chocolate

Mild and creamy, milk chocolate is made with up
to 40% milk or milk products and contains less
cocoa solids than dark chocolate. Because it has a
mild flavour, you will need to add more than
when using dark (bittersweet) chocolate. You can
use a combination of melted milk chocolate and
chopped milk chocolate. As with white chocolate,
the addition of milk products means that it
requires more careful heating than dark chocolate.

## Carob

Although not a true chocolate, carob is viewed
by many as an acceptable alternative. It is the
ground seedpod of the carob or locust tree and
can be used as a chocolate substitute. Usually
available from health food shops and sold in
bars or in a powdered form as a flour.
If you are using a bar, be cautious as it is highly
concentrated. The flour can be used in a similar
way to cocoa.

### STORING CHOCOLATE

Wrap opened packs of chocolate well or
pack them in a plastic box. Store in a cool,
dry place away from foods with very strong
flavours, such as spices, which may taint
the chocolate. Avoid very cold places or the
chocolate may develop a dull whitish
bloom. Chocolate has a long shelf life, but
check use-by dates before cooking.

# Fruits

### Soft berry fruits

**TYPES/FORMS:** Berry fruits make marvellous ice creams and sorbets. You can choose from standard raspberries, larger tayberries and loganberries, bright red strawberries and tiny alpine and Hautbois strawberries, blueberries and blackberries. Look out for golden raspberries, too. These tend to be grown in small quantities by keen gardeners and are often difficult to find in the shops, but they are well worth trying when available.

**USES:** Delicious in ice creams, sorbets and sherbets, berry fruits can easily be transformed into superb sauces. Melba sauce is an obvious example, but there are plenty more to choose from. A delectable iced summer pudding that teams sliced strawberries with strawberry ice cream and soft fruit sorbet makes perfect use of summer fruits. Blueberries and red berries look most attractive sprinkled over ice cream sundaes or crushed and added to just setting ice cream for added texture and colour. Expensive alpine and Hautbois strawberries can be used for decoration only.

**PREPARATION:** Purée ripe fruits, then strain to remove the seeds, then use the purée in ice creams, sherbets or sorbets. Berry fruit purées are also delicious spooned over ice cream or mixed with a sugar syrup and lemon juice for a refreshing ice cream sauce.

*RIGHT: Redcurrants.*

---

### MAKING A PURÉE

Purée berry fruits in a food processor or blender until smooth, then strain the purée into a large bowl, using the back of a large spoon or ladle.

---

### Cane fruits

**TYPES/FORMS:** This category includes black, red and white currants, green gooseberries and the more unusual red gooseberries. As their short midsummer season is soon over, enjoy them while they are available fresh and bursting with rich flavour.

**USES:** All cane fruits make good ice creams, sherbets and sorbets. They can also be used to make coulis and sauces. Currants look beautiful and are often used for decoration.

**PREPARATION:** Gently remove currants from their stems, using the tines of a fork. As blackcurrants have such a sharp flavour, it is wise to poach them first with sugar and a little water until just tender. Red and white currants can be eaten raw or lightly poached. Gooseberries should be topped and tailed with scissors before being cooked. Purée and strain currants or cooked gooseberries if adding to ice cream, sorbet or sherbet. Gooseberry and ice cream made with clotted cream is a wonderful summertime treat.

### Orchard fruits

**TYPES/FORMS:** Choose from apples, pears, plums, damsons, cherries, apricots, peaches and nectarines.

**USES:** Orchard fruits, particularly peaches and nectarines, make irresistible ices. Use them in creamy ice creams, sorbets and similar desserts, with a little liqueur, if you like.

**PREPARATION:** Apples and pears should be peeled and cored; plums, peaches and apricots should be halved and stoned. The fruit should then be poached in a little water and sugar until tender before being processed to a smooth purée. Ripe peaches, nectarines and apricots can be puréed raw, then strained to remove the skins. Damsons are small and fiddly to prepare, so poach, then scoop out the stones. Alternatively, press the cooked fruit through a sieve to remove the stones (pits). Use stoned (pitted) cherries whole or chopped. Larger fruits can be used for decoration, provided they are ripe. Slice or chop them if necessary, and toss apples and pears in a little lemon juice to prevent discoloration.

## How to stone (pit) and string cherries

**1** Remove cherry stones (pits) easily with this handy gadget which pushes the stones out of the fruit. Usually available from good cookshops.

**2** Cherries threaded on a skewer or cocktail stick make an attractive decoration, especially for an iced drink.

## Citrus fruits

**TYPES/FORMS:** Choose from lemons, limes, oranges, tangerines, clementines, kumquats and grapefruit.

**USES:** All citrus fruit can be used to make sorbets, granitas and sherbets. In addition, oranges make a very good ice cream. Citrus fruit can also be used to make sauces, and the rind is frequently used as a decoration.

**PREPARATION:** Grate the rind or pare it thinly, taking care to remove only the coloured skin, leaving the bitter white pith behind. Cut the fruit in half and squeeze it, then strain the juice to remove any pips. Mix it with cream and custard for ice cream or with sugar syrup for sorbets, sherbets and granitas. Kumquats can be poached whole or in slices and used to accompany iced desserts.

**RIGHT:** *Halved lemons and limes.*

## Rhubarb

**TYPES/FORMS:** Strictly speaking, these pretty pink stems are not a fruit at all but a vegetable. For making iced desserts, choose the early forced rhubarb with its delicate flavour and baby-pink stems. Maincrop rhubarb has thicker, darker stems and a coarser texture.

**USES:** Puréed cooked rhubarb makes an excellent sorbet and granita, or flavour it with ginger for an old-fashioned ice cream. Lightly poached rhubarb can be served as an accompaniment to vanilla, cinnamon or goat's milk ice cream.

**PREPARATION:** Both early forced and maincrop rhubarb need to be cooked with sugar and just a tablespoon or two of water.

## Melons

**TYPES/FORMS:** Choose from Canteloupe, Charantais, Galia and Ogen melons. Test them for ripeness by pressing the stalk area of the skin. The melon should smell quite perfumed.

**USES:** With their delicate perfume, melons make the most wonderfully refreshing sorbets and granitas. The shells make excellent and attractive containers for serving melon ices.

**PREPARATION:** Cut them in half, scoop out the seeds, then purée the flesh before use. Watermelons can also be used, but as the seeds are speckled throughout the flesh it is often easier to leave them in when processing the fruit. Straining the purée will remove them. As watermelons have rather a bland flavour, mix the purée with grated lime rind and juice.

## How to segment an orange or grapefruit

**1** Using a sharp knife, start by cutting a slice off the top and bottom of the orange or grapefruit.

**2** Using a small serrated knife, slice off the skin and pith cleanly. Work your way from the top down to the base of the fruit.

**3** Holding the fruit over a bowl to catch the juices, carefully cut between the membranes to remove the whole fruit segments.

## Tropical fruits

**TYPES/FORMS:** Choose from bananas, pineapples, mangoes, passion fruit, grapes and kiwi fruit. These fruits are available year-round and are a welcome alternative to seasonal fruits.

**USES:** Mash peeled bananas or purée them with a little lemon or lime rind to prevent discoloration and make them into smooth ice creams with honey, ginger, chocolate or cinnamon. Puréed or chopped pineapple flesh makes wonderful ice cream, especially when chunky pieces of crushed meringue or a few tablespoons of rum are added. Pineapple can also be puréed and made into sorbets. Look out for the extra sweet varieties, with their bright yellow flesh. Mix puréed mango with ginger, lime or coconut for a sorbet with a Caribbean flavour. Grapes and kiwi fruit are best served as an attractive accompaniment to iced desserts, although both can be made into sorbet.

**PREPARATION:** Sliced or diced tropical fruits can be used as a decoration or sautéed in a little butter and sugar and then flamed in a little brandy, rum or orange liqueur for an easy ice cream accompaniment.

### PREPARING PASSION FRUITS AND PINEAPPLES

Passion fruits are easy to prepare. Just slice them in half and scoop out the seeds with a teaspoon. If necessary, strain the pulp.

To prepare pineapples, slice the top off the pineapple, then cut it into slices of the desired width. Cut away the rind with a small sharp knife. Cut away any remaining eyes from the edges of the pineapple slices.

Remove the central core of each slice with an apple corer, pastry (cookie) cutter or knife.

## Preparing a mango

**1** Place the mango, narrow side down, on a board. Cut a thick, lengthways slice off the sides, keeping the knife blade as close to the central stone (pit) as possible. Turn the mango round and repeat on the other side.

**2** Make criss-cross cuts in the mango flesh, cutting down only as far as the skin, then turn the large slices of mango inside out so that the diced flesh stands proud. Scoop it into a bowl.

**3** Cut all the remaining fruit away from the stone (pit), remove the skin and dice the flesh.

## Dried fruits

**TYPES/FORMS:** Sultanas (golden raisins), raisins, prunes, apricots, peaches, dates and figs are all suitable, as are dried apples and pears, although these are seldom used for making ice creams and sorbets. Several types of dried fruit are sold in vacuum packs labelled "ready to eat" and these do not need soaking before use, although they are sometimes macerated in wine or liqueur for extra flavour. More unusual dried fruit includes mango, cranberries and blueberries.

**USES:** Using dried fruits in ice creams is nothing new – rum and raisin is a classic combination. Drying fruits such as peaches and apricots intensifies their flavour, so they make excellent purées. These can either be incorporated in ice creams or sorbets, or used as sauces for any ice cream dessert.

**PREPARATION:** Use the smaller varieties of dried fruit whole or chopped, and steep them in fruit juice, wine, spirits or liqueur if you like. Larger fruits such as apricots and peaches need to be soaked and puréed before being added to ice cream, although chopped fruit can be added when the ice cream is partially frozen to give extra texture and colour.

## Glacé fruits and candied peel

These vibrant, jewel-like fruits make a pretty addition to partially frozen ice cream, and are the traditional flavouring in the classic Italian Tutti Frutti Ice Cream. They can also be used to decorate elaborate ice cream sundaes. Most fruits can be glacéd (candied) and a wide selection is available in supermarkets and cookshops. Choose from glacé cherries of various colours, glacé or candied pineapple and candied fruit peels. Large whole or sliced glacé fruits tend to be expensive, but are great for special occasion desserts. Sugar is a natural preservative and glacé fruits will keep well in an airtight container, but they are best used as soon as possible and purchased fresh as needed.

### Using glacé (candied) fruits

Use a small, sharp knife to finely chop the glacé fruits, then fold on to just setting vanilla ice cream for a classic Tutti Frutti.

# Nuts

## Nuts

**TYPES/FORMS:** Choose from a wide range of whole nuts such as almonds, hazelnuts, pistachios, walnuts and pecans, plus the less widely used macadamias, Brazil nuts and unsalted peanuts.

**USES:** Nuts are most popular in cream-based ice creams and are seldom added to water ices. Add chunky toasted nuts or praline for extra crunch in ice creams, or sprinkle them over elaborate ice cream sundaes. Roughly chopped sugared almonds with pastel-coloured coatings look good and make an easy decoration. Ground nuts infused in milk or cream give a delicate flavour to ice creams that are inspired by recipes from the Middle East.

**PREPARATION:** Toast the nuts, chop them roughly and fold them into partially frozen ice cream. Alternatively, use them to make praline, which can be broken up and folded into ice cream that is on the verge of setting. Finely ground almonds or cashews can be added to just boiled milk or cream, then left to cool. The flavoured milk can be strained or used as is to make a custard-based ice cream.

**BELOW:** *Pistachio nuts are an attractive addition to ice cream.*

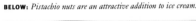

## Blanched nuts

**1** Put nuts such as pistachios or almonds into a bowl and pour over just enough boiling water to cover. Leave to stand for a minute or two until the skins expand and soften.

**COOK'S TIP** *Canned coconut milk combines convenience and full flavour for an ice cream that tastes good and is very easy to make.*

**2** Drain the nuts. To pop nuts such as almonds out of their skins, simply pinch them. Skin pistachios by tipping them into a dish towel and rubbing them together.

## Toasted nuts

For maximum flavour, toast whole or roughly chopped nuts in a dry frying pan on the hob, in a shallow cake tin (pan) under the grill (broiler) or on a baking sheet in a medium oven until golden and lightly roasted. There is no need to add oil, as they have such a high natural oil content. Desiccated (dry unsweetened shredded) coconut can also be toasted in this way but because it is so finely processed you will need to keep a very close eye on it. It browns in a matter of seconds.

Spread out whole, sliced or roughly chopped nuts on a baking pan or sheet. Grill (broil) for 3–4 minutes, shaking the pan or sheet frequently so that the nuts brown evenly.

**1** Put granulated (white) sugar, whole nuts and a little water into a heavy frying pan. Heat gently, without stirring. Do not use caster (superfine) sugar and do not stir as this would cause the sugar to crystallize, making it solidify and opaque. Continue to heat the sugar, but don't be tempted to stir the mixture with a spoon. Tilt the pan gently if necessary, to mix any sugar that has not dissolved completely.

**2** Keep a watchful eye over the nuts as the sugar and nuts begin to turn golden. Remember to keep the heat low.

**3** Quickly pour the praline on to an oiled baking sheet. Leave to cool and harden.

**4** Cover the cooled praline with clear film (plastic wrap) or put it in a plastic bag. Break it into rough pieces by tapping with a rolling pin.

**5** If finely ground praline is needed, crush it in a food processor or coffee grinder.

# Other flavourings

### Coffee

Iced desserts can be made successfully with freshly-made filter coffee or good instant coffee. Strong filter or espresso coffee is preferable for coffee granita, while coffee ice cream can be made with cracked coffee beans. Bring milk or cream to the boil, add the beans and infuse them, then strain the mixture and use the flavoured milk as the basis for the custard in the ice cream. Another way to make coffee ice cream is by blending cold, strong filter coffee or instant coffee dissolved in a very small amount of water with thick custard and cream. While cracked coffee beans give perhaps the best flavour and a pretty speckled finish (after straining) it can be difficult to judge quantities, so this method is more demanding. If too many beans are used or the custard is overcooked, the finished ice cream can be bitter.

### Spirits and liqueurs

The addition of a favourite spirit such as brandy, Calvados or whisky to ice cream, gin or vodka to sorbet, or an orange-flavoured liqueur to a fruity granita can lift a simple iced dessert into the realms of gourmet dining. While it is important to add sufficient alcohol to flavour the mixture (bearing in mind that freezing will dull the flavour), it is also vital to note that too much alcohol can prevent the ice cream or sorbet from freezing hard.

Purists or professional ice cream makers test the density and balance of an ice cream before freezing, using a saccharometer, but a beer-making hydrometer may also be used. This enables the level of sugar to liquid to be checked, ensuring satisfactory freezing. The home cook is unlikely to go to these lengths and the best guide when adapting or making up

recipes is to taste the mixture before freezing. If it is bland, don't add extra spirit, but pour a little over the ice cream just before serving.

> **FLAVOURING DURING FREEZING**
>
> To add additional flavour and texture, praline, sugared breadcrumbs, crumbled cookies, diced chocolate, diced glacé (candied) fruits or brandy-soaked dried fruits can be folded into semi-frozen ice cream. If you are using an ice cream maker, transfer the ice cream to a plastic tub or similar freezerproof container when it is thick, but still soft, before folding in the chosen flavouring. If you are making the ice cream by hand, fold in the flavouring after the second beating.

**ABOVE:** *Spirits and liqueurs can be used in small quantities to add flavour to ice creams.*

### Honey

For a single pot of honey, bees have to visit more than two million flowers. The type of flowers and the time of harvest determine the flavour, colour and texture of the finished honey. You can choose from clover, lavender or heather honey, and cheaper blends are also available that include honey from more than one country. Clear heather honey has the best flavour for making ice cream and tastes especially delicious mixed with goat's milk.

**ABOVE:** *Alcohol is an excellent flavouring for all iced desserts.*

# Using moulds

*There is no need to buy specialist equipment unless you plan to make moulded ice creams on a regular basis or you have a particular favourite. Look through your kitchen cupboards and you may be surprised to find that an item you use regularly or had forgotten about is just the shape you need. Any item not specifically designed to be used for ice cream making should be lined with clear film (plastic wrap). Use a generous amount, so that there is enough overlap to cover the exposed surface of the ice cream to stop it drying out in the freezer.*

## TRANSFORMING EVERYDAY EQUIPMENT

- For rectangular ice cream bombes or terrines, metal loaf tins (pans) can be used. Both the 450g|1lb and the 900g|2lb sizes are suitable, or you can experiment with the larger, hinged metal pâté tins. Unless tins have a non-stick finish, line them with clear film (plastic wrap). If all your loaf tins have sloping sides, don't despair. Simply cut a piece of cardboard the length and height of the tin and use it to make the shape rectangular. Line this with clear film, pushing it carefully into the corners.

- For bombes or cassatas you may have a plastic pudding basin with a lid left over from last year's bought Christmas pudding, or you may have bought such a basin for refrigerator storage. These make ideal moulds, as the thin plastic conducts the cold well in the freezer and the plastic can be flexed to aid turning out.

- For kulfi, use conical-shaped lolly moulds without their lids or sticks. New disposable plastic cups also work well.

- For individual moulds, old china cups can be lined with clear film (plastic wrap). The tiny plastic pots with lids used for freezing baby food are ideal.

- New disposable plastic cups or small, well-washed cream cartons that have lids also make good containers. Metal dariole moulds or individual metal steamed pudding moulds can be used if lined with clear film (plastic wrap). This ensures turning out the finished ice.

- If you don't have an ice cream cone mould, make a cardboard cone from an empty cereal packet and cover it with foil. Alternatively, stuff cone shapes made from crumpled foil into cream horn tins so that they become one-third longer.

**LEFT:** *Specialized bombe, dariole and ring moulds will ensure a professional finish but they can be an expensive piece of kitchen equipment.*

**BELOW:** *Individual metal steamed-pudding moulds can be used if lined with clear film.*

- If you have used an ordinary glass or china basin, do not dip it in hot water or the mould may break. Simply insert a knife between the clear film (plastic wrap) and the side of the basin to release the vacuum. Invert the basin on a serving plate, then warm the outside by covering it with a hot dish cloth. Count to 20 and then lift the basin off. Glass and china are poor conductors of heat so will require longer and more gradual warming than metal. When dipping moulds, use hot tap water rather than boiling water from the kettle, which would cause the outside of the ice cream to melt instantly and run over the plate when turned out.

## Improvising shaped moulds

Individual ice cream moulds can also be shaped from 2.5–4cm | 1–1½in strips of flexible cardboard which have been wrapped in a layer of foil. These covered strips are folded or curved and then stapled into the desired shape. You might try making hearts, circles or ovals, or fold the edges of the cardboard and make into squares or triangles.

**1** Wrap a sheet of foil around a strip of cardboard cut to the desired height.

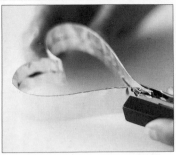

**2** Bend the cardboard into a heart shape, then staple the two ends together.

**3** Support the shape on a baking sheet, fill with ice cream that is on the point of setting, then level the surface with a knife and freeze until completely firm.

**4** Cut the foil-covered card with scissors and peel it away. Slide a metal spatula under the shaped ice cream, lift it on to a serving plate and decorate with fruit or chocolate curls.

---

### ADDING INTEREST TO LAYERS

Ice cream layers in a moulded dessert don't have to be restricted to horizontal lines but can be set at angles by propping up the mould as it freezes. The ice cream can be frozen in one layer to form a triangle or frozen as three layers, each set at opposing angles for a zigzag effect. Terrine or loaf-shaped tins (pans), and square shapes are ideal. Make sure that there is room in the freezer before you begin, as the angled mould and its supports take up quite a lot of space. Bags of frozen vegetables or small boxes of frozen fruit are ideal for wedging the tin at a 45° angle. When the first layer is frozen add the next on the opposite side of the mould and wedge in position.

---

## Unmoulding an iced dessert

**1** Dip the filled metal or plastic mould into hot water and leave it for a couple of seconds. Lift it out and blot the excess water. If the mould is lined with clear film (plastic wrap), carefully insert a knife between the film and the mould to loosen the ice cream.

**2** Invert the dessert on a serving plate, lift off the mould and peel away the clear film (plastic wrap). If you have difficulty turning out the dessert, try dipping the mould into the hot water for a few seconds more and repeat the process as before.

**3** Another way to ease an iced pudding from its mould is to invert it on the serving plate and cover the mould with a clean dish towel which has been dipped in boiling water, and then wrung out. Leave the dish towel in place for a few seconds, and lift off the mould.

# Layering and rippling

*For a professional look and a dramatic effect, create different layers of harmonizing ice creams in large or small, rectangular or round moulds. There are plenty of possibilities — just let your imagination take over.*

## How to layer ices

### Simple three-tier ice cream

**1** When the first flavour has thickened and is semi-frozen, pour it into a 25 x 7.5 x 7.5cm | 10 x 3 x 3in terrine or loaf tin (pan) that has been lined with clear film (plastic wrap). Spread it in an even layer and freeze it in the coldest part of the freezer for 1 hour or until firm.

**2** Pour in the second layer of semi-frozen ice cream and spread it out evenly. Freeze until firm, then add the final ice cream layer and freeze for 4–5 hours until hard. When ready to serve, turn out the ice cream from the mould, peel off the clear film (plastic wrap) and cut the terrine into slices, using a warm knife.

### Chequerboard

**1** Make a two-tier terrine, using two of your favourite ice creams layered in a terrine or straight sided 900g | 2lb loaf tin (pan). Turn out the two-tier terrine on a board and cut it in half lengthways, using a hot knife.

**2** Turn one of the halves over to reverse the colour sequence and wrap tightly in clear film (plastic wrap) to stick them together. Refreeze to harden. To serve, peel away the clear film and slice with a hot knife.

### Iced roulade

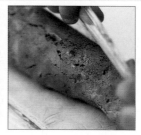

**1** Prepare two quantities of semi-frozen ice cream with flavours that complement each other well. Line a 30 x 23cm | 12 x 9in baking sheet with clear film (plastic wrap) or waxed paper. Spread one quantity of thick, semi-frozen, flavoured ice cream. Freeze for 20 minutes.

**2** Spoon the second batch of semi-frozen ice cream over a second piece of clear film (plastic wrap) or waxed paper to make a rectangle a little smaller than the first. Freeze for 20 minutes. Place this sheet of ice cream over the first layer, then peel off the clear film or waxed paper.

**3** Roll the layered ice cream, as if making a Swiss roll, starting from the longest edge and using the clear film (plastic wrap) or paper to roll it. Pat the ice cream into a neat cylinder, then wrap it in more clear film. Freeze for several hours, until the roll is hard.

**4** Peel off the clear film (plastic wrap) or paper and put the roll on a board. Cut it into thick slices, using a warmed knife.

## Classic cassata

This classic Italian iced dessert is traditionally made in a rounded metal mould with a lid. Some think that it is modelled on the dome of the Brunelleschi cathedral in Florence; others believe that the famous dessert was the result of a culinary accident when cream and wine were accidentally spilled into a soldier's metal helmet which was being stored in a chilly cave. Whatever its true origins, cassata is traditionally served in Italy at weddings and Easter celebrations and comprises two or three layers of ice cream, depending on the size of the mould in which it is made. If you don't have a metal mould, a plastic or thick glass pudding basin can be used instead.

**1** Line a 1.2 litre | 2 pint | 5 cup pudding basin with clear film (plastic wrap). Line it with a 2cm | ¾in thick layer of semi-frozen strawberry ice cream, using the back of a metal spoon to press the ice cream against the sides and bottom of the basin. Cover and freeze for 1–2 hours or until the ice cream lining is firm.

**2** Again using the back of a metal spoon, press chocolate ice cream on to the strawberry ice cream in the mould to make a second 2cm | ¾in thick layer of chocolate ice cream against the frozen strawberry layer. Leave a space in the middle. Cover and freeze for 1–2 hours more or until the chocolate ice cream is firm.

**3** Pack the middle of the mould with tutti frutti ice cream and smooth the top. Cover and freeze the dessert overnight until firm. Dip the mould in hot water for 10 seconds, insert a knife between the clear film (plastic wrap) and the basin to loosen the cassata, then invert it on to a serving plate. Lift off the basin and peel away the clear film before decorating the dessert with glacé (candied) fruits or chocolate caraque. Serve in wedges.

## Individual bombes

**1** Line four individual metal moulds with clear film (plastic wrap), then press a 1cm | ½in layer of dark chocolate ice cream over the bottom and sides of each mould, smoothing the ice cream with the back of a teaspoon. Cover and freeze for 30 minutes or until the ice cream is firm.

**2** Add a scoop of vanilla ice cream to the middle of each lined mould and insert a brandy-soaked prune or cherry into the middle. Smooth the surface, cover and freeze for 4 hours until firm.

**3** Dip the filled moulds into a roasting pan filled with hot water for 2 seconds. Invert the moulds on to serving plates and quickly remove the tins and clear film.

**4** Decorate the top and sides of each individual bombe with long sweeping lines of piped white chocolate. Serve immediately.

# How to ripple ices

This dramatic and eye-catching effect is surprisingly easy to achieve, using ice creams and sauces in contrasting colours, which are lightly swirled together while the ice cream is semi-frozen.

### Flavoured ice cream

Choose softly set ice cream that is too soft to scoop but thick enough to hold its shape. The colours should be markedly different for the most dramatic effect.

### Sauces

Marble a chocolate, toffee or fruit sauce through ice cream that is on the verge of setting. Be careful with toffee sauces as they can dissolve into the ice cream, so losing the effect.

### Raspberry ripple ice cream

### Fruit purée

Puréed and sieved fruit purées can be used unsweetened but can taste rather icy. It is better to mix them with a thick sugar syrup before swirling them with semi-frozen ice cream.

### Jam

For the easiest rippled ice cream of all, use softly set extra fruit jam straight from the jar. You can use firmer jams, but they will need to be mixed with a little boiling water to soften before being used. Make sure the jam is cold when you use it, or it will melt the ice cream. Any fruit jam can be used but the contrast of berry fruits looks the most attractive.

**LEFT:** *Use softly set jam for ice creams.*

**1** Make the vanilla ice cream by hand or churn it in an ice cream maker until it is thick but too soft to scoop.

**2** Mix 75g | 3oz | 6 tbsp caster (superfine) sugar with 60ml | 4 tbsp water in a pan. Heat until the sugar has dissolved, then boil for 3 minutes until syrupy, but not coloured. Cool slightly. Purée 250g | 9oz | 1½ cups fresh raspberries in a food processor or blender then strain into a bowl. Stir in the syrup and chill well.

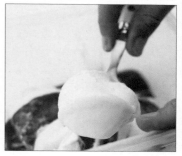

**3** Add alternate spoonfuls of the soft, partially frozen vanilla ice cream and the chilled raspberry syrup to a 1 litre | 1¾ pint | 4 cup plastic tub or similar freezerproof container. Don't be alarmed if the contrasting layers look a little messy to begin with.

**4** Stir through the syrup and ice cream two or three times to create a rippled effect. Freeze.

---

### CLASSIC COMBINATIONS

Ripple one of the basic recipes in this book with one of your own favourite flavours. Use the same basic technique as for raspberry ripple.

**Mixed berry swirl** – strawberry ice cream with raspberry syrup.

**Coffee toffee swirl** – dark classic coffee ice cream swirled with a rich toffee sauce.

**Double chocolate** – smooth dark (bittersweet) chocolate ice cream rippled with smooth white chocolate ice cream.

**Apricot and orange ripple** – orange and yogurt ice rippled with apricot sauce.

**Creamy toffee ripple** – rich toffee sauce rippled through creamy vanilla ice cream.

**Raspberry ripple** – try the home-made version made with the very best of ingredients for a truly timeless classic.

## Marbling ice cream

Although very similar to the technique used when making a rippled ice cream, marbling creates softer, less defined swirls. The same combinations of ice cream and syrup, sauce or purée can be used as for making rippled ice creams, but the softer effect is achieved by mixing together more thoroughly.

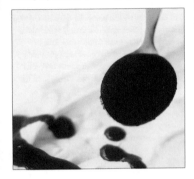

**1** To achieve this effect, spoon alternate layers of partially frozen ice cream into a plastic tub or similar freezerproof container. Drizzle coloured liquid flavouring or syrup, over each layer, using a spoon.

**2** Pass the handle of a wooden spoon through the ice cream and liquid flavouring five or six times to produce a lightly marbled effect. Freeze the ice cream for 4–5 hours or overnight, until firm.

**COOK'S TIP** *Soft marbled ice cream need only be lightly swirled with the end of a spoon to create the required effect. Choose a coloured liquid flavouring that complements the base ice cream in colour and taste.*

**ABOVE:** *A single scoop of marbled ice cream.*

### SECRETS OF SUCCESS

- Line the mould with clear film (plastic wrap) so that it is easy to remove the frozen dessert.

- Choose flavours that contrast or complement each other, such as dark (bittersweet) chocolate with pistachio, or vanilla and strawberry.

- Freeze ice cream after each layer has been added so that soft mixtures do not merge together. That way, the finished dessert will have well-defined layers.

- Make sure that the colours of the ice cream are in harmony, but are strong enough to be visible.

- Freeze the mould thoroughly after layering, preferably overnight, so that the layers will not separate when the ice cream is sliced.

- Dip the mould in hot water for 10–15 seconds so that the dessert will turn out easily. Peel off the clear film and use a knife dipped into warm water for slicing.

# Baskets, biscuits and cones

*Not only beautiful to look at, these sensational edible containers are easy to make and bound to impress your guests. They are the ultimate stylish and professional presentation.*

## How to make baskets

**Spun sugar baskets**

These impressive baskets look stunning filled with ice cream or upturned and placed over a single scoop of ice cream to form a cage and arranged in the middle of a large white dinner plate. Use an oiled soup ladle instead of oranges for slightly flatter baskets, and loosen with the tip of a small knife before removing. Add rich colour by decorating the plate with tiny clusters of blueberries, a few raspberries and a sprig or two of redcurrants or any combination of summer fruits. Dust lightly with icing (confectioners') sugar for the final effect.

**MAKES SIX**

**INGREDIENTS**

3 ORANGES, to serve as moulds

a little OIL for greasing

250g | 9oz | generous 1 cup GRANULATED (WHITE) SUGAR

75ml | 5 tbsp WATER

VANILLA ICE CREAM and
FRESH SUMMER FRUITS, to serve

**1** Smooth squares of foil over three oranges and brush lightly with oil. Put the granulated sugar and water in a pan and heat gently, without stirring, until the sugar has completely dissolved. Increase the heat and boil the syrup until it turns golden and starts to caramelize.

**2** Take the pan off the heat and plunge the bottom of it into a bowl of cold water to prevent the caramel from overbrowning. Allow the caramel to cool for 15–30 seconds, stirring it gently until it starts to thicken, then lift the pan out of the water.

**3** Hold a foil-wrapped orange over the pan and quickly drizzle caramel from a teaspoon over half the orange, making squiggly lines and gradually building up layers to make the basket shape. Leave the caramel to set and make a second and third basket in the same way. Warm the caramel when it gets too stiff to drizzle.

**4** Ease the foil off the first orange. Carefully peel the foil away and put the finished sugar basket on a lightly oiled baking sheet. Repeat with the remaining baskets, then make three more in the same way, reheating the caramel as needed and adding a little boiling water if it gets too thick to drizzle.

**5** Use the baskets on the day you make them, filling them with vanilla ice cream and summer fruits and adding a dusting of sifted icing (confectioners') sugar. The baskets are extremely fragile, so scoop the ice cream on to a plate or baking sheet first and lower it carefully into each basket with the aid of two forks.

## Chocolate tulips

These easy-to-make tulip baskets take only minutes to prepare and can then be set aside to harden. Fill with one large scoop of ice cream and decorate with blueberries and halved strawberries, or fill with tiny scoops of ice cream shaped with a melon baller and decorate with tiny chocolate shapes.

**VARIATIONS** *Any of the chocolate basket ideas suggested here are a perfect way of setting off your favourite chocolate, coffee or vanilla ice cream. You do not have to use dark (bittersweet) chocolate to make the baskets – Belgian white or milk chocolate work just as well.*

**1** Using the back of a teaspoon, spread 175g | 6oz melted dark (bittersweet) chocolate over six 13cm | 5in circles of non-stick baking parchment, taking it almost, but not completely, to the edge, and giving it a swirly, wave-like edge.

**2** Drape each paper circle, chocolate side outwards, over an upturned glass tumbler set on a baking sheet. Ease the paper into soft pleats and leave the baskets in a cool place to set. When ready to serve, lift the baskets off the glasses and carefully peel away the paper.

## A large chocolate bowl

**3** Chill well until set, then carefully peel away the foil and place the bowl on a plate. Store in the refrigerator until ready to fill with ice cream.

**COOK'S TIP** *This bowl can be made in any size. Small ones are perfect for individual portions, while larger bowls can serve up to four. Make it thicker than the other bowls and don't fill it too full or the weight of the ice cream might cause the chocolate to crack.*

**1** Smooth a double thickness of foil into a suitably sized mixing bowl or basin, so that it takes on the shape of the container. Carefully lift the foil out of the bowl.

**2** Spoon melted chocolate into the bottom of the foil bowl. Spread it to an even, fairly thick layer, taking it over the base and sides with the back of a spoon or a pastry brush.

## Individual chocolate cups

**3** Fill each of the set chocolate cups with parfait. Chill again in the freezer, then carefully peel away the paper from each cup. Using a palette knife to transfer each filled cup to a plate, decorate them with a light dusting of sifted cocoa and serve.

**COOK'S TIP** *When melting chocolate, it is important that the chocolate isn't overheated or allowed to come into contact with steam or small amounts of moisture, as these will cause it to stiffen or "seize". Make sure that the base of the bowl doesn't touch the water and don't allow the water to boil.*

**1** Cut six 30 x 15cm | 12 x 6in strips of baking parchment. Fold each strip in half lengthways, roll into a circle and fit it inside a 7.5cm | 3in plain biscuit (cookie) cutter to make a collar. Secure with tape. Ease the biscuit cutter away and make five more collars, leaving the last collar inside the cutter. Place on a baking sheet.

**2** Melt 250g/9oz dark (bittersweet) chocolate in a heatproof bowl over a pan of hot water. Brush chocolate evenly over the base and sides of the paper collar, supported by the biscuit cutter, and make the top edge jagged. Carefully lift off the biscuit cutter and slide over the next paper collar. Make six cups and leave to set.

# Toppings and decorations

*Complete the simplest dish of beautifully scooped ice cream or a party-style sundae with one of these professional looking decorations and you will be sure to impress your dinner guests.*

## How to make decorations

### Plain chocolate caraque

**1** Using a palette knife or the back of a spoon spread melted dark (bittersweet) chocolate over a marble slab or cheese board, or an offcut of kitchen work surface, to a depth of about 5mm | ¼in. Leave in a cool place to set.

**2** Draw a long, fine-bladed cook's knife across the chocolate at a 45° angle, using a see-saw action to pare away long curls. If the chocolate is too soft, put it in the refrigerator for 5 minutes or in a cold place for 15 minutes. Do not overchill.

### Two-tone caraque

**1** Spoon alternate lines of melted white and dark (bittersweet) chocolate over a marble slab or cheese board, or an offcut of work surface and spread lightly so that all the chocolate is the same height. Leave to cool and harden.

**2** Pare away long, thin curls of chocolate with a fine-bladed cook's knife in the same way that you do when making plain chocolate caraque.

### Simple chocolate curls

Holding a bar of dark (bittersweet), white or milk chocolate over a plate, pare curls away from the edge of the bar, using a swivel-blade vegetable peeler. Lift the pared curls carefully with a flat blade or a palette knife and arrange as desired.

### Piped chocolate shapes

Spoon a little melted dark (bittersweet) chocolate into a paper piping (pastry) bag and snip off the tip. Pipe squiggly shapes, stars, hearts, butterflies, musical notes or even initials on to a lined baking sheet. Peel off when cool and chill until required.

### Chocolate rose leaves

Brush melted dark chocolate, as evenly as possible, over the underside of clean, dry rose leaves. Avoid brushing over the edges. Put the leaf onto a baking parchment-lined baking sheet and leave in a cool place to set. Carefully peel each leaf away and chill until required.

**COOK'S TIP** *If the chocolate used for decoration is not at the right temperature the curls will either be too brittle or won't hold their shape. Set the chocolate aside at room temperature for 20 minutes before working with it.*

## How to make dipped fruits

Fruit looks and tastes fabulous when half dipped in melted dark (bittersweet) or white chocolate. Choose from tiny strawberries (still with their green hulls attached), tiny clusters of green or red grapes, physalis or cherries, with their stalks. It can also look very effective if you dip half the fruits in dark chocolate and the remainder in white chocolate. Leave the fruits to set on a baking sheet lined with baking parchment.

## Caramel-dipped fruits

For a more unusual fruit decoration for ice cream dishes, half-dip peeled physalis, whole strawberries or cherries (with the stalks intact) into the warm syrup, then leave to cool and harden on an oiled baking sheet.

**COOK'S TIP**  *Always carefully select fruit used for decoration and check that the fruit is perfect and free of any bruising as this will quickly spoil the decoration. Wipe them over with a damp cloth to remove any dust. A more even effect can be achieved if the stalks are still firmly attached to the fruit.*

### DECORATING WITH EXOTIC FRUITS

The pretty addition of a few exotic fruits can transform ice cream into a gourmet feast. Physalis look marvellous with their papery cases twisted back to reveal the berry fruit, while pearly white lychees add a dramatic note if the red skin is torn off into a spiral. Try using a quartered fig, with its delicate ruby flesh, or a few jewel-like pomegranate seeds or perfumed passion fruit seeds.

## Caramel shapes

The caramel used for making baskets is also suitable for making fancy shapes to decorate ice cream sundaes. Instead of drizzling the caramel on to foil-covered oranges, drizzle shapes such as treble clefs, graduated zigzags, spirals, curly scribbles, initials, stars or hearts on to a lightly oiled baking sheet. Vary the sizes, from small decorations about 5cm|2in long to larger 10cm|4in long shapes.

## Using coloured chocolate

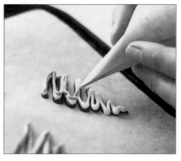

**1** Pipe random lines of melted dark (bittersweet) chocolate over a piece of baking parchment. Overpipe with piped white chocolate. Using pink liquid food colouring, tint a little of the melted white chocolate.

**2** Pipe a third layer of chocolate squiggles, this time in pink, over the dark and white layers. Chill in the refrigerator until set.

**3** Break the coloured shapes into jagged fragments of varying sizes and stick them into ice cream to decorate. They look particularly good on top of ice cream sundaes.

### Frosted flowers

**1** Lightly beat an egg white, then brush a very thin layer over edible flowers such as pansies, violas, nasturtiums, tiny rose buds or petals. Herb flowers can also be used, as can strawberries, seedless grapes or cherries.

**2** Sprinkle the flower or fruit with caster (superfine) sugar and leave to dry on a large plate. Use on the day of making.

### Citrus curls

**1** Using a zester, pare the rind of an orange, lemon or lime, removing just the coloured rind of the skin and leaving the bitter white pith on the fruit.

**2** Dust the citrus curls with a little caster (superfine) sugar and use them to sprinkle over citrus-based ices such as lemon sorbet.

### Corkscrews

**1** Use a canelle knife (zester) to pare long strips of orange, lemon or lime rind. The strips should be as long as possible and very narrow.

**2** Twist the strips of rind tightly around cocktail sticks so that they curl into corkscrews. Slide the sticks out and hang the corkscrew curls over the edge of ice cream dishes.

### Meringue dainties

**1** Make a meringue mixture using 2 eggs and 115g | 4oz | generous ½ cup caster (superfine) sugar. Spoon it into a piping (icing) bag fitted with either a plain 5mm | ¼ in or a 9mm | ⅜in nozzle.

**2** Pipe heart shapes, zigzags, shooting stars or geometric shapes on to baking sheets lined with baking parchment.

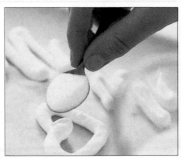

**3** Sprinkle the shapes lightly with caster (superfine) sugar and bake at low heat until they are firm enough to be lifted off the paper easily. Cool, then store for up to 1 week or until required.

# Decorative effects with sauces

Spooning sauces over ice cream is a quick and simple method of decorating ices and can look particularly pretty over ice cream sundaes, but sauces can also be piped in decorative shapes and patterns or used to create elaborate or dramatic backdrops against which to display your favourite ice creams.

### Creating teardrops

**1** Spoon a little Melba sauce over the base of a plate, tilt to cover then pipe or spoon small dots of unwhipped double (heavy) cream around the edge of the plate.

**2** Draw a skewer or cocktail stick through the dots to form teardrops. Scoop the ice cream into the middle of the plate.

### Feathering

**1** Spoon a little chocolate or butterscotch sauce over the base of a plate, then pipe a central dot and one or more circles of melted white chocolate or double (heavy) cream on the sauce, starting at the middle and working outwards.

**2** Draw a skewer or cocktail stick in lines from the middle of the plate to the rim, like the spokes of a wheel. Or mark lines in alternate directions for a spider's web effect.

### Piping zigzag lines

Arrange scoops of ice cream on a plate. Spoon a little cooled chocolate sauce into a piping (icing) bag, snip the tip, and pipe long zigzag lines over the plate and ice cream. Dust with a little sifted unsweetened cocoa powder.

### Piped border

**1** Pipe a swirly border of strained strawberry or apricot jam around the edge of a plate. Alternatively, use melted white or dark (bittersweet) chocolate and leave chocolate to set.

**2** Using the jam or chocolate as a border, flood the middle of the design with fruit, chocolate or butterscotch sauce, or cream. Arrange the ice cream on top, keeping it within the border.

### Decorative squiggles

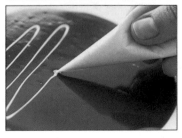

Spoon a little butterscotch or chocolate sauce over the base of a flat plate and tilt the plate to cover the bottom completely. Spoon melted white chocolate into a piping (icing) bag, snip off the tip and pipe squiggly lines over the sauce. Leave to set, then arrange the ice cream.

# the recipes

This section contains over 150 recipes for the most exquisite ice cream desserts. Beautifully presented with easy-to-follow steps they range from the traditional flavours in ice cream and sorbets to imaginative low-fat, elegant, and even hot ice cream desserts. With new and exciting combinations, every recipe will bring certain success.

# classic sorbets, water ices & granitas

After a rich main course, nothing refreshes the palate better than a clean-tasting sorbet or water ice. Stock up the freezer when fruits are plentiful to make effortless desserts throughout the year. Slushy granitas are even easier, and introduce robust flavours such as coffee and ginger.

# Lemon Sorbet

*This is probably the most classic sorbet of all. Refreshingly tangy and yet deliciously smooth, it quite literally melts in the mouth.*

**SERVES SIX**

**INGREDIENTS**

200g | 7oz | 1 cup
CASTER (SUPERFINE) SUGAR

300ml | ½ pint | 1¼ cups WATER

4 LEMONS, well scrubbed

1 EGG WHITE

SUGARED LEMON RIND,
to decorate

**1** Put the sugar and water into a pan and bring to the boil, stirring occasionally until the sugar has just dissolved.

**2** Using a swivel vegetable peeler pare the rind thinly from two of the lemons so that it falls straight into the pan.

**3** Simmer for 2 minutes without stirring, then take the pan off the heat. Leave to cool, then chill.

**4** Squeeze the juice from all the lemons and add it to the syrup.

**BY HAND:** Strain the syrup into a shallow freezerproof container, reserving the rind. Freeze the mixture for 4 hours until it is mushy.

**USING AN ICE CREAM MAKER:** Strain the syrup and lemon juice and churn the mixture until thick.

**5 BY HAND:** Scoop the sorbet into a food processor and beat it until smooth. Lightly whisk the egg white with a fork until it is just frothy. Spoon the sorbet back into the tub, beat in the egg white and return the mixture to the freezer for 4 hours.

**USING AN ICE CREAM MAKER:** Add the egg white to the mixture and continue to churn for 10–15 minutes until firm enough to scoop.

**6** Scoop into bowls or glasses and decorate with sugared lemon rind.

**COOK'S TIP** *Cut one third off the top of a lemon and retain as a lid. Squeeze the juice out of the larger portion. Remove any membrane and use the shell as a ready-made container. Scoop or pipe sorbet into the shell, top with lid and add lemon leaves or small bay leaves. Serve on a bed of crushed ice allowing one lemon per person.*

**VARIATION** *Sorbet can be made from any citrus fruit. As a guide you will need 300ml | ½ pint | 1¼ cups fresh fruit juice and the pared rind of half the squeezed fruits. Use 4 oranges or 2 oranges and 2 lemons, or, for a grapefruit sorbet, use the rind of one ruby grapefruit and the juice of two. For lime sorbet, combine the rind of three limes with the juice of six.*

# Pear and Sauternes Sorbet

*Based on a traditional sorbet that would have been served between dinner courses,*

*this fruity ice is delicately flavoured with the honied bouquet of*

*Sauternes wine, spiked with brandy.*

**SERVES SIX**

**INGREDIENTS**

675g | 1½lb RIPE PEARS

50g | 2oz | ¼ cup CASTER (SUPERFINE) SUGAR

250ml | 8fl oz | 1 cup WATER plus 60ml | 4 tbsp extra

250ml | 8fl oz | 1 cup SAUTERNES WINE, plus extra to serve

30ml | 2 tbsp BRANDY

juice of ½ LEMON

1 EGG WHITE

FRESH MINT SPRIGS, dusted with icing (confectioners') sugar, to decorate

**1** Quarter the pears, peel them and cut out the cores. Slice them into a pan and add the sugar and 60ml | 4 tbsp of the measured water. Cover and simmer for 10 minutes, or until the pears are just tender.

**2** Tip the pear mixture into a food processor or blender and process until smooth, then scrape into a bowl. Leave to cool, then chill.

**3** Stir the wine, brandy and lemon juice into the chilled pear purée with the remaining water.

**4 BY HAND:** Pour the mixture into a plastic tub or similar freezerproof container, freeze for 4 hours, then beat in a food processor or blender until smooth. Return the sorbet to the tub.

**USING AN ICE CREAM MAKER:** Simply churn the pear mixture in an ice cream maker until thick.

**5** Lightly whisk the egg white with a fork until just frothy. Either add to the sorbet in the ice cream maker, or stir into the sorbet in the tub. Churn or return to the freezer until the sorbet is firm enough to scoop. Serve the sorbet in small dessert glasses, with a little extra Sauternes poured over each portion. Decorate with the sugared mint sprigs.

**COOK'S TIP** *Sorbets that contain alcohol tend to take a long time to freeze, especially when made in an ice cream maker. To save time, transfer it to a tub as soon as it thickens and finish freezing it in the freezer. If you make the sorbet by hand, freeze the mixture in a stainless steel roasting pan to begin with. Transfer the sorbet to a plastic tub only after the egg white has been added.*

# Red Berry Sorbet

*This vibrant red sorbet seems to capture the true flavour of summer. Pick your own berries, if you can, and use them as soon as possible.*

**SERVES SIX**

**INGREDIENTS**

150g | 5oz | ¾ cup CASTER (SUPERFINE) SUGAR

200ml | 7fl oz | scant 1 cup WATER

500g | 1¼lb | 5 cups MIXED RIPE BERRIES, hulled, including two or more of the following: STRAWBERRIES, RASPBERRIES, TAYBERRIES or LOGANBERRIES

juice of ½ LEMON

1 EGG WHITE

small whole and halved STRAWBERRIES and STRAWBERRY LEAVES and FLOWERS, to decorate

**1** Put the sugar and water into a pan and bring to the boil, stirring until the sugar has dissolved. Pour the syrup into a bowl, leave to cool, then chill.

**2** Purée the fruits in a food processor or blender, then strain into a large bowl. Stir in the syrup and lemon juice.

**3 BY HAND:** Pour the mixture into a plastic tub or similar freezerproof container and freeze for 4 hours until mushy. Transfer to a food processor, process until smooth, then return to the tub. Lightly whisk the egg white and stir into the mixture. Freeze for 4 hours.

**USING AN ICE CREAM MAKER:** Churn until thick, then add the whisked egg white. Continue to churn until firm enough to scoop.

**4** Scoop onto plates or bowls, and decorate with fresh strawberries, leaves and flowers.

**VARIATION** *For a fruity sorbet with a hidden kick, add 45ml | 3 tbsp vodka or cassis. Don't be too generous with the spirits or the sorbet will not freeze firm.*

# Blackcurrant Sorbet

*Wonderfully sharp and bursting with flavour, this is a very popular sorbet. If you find it a bit tart, add a little more sugar before freezing.*

**SERVES SIX**

**INGREDIENTS**

500g | 1¼lb | 5 cups BLACKCURRANTS, trimmed

350ml | 12fl oz | 1½ cups WATER

150g | 5oz | ¾ cup CASTER (SUPERFINE) SUGAR

1 EGG WHITE

SPRIGS OF BLACKCURRANTS, to decorate

**1** Put the blackcurrants in a pan and add 150ml | ¼ pint | ⅔ cup of the measured water.

**2** Cover the pan and simmer for 5 minutes or until the fruit is soft. Cool slightly, then purée in a food processor or blender.

**3** Strain the purée over a bowl, pressing it through the mesh with the back of a spoon.

**4** Pour the remaining measured water into the clean pan. Add the sugar and bring to the boil, stirring until the sugar has dissolved. Pour the syrup into a bowl. Cool, then chill. Mix the blackcurrant purée and sugar syrup together.

**5 BY HAND:** Spoon into a plastic tub or similar freezerproof container and freeze until mushy. Lightly whisk the egg white until just frothy. Spoon the sorbet into a food processor, process until smooth, then return it to the tub and stir in the egg white. Freeze for 4 hours or until firm.

**USING AN ICE CREAM MAKER:** Churn until thick. Add the egg white and continue churning until it is firm enough to scoop.

**6** Serve decorated with the blackcurrant sprigs.

# Strawberry and Lavender Sorbet

*Delicately perfumed with just a hint of lavender, this delightful pastel pink sorbet is perfect for a special-occasion dinner.*

**SERVES SIX**

**INGREDIENTS**

150g | 5oz | ¾ cup CASTER (SUPERFINE) SUGAR

300ml | ½ pint | 1¼ cups WATER

6 FRESH LAVENDER FLOWERS

500g | 1¼lb | 5 cups STRAWBERRIES, hulled

1 EGG WHITE

LAVENDER FLOWERS, to decorate

**1** Bring the sugar and water to the boil in a pan, stirring until the sugar has dissolved.

**2** Take the pan off the heat, add the lavender flowers and leave to infuse for 1 hour. If time permits, chill the syrup before using.

**3** Purée the strawberries in a food processor or in batches in a blender, then strain the purée into a large bowl.

**4 BY HAND:** Pour the purée into a plastic tub, strain in the syrup and freeze for 4 hours until mushy. Transfer to a food processor and process until smooth. Whisk the egg white until frothy, and stir into the sorbet. Spoon the sorbet back into the tub and freeze until firm.

**USING AN ICE CREAM MAKER:** Pour the strawberry purée into the bowl and strain in the lavender syrup. Churn until thick. Add the whisked egg white to the ice cream maker and continue to churn until the sorbet is firm enough to scoop.

**5** Serve in scoops, piled into tall glasses, and decorate with sprigs of lavender flowers.

**COOK'S TIP** *The size of the lavender flowers can vary; if they are very small you may need to use eight. To double check, taste a little of the cooled lavender syrup. If you think the flavour is a little mild, add 2–3 more flowers, reheat and cool again before using.*

# Minted Earl Grey Sorbet

*Originally favoured by the Georgians at grand summer balls, this refreshing, slightly tart sorbet is perfect for a lazy afternoon in the garden.*

**SERVES SIX**

**INGREDIENTS**

200g | 7oz | 1 cup
CASTER (SUPERFINE) SUGAR

300ml | ½ pint | 1¼ cups WATER

1 LEMON, well scrubbed

45ml | 3 tbsp EARL GREY
TEA LEAVES

450ml | ¾ pint | 2 cups
BOILING WATER

1 EGG WHITE

30ml | 2 tbsp chopped fresh
MINT LEAVES

FRESH MINT SPRIGS or
FROSTED MINT,
to decorate

**1** Put the caster sugar and water into a pan and bring the mixture to the boil, stirring until the sugar has dissolved.

**2** Thinly pare the rind from the lemon so that it falls straight into the pan of syrup. Simmer for 2 minutes then pour into a bowl. Cool, then chill.

**3** Put the tea into a pan and pour on the boiling water. Cover and leave to stand for 5 minutes, then strain into a bowl. Cool, then chill.

**4 BY HAND:** Pour the tea into a plastic tub or similar freezerproof container. Strain in the chilled syrup. Freeze for 4 hours.

**USING AN ICE CREAM MAKER:** Combine the tea and syrup and churn the mixture until thick.

**5 BY HAND:** Lightly whisk the egg white until just frothy. Scoop the sorbet into a food processor, process until smooth and mix in the mint and egg white. Spoon back into the tub and freeze for 4 hours until firm.

**USING AN ICE CREAM MAKER:** Add the mint to the mixture. Lightly whisk the egg white until just frothy, then tip it into the ice cream maker and continue to churn until firm enough to scoop.

**6** Serve in scoops, decorated with a few fresh or frosted mint leaves.

**COOK'S TIP** *If you only have Earl Grey tea bags these can be used instead, but add enough to make 450ml | ¾ pint | scant 2 cups strong tea. Make frosted mint leaves by dipping the leaves in egg white and sprinkling them with caster (superfine) sugar.*

# Coffee Granita

*The most famous of all granitas, this originated in Mexico. It consists of full-bodied coffee frozen into tiny ice flakes.*

**SERVES SIX**

**INGREDIENTS**

75ml | 5 tbsp good quality
GROUND FILTER COFFEE

1 litre | 1¾ pints | 4 cups BOILING WATER

150g | 5oz | ¾ cup CASTER
(SUPERFINE) SUGAR

150ml | ¼ pint | ⅔ cup
DOUBLE (HEAVY) CREAM (optional)

**1** Spoon the coffee into a cafetière (press pot) or jug (pitcher), pour on the boiling water and leave to stand for 5 minutes. Plunge the cafetière or strain from the jug, then into a large plastic container, to a depth of 2.5cm | 1in.

**2** Add the sugar and stir until it has dissolved completely. Leave the mixture to cool.

**3** Cover and freeze for 2 hours or until the coffee mixture around the sides of the container is starting to become mushy.

**4** Using a fork, break up the ice crystals and mash the mixture finely. Return the granita to the freezer for 2 hours more, beating every 30 minutes until the ice becomes fine, even crystals.

**5** After the final beating return the now slushy granita to the freezer. When ready to serve, spoon the granita into glass dishes. Whip the cream and offer it separately, if you like.

**COOK'S TIP** *If you taste the coffee before freezing, don't be alarmed by its strength; the change from liquid to ice mysteriously dulls the flavour, so the finished taste is just right.*

# Raspberry Granita

*This vibrant bright red granita looks spectacular. Served solo, it is an excellent dessert for*

*anyone on a fat-free diet. For something a little more indulgent, serve with whole berries and crème fraîche*

*or clotted cream, for an elegant and contemporary Knickerbocker Glory style dessert.*

**SERVES SIX**

**INGREDIENTS**

115g | 4oz | ½ cup CASTER (SUPERFINE) SUGAR

300ml | ½ pint | 1¼ cups WATER

500g | 1¼lb | 3½ cups RASPBERRIES, hulled, plus extra, to decorate

juice of 1 LEMON

little SIFTED ICING (CONFECTIONERS') SUGAR, for dusting

**1** Tip the sugar and water into a large pan and bring to the boil, stirring occasionally until the sugar has dissolved. Pour the sugar syrup into a bowl, leave to cool, then chill.

**2** Purée the raspberries in a food processor or in batches in a blender. Strain the purée over a large bowl. Press the purée through with the back of the spoon and then discard the seeds.

**3** Scrape the purée into a large measuring jug (pitcher), stir in the sugar syrup and lemon juice and top up to 1 litre | 1¾ pints | 4 cups with cold water.

**4** Pour the mixture into a large plastic container so that the depth is no more than 2.5cm | 1in. Cover and freeze for 2 hours until the mixture around the sides of the container is mushy.

**5** Using a fork, break up the ice crystals and mash finely. Return to the freezer for 2 hours, beating every 30 minutes until the ice forms fine, even crystals.

**6** Spoon into tall glass dishes and decorate with extra raspberries dusted with a little sifted icing sugar, if you wish.

**COOK'S TIP** *For a granita with a little extra oomph, stir in 45ml | 3 tbsp cassis, but don't be tempted to add more or the granita will not freeze. If you miss one of the beatings, don't panic. Leave the granita at room temperature for 10–15 minutes to soften slightly, then beat thoroughly with a fork until it is the required consistency. Return it to the freezer and continue with the recipe.*

# Watermelon Granita

*Pastel pink flakes of ice, subtly blended with the citrus freshness of lime and the delicate flavour of watermelon, make this granita a rare treat for the eye and the tastebuds.*

**SERVES SIX**

**INGREDIENTS**

150g | 5oz | ⅔ cup CASTER (SUPERFINE) SUGAR

150ml | ¼ pint | ⅔ cup WATER

1 whole WATERMELON, about 1.75kg | 4–4½lb

FINELY GRATED RIND and JUICE of 2 LIMES, plus LIME WEDGES, for serving

**1** Bring the sugar and water to the boil in a pan, stirring until the sugar has dissolved. Pour into a bowl. Cool, then chill. Cut the watermelon into quarters.

**2** Discard most of the seeds, scoop the flesh into a food processor and process briefly until smooth. Alternatively, use a blender, and process the watermelon quarters in small batches.

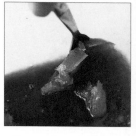

**3** Strain the purée into a large plastic container. Discard the seeds. Pour in the chilled syrup, lime rind and juice and mix well.

**4** Cover and freeze for 2 hours until the mixture around the sides of the container is mushy. Mash the ice finely with a fork and return the granita to the freezer.

**5** Freeze for 2 hours more, mashing the mixture every 30 minutes, until the granita has a fine slushy consistency. Scoop it into dishes and serve with the wedges of extra lime.

**VARIATION** *To serve this granita cocktail-style, dip the rim of each glass serving dish in a little water or beaten egg white, then dip it into sugar. Spoon in the granita, pour over a little Cointreau, Tequila or white rum and decorate with lime wedges or thin strips of lime rind removed with a cannelle knife and twisted around a cocktail stick.*

# Tequila and Orange Granita

*Full of flavour, this distinctive Mexican granita will have guests clamouring for more. Serve simply with wedges of citrus fruit or spoon over a little grenadine.*

**SERVES SIX**

**INGREDIENTS**

115g | 4oz | ½ cup CASTER (SUPERFINE) SUGAR

300ml | ½ pint | 1¼ cups WATER

6 ORANGES, well scrubbed

90ml | 6 tbsp TEQUILA

ORANGE and LIME WEDGES to decorate

**1** Put the sugar and water into a pan. Using a vegetable peeler, thinly pare the rind from three of the oranges, letting it fall into the pan. Bring to the boil, stirring to dissolve the sugar. Pour the syrup into a bowl, cool, then chill.

**2** Strain the syrup into a shallow plastic container. Squeeze all the oranges, strain the juice into the syrup then stir in the tequila. Check that the mixture is no more than 2.5cm | 1in deep; transfer to a larger container if needed.

**3** Cover and freeze for 2 hours until the mixture around the sides of the container is mushy. Mash well with a fork and return the granita to the freezer.

**4** Freeze for 2 hours more, mashing the mixture with a fork every 30 minutes until the granita has a fine slushy consistency. Scoop it into dishes and serve with the orange and lime wedges.

**COOK'S TIP** *If you don't have any tequila, make the granita with vodka, Cointreau, or even white rum. Don't be tempted to add more than the recommended amount; too much alcohol will stop the granita from freezing.*

# Ruby Grapefruit Granita

*This is slightly sharper than the other granitas, but is very refreshing. It's the ideal choice for serving after a rich or very filling main course.*

**SERVES SIX**

**INGREDIENTS**

200g | 7oz | 1 cup
CASTER (SUPERFINE) SUGAR

300ml | ½ pint | 1¼ cups WATER

4 RUBY GRAPEFRUIT

TINY MINT LEAVES,
to decorate

**1** Put the sugar and water into a pan. Bring the water to the boil, stirring until the sugar has dissolved. Pour the syrup into a bowl, cool, then chill.

**COOK'S TIP** *Grapefruit shells make very good serving dishes. For a more modern treatment, consider the effect you would like to achieve when halving the grapefruit. They look great when tilted at an angle. Having squeezed the juice and removed the membrane, trim a little off the base of each shell so that it will remain stable when filled with granita.*

**2** Cut the grapefruit in half. Squeeze the juice, taking care not to damage the grapefruit shells. Set these aside. Strain the juice into a large plastic container. Stir in the chilled syrup, making sure that the depth of the mixture does not exceed 2.5cm | 1in.

**3** Cover and freeze for 2 hours or until the mixture around the sides of the container is mushy. Using a fork, break up the ice crystals and mash the granita finely.

**4** Freeze for 2 hours more, mashing the mixture every 30 minutes until the granita consists of fine, even crystals.

**5** Select the six best grapefruit shells for use as the serving dishes. Using a sharp knife, remove the grapefruit pulp, leaving the shells as clean as possible.

**6** Scoop the sorbet into the grapefruit shells, decorate with the tiny mint leaves and serve.

# Ginger Granita

*This full-bodied granita is a must for ginger lovers. Served solo, it is a simple and inexpensive dessert, yet is smart enough to serve to the most sophisticated guests.*

**SERVES SIX**

**INGREDIENTS**

150g | 5oz | ¼ cup CASTER (SUPERFINE) SUGAR

1 litre | 1¾ pints | 4 cups WATER

75g | 3oz ROOT GINGER

a little GROUND CINNAMON,
to decorate

**1** Put the sugar and water into a pan. Bring to the boil, stirring until the sugar has dissolved. Take the pan off the heat.

**2** Peel the ginger, chop it finely, then stir it into the hot sugar syrup. Leave for at least 1 hour to infuse and cool, then pour into a bowl and chill.

**3** Strain the chilled syrup into a large, shallow plastic container, making sure the depth is no more than 2.5cm | 1in. Cover and freeze for 2 hours or until the mixture around the sides of the container has become mushy.

**4** Using a fork, break up the ice crystals and mash finely. Return the granita to the freezer for 2 hours more, beating every 30 minutes until the ice becomes soft and very fine with evenly sized ice crystals.

**COOK'S TIP** *You will be able to maintain the right texture for an hour or so but after that it will become too firm. To serve, spoon into tall glasses and dust with ground cinnamon.*

**5** After the final beating, return the now slushy granita to the freezer. Serve in tall glasses decorated with ground cinnamon.

**VARIATION** *Whip 150ml | ¼ pint | ⅔ cup double (heavy) cream and pipe it on top of each portion of granita. Then decorate with crystallized (candied) ginger.*

# Damson Water Ice

*Use ripe fruits for natural sweetness. If you can't find damsons, use another deep-red variety of plum or extra-juicy Victoria plums.*

**SERVES SIX**

**INGREDIENTS**

500g | 1¼lb RIPE DAMSONS, washed

450ml | ¾ pint | scant 2 cups WATER

150g | 5oz | ⅔ cup CASTER (SUPERFINE) SUGAR

**1** Put the damsons into a pan and add 150ml | ¼ pint | ⅔ cup of the water. Cover and simmer for 10 minutes or until the damsons are tender.

**2** Pour the remaining water into a second pan. Add the sugar and bring to the boil, stirring until the sugar has dissolved. Pour the syrup into a bowl, leave to cool, then chill.

**3** Break up the cooked damsons in the pan with a wooden spoon and scoop out any free stones (pits). Strain the fruit and juices into a large bowl. Press the fruit through with the wooden spoon and discard the skins and any remaining stones.

**4 BY HAND:** Pour the damson purée into a shallow plastic container. Stir in the syrup and freeze for 6 hours, beating once or twice to break up the ice crystals.

**USING AN ICE CREAM MAKER:** Mix the purée with the syrup and churn until firm enough to scoop.

**5** Spoon into tall glasses or dishes and serve with wafer biscuits.

**VARIATIONS** *Apricot water ice can be made in the same way. Flavour the water ice with a little lemon or orange rind or add a broken cinnamon stick to the pan when poaching the fruit.*

# Apple and Cider Water Ice

*This very English combination has a subtle apple flavour with just a hint of cider. As the apple purée is very pale, almost white, add a few drops of green food colouring to echo the pale green skin of the Granny Smith apples.*

**SERVES SIX**

**INGREDIENTS**

500g | 1¼lb EATING APPLES

150g | 5oz | ¾ cup CASTER
(SUPERFINE) SUGAR

300ml | ½ pint | 1¼ cups WATER

250ml | 8fl oz | 1 cup
STRONG DRY CIDER

few drops of GREEN FOOD
COLOURING
(optional)

strips of thinly pared
LIME RIND, to decorate

**1** Quarter, core and roughly chop the apples. Put them into a pan. Add the caster sugar and half the water. Cover and simmer for 10 minutes or until the apples are soft.

**2** Strain the mixture over a large bowl. Discard the apple skins and seeds. Stir the cider and the remaining water into the apple purée and add a little colouring, if you like.

**3 BY HAND:** Pour into a shallow plastic container and freeze for 6 hours, beating with a fork once or twice to break up the ice crystals.

**USING AN ICE CREAM MAKER:** Churn until firm enough to scoop.

**4** Scoop into dishes and decorate with twists of thinly pared lime rind.

**COOK'S TIP** *Add the food colouring gradually, making the mixture a little darker than you would like the finished sorbet to be as freezing lightens the colour slightly.*

# classic vanilla, chocolate & coffee ice creams

This chapter provides the best classic vanilla ice cream recipes plus some imaginative variations using ingredients such as brandied fruits, crumbled cookies, saffron, and cinnamon. The principle flavours of chocolate, coffee and toffee ice cream are many people's favourites, making this selection the ultimate collection of classic ice creams.

# Classic Vanilla Ice Cream

*Nothing beats the creamy simplicity of true vanilla ice cream. Vanilla pods are expensive, but well worth buying for the superb flavour they impart.*

**2** Lift the vanilla pod up. Holding it over the pan, scrape the black seeds out of the pod with a small knife so that they fall back into the milk. Set the vanilla pod aside and bring the milk back to the boil.

**4** When the custard thickens and is smooth, pour it back into the bowl. Cool it, then chill.

**SERVES FOUR**

**INGREDIENTS**

1 VANILLA POD (BEAN)

300ml | ½ pint | 1¼ cups
SEMI-SKIMMED
(LOW-FAT) MILK

4 EGG YOLKS

75g | 3oz | 6 tbsp CASTER
(SUPERFINE) SUGAR

5ml | 1 tsp CORNFLOUR
(CORNSTARCH)

300ml | ½ pint | 1¼ cups
DOUBLE (HEAVY) CREAM

**1** Using a small knife slit the vanilla pod lengthways. Pour the milk into a heavy pan, add the vanilla pod and bring to the boil. Remove from the heat and leave for 15 minutes to allow the flavours to infuse.

**3** Whisk the egg yolks, sugar and cornflour in a bowl until the mixture is thick and foamy. Gradually pour on the hot milk, whisking constantly. Return the mixture to the pan and cook over a gentle heat, stirring all the time.

**5 BY HAND:** Whip the cream until it has thickened but still falls from a spoon. Fold it into the custard and pour into a plastic tub or similar freezerproof container. Freeze for 6 hours or until firm enough to scoop, beating twice with a fork, or in a food processor.

**USING AN ICE CREAM MAKER:** Stir the cream into the custard and churn the mixture until thick.

**6** Scoop into dishes, bowls or bought cones – or eat straight from the tub.

**COOK'S TIP** *Don't throw the vanilla pod away after use. Instead, rinse it in cold water, dry and store in the sugar jar. After a week or so the sugar will take on the wonderful aroma and flavour of the vanilla and will be delicious sprinkled over summer fruits. Use it to sweeten whipped cream, custard, biscuits (cookies) and shortbread.*

# Brown Bread Ice Cream

*This classic and very English ice cream is flecked with tiny clusters of crisp, crunchy caramelized brown breadcrumbs and tastes rather like the more modern American style cookies-and-cream ice cream.*

**SERVES FOUR TO SIX**

**INGREDIENTS**

4 EGG YOLKS

75g | 3oz | 6 tbsp CASTER (SUPERFINE) SUGAR

5ml | 1 tsp CORNFLOUR (CORNSTARCH)

300ml | ½ pint | 1¼ cups SEMI-SKIMMED (LOW-FAT) MILK

40g | 1½oz | 3 tbsp BUTTER

75g | 3oz | 1½ cups FRESH BROWN BREADCRUMBS

50g | 2oz | ¼ cup SOFT LIGHT BROWN SUGAR

5ml | 1 tsp NATURAL VANILLA EXTRACT

300ml | ½ pint | 1¼ cups DOUBLE (HEAVY) CREAM

**1** Whisk the egg yolks, sugar and cornflour together in a bowl until thick and pale. Pour the milk into a heavy pan, bring it just to the boil, then gradually pour it on to the egg yolk mixture, whisking constantly.

**2** Return the mixture to the pan and cook over a gentle heat, stirring constantly until the custard thickens and is smooth. Pour it back into the bowl, leave to cool, then chill.

**COOK'S TIP** *Watch the breadcrumbs carefully when frying. Like almonds, they have a habit of burning if you turn your back on them for a moment, and burnt crumbs will give the ice cream a bitter taste. The crumbs should darken only slightly.*

**3** Melt the butter in a large frying pan. Add the breadcrumbs, stir until evenly coated in butter, then sprinkle the sugar over. Fry gently for 4–5 minutes, stirring until lightly browned. Remove from the heat and leave until cool and crisp.

**4 BY HAND:** Add the vanilla extract to the custard and mix well. Whip the cream until thick then fold into the custard. Pour into a plastic tub or similar freezerproof container. Freeze for 4 hours, beating once with a fork to break up the crystals.

**USING AN ICE CREAM MAKER:** Add the vanilla extract to the custard and mix well. Stir in the cream. Transfer to the ice cream maker and churn until thick.

**5 BY HAND:** Break up the breadcrumbs with your fingers. Beat the ice cream briefly, then stir in the breadcrumbs. Return the tub to the freezer and leave until firm enough to scoop.

**USING AN ICE CREAM MAKER:** Rub the breadcrumbs between your fingers to break up any lumps. Stir the breadcrumbs into the mixture, churn for 5–10 minutes until ready to serve in scoops.

# Crème Fraîche and Honey Ice

*This delicately flavoured vanilla ice cream is delicious either served on its own or with slices of hot apple or cherry pie.*

**SERVES FOUR**

**INGREDIENTS**

4 EGG YOLKS

60ml | 4 tbsp CLEAR FLOWER HONEY

5ml | 1 tsp CORNFLOUR (CORNSTARCH)

300ml | ½ pint | 1¼ cups SEMI-SKIMMED (LOW-FAT) MILK

7.5ml | 1½ tsp NATURAL VANILLA EXTRACT

250g | 9oz | generous 1 cup CRÈME FRAÎCHE

NASTURTIUM, PANSY or HERB FLOWERS, to decorate

**1** Whisk the egg yolks, honey and cornflour in a bowl until thick and foamy. Pour the milk into a heavy pan, bring to the boil, then gradually pour on to the yolk mixture, whisking constantly.

**2** Return the mixture to the pan and cook over a gentle heat, stirring all the time until the custard thickens and is smooth. Pour it back into the bowl, then chill.

**3 BY HAND:** Stir in the vanilla extract and crème fraîche. Pour into a plastic tub or similar freezerproof container. Freeze for 6 hours or until firm enough to scoop, beating once or twice with a fork or in a food processor to break up the ice crystals.

**USING AN ICE CREAM MAKER:** Stir the vanilla extract and crème fraîche into the custard mix and churn until thick and firm enough to scoop.

**4** Serve in glass dishes and decorate with nasturtiums, pansies or herb flowers.

**COOK'S TIP** *Measure the honey carefully and use level spoonfuls; if you are over-generous, the honey flavour will dominate and the ice cream will be too sweet.*

# Tutti frutti

*This Italian fruit ice cream takes its name from an expression meaning "all the fruits".*

*Four fruits have been used here but you can make up your own blend of candied*

*or glacé fruits, including exotics such as papaya or mango.*

**SERVES FOUR TO SIX**

**INGREDIENTS**

300ml | ½ pint | 1¼ cups
SEMI-SKIMMED (LOW-FAT)
MILK

1 VANILLA POD (BEAN)

4 EGG YOLKS

75g | 3oz | 6 tbsp CASTER
(SUPERFINE) SUGAR

5ml | 1 tsp CORNFLOUR
(CORNSTARCH)

300ml | ½ pint | 1¼ cups
WHIPPING CREAM

150g | 5oz | ⅔ cup
MULTI-COLOURED
GLACÉ (CANDIED) CHERRIES

50g | 2oz | ⅓ cup
SLICED CANDIED LIME and
ORANGE PEEL

50g | 2oz | ⅓ cup
CANDIED PINEAPPLE

**1** Pour the milk into a heavy pan. Slit the vanilla pod lengthways, add it to the milk and bring to the boil. Immediately remove the pan from the heat and leave the milk for 15 minutes to allow to infuse.

**2** Lift up the vanilla pod. Holding it over the pan of milk, scrape out the small black seeds with a knife so that they fall into the milk. Set aside, for later re-use, and bring the flavoured milk back to the boil over a gentle heat.

**3** Meanwhile, whisk the egg yolks, sugar and cornflour in a bowl until thick and foamy. Gradually whisk in the flavoured milk.

**4** Pour the milk mixture back into the pan. Cook over a gentle heat, stirring constantly until the custard thickens. Pour it back into the bowl and cover. Cool, then chill.

**5 BY HAND:** Whip the cream until it has thickened but is still soft enough to fall from a spoon, then fold it into the custard.

**USING AN ICE CREAM MAKER:** Mix the thickened custard with the cream. There is no need to whip the cream first. Churn the custard and cream mixture until it is thick.

**6 BY HAND:** Pour the mixture into a plastic tub or similar freezerproof container. Freeze for 4 hours, beating once with a fork or electric mixer to break up the ice crystals. If you prefer, break up the crystals by blending the mixture briefly in a food processor.

**7** Finely chop the glacé cherries, candied peel and pineapple and fold into the ice cream. Return to the freezer for 2–3 hours or churn in the ice cream maker for 5–10 minutes until firm enough to scoop.

**VARIATION** *Steep the glacé fruits in a little Kirsch for 3 hours before adding.*

**classic vanilla, chocolate & coffee ice creams** 83

# Cookies and Cream

*This wickedly indulgent ice cream is a favourite in the USA. To make the result even more luxurious, use freshly baked home-made cookies with large chunks of chocolate and nuts.*

**SERVES FOUR TO SIX**

**INGREDIENTS**

4 EGG YOLKS

75g | 3oz | 6 tbsp CASTER (SUPERFINE) SUGAR

5ml | 1 tsp CORNFLOUR (CORNSTARCH)

300ml | ½ pint | 1¼ cups SEMI-SKIMMED (LOW-FAT) MILK

5ml | 1 tsp NATURAL VANILLA EXTRACT

300ml | ½ pint | 1¼ cups WHIPPING CREAM

150g | 5oz CHOCOLATE AND HAZELNUT BISCUITS, crumbled

**1** Whisk the egg yolks, sugar and cornflour in a bowl until the mixture is thick and foamy. Pour the milk into a pan, bring it just to the boil, then pour it on to the yolk mixture, whisking constantly.

**2** Return to the pan and cook over a gentle heat, stirring until the custard thickens and is smooth. Pour it back into the bowl and cover closely. Leave to cool, then chill.

**3 BY HAND:** Stir the vanilla extract into the custard. Whip the cream until it is thickened but is still soft.

**USING AN ICE CREAM MAKER:** Stir the vanilla extract into the custard. Stir in the whipping cream and churn until thick.

**4 BY HAND:** Fold the cream into the chilled custard, then pour into a plastic tub or similar freezerproof container. Freeze for 4 hours, beating once with a fork, electric whisk or in a food processor to break up the ice crystals. Beat one more time, then fold in the biscuit chunks. Cover and return to the freezer until firm.

**USING AN ICE CREAM MAKER:** Churn until thick enough to scoop then scrape the ice cream into a freezerproof container. Fold in the biscuit chunks and freeze for 2–3 hours until firm.

**COOK'S TIP** *Experiment with different types of cookies to find the type that gives the best results.*

# Brandied Fruit and Rice Ice Cream

*Based on a favourite Victorian rice ice cream, this rich dessert combines spicy rice pudding with a creamy egg custard flecked with brandy-soaked fruits. The mixture is then frozen until it is just firm enough to scoop.*

**SERVES FOUR TO SIX**

**INGREDIENTS**

50g | 2oz | ⅓ cup
READY-TO-EAT
PITTED PRUNES

50g | 2oz | ⅓ cup
READY-TO-EAT
DRIED APRICOTS

50g | 2oz | ¼ cup
GLACÉ (CANDIED) CHERRIES

30ml | 2 tbsp BRANDY

150ml | ¼ pint | ⅔ cup
SINGLE (LIGHT) CREAM

**For the rice mixture**

40g | 1½oz | generous ¼ cup
PUDDING (DESSERT) RICE

450ml | ¾ pint | scant 2 cups
FULL-CREAM (WHOLE) MILK

1 CINNAMON STICK,
halved, plus extra CINNAMON
STICKS, to decorate

4 CLOVES

**For the custard**

4 EGG YOLKS

75g | 3oz | 6 tbsp CASTER
(SUPERFINE) SUGAR

5ml | 1 tsp CORNFLOUR
(CORNSTARCH)

300ml | ½ pint | 1¼ cups
FULL-CREAM (WHOLE) MILK

**1** Chop the prunes, apricots and glacé cherries finely and put them in a bowl. Pour over the brandy. Cover and leave to soak for 3 hours or overnight if possible.

**2** Put the rice, milk and whole spices in a large pan. Bring to the boil, then simmer gently for 30 minutes, stirring occasionally until most of the milk has been absorbed. Lift out the spices and leave the rice to cool.

**3** Whisk the egg yolks, sugar and cornflour in a bowl until thick and foamy. Heat the milk in a heavy pan then gradually pour it on to the yolks, whisking constantly. Pour back into the pan and cook, stirring until the custard thickens. Leave to cool, then chill.

**4 BY HAND:** Mix the chilled custard, rice and cream together. Pour into a plastic tub or similar freezerproof container and freeze for 4–5 hours until mushy then beat the ice cream lightly with a fork to break up the ice crystals.

**USING AN ICE CREAM MAKER:** Mix the chilled custard, rice and cream together. Churn until thick.

**5 BY HAND:** Fold in the fruits then freeze for 2–3 hours until firm enough to scoop.

**USING AN ICE CREAM MAKER:** Spoon the ice cream into a freezerproof container and fold in the fruits. Freeze for 2–3 hours until firm.

**6** Serve the ice cream in scoops decorated with cinnamon sticks.

**COOK'S TIP** *As the brandy-soaked fruits are so soft, it is better to remove the ice cream from the ice cream maker, fold in the fruits and then freeze the mixture in a tub until firm enough to scoop. This way, the fruits do not disintegrate and their colours are preserved. If you make the ice cream by hand, do not process it to break up ice crystals or the texture of the rice will be lost.*

# Cinnamon and Coffee Parfait

*This French-style ice cream is flecked with cinnamon and mixed with just a hint of coffee. As it is made with a boiling sugar syrup it doesn't require beating during freezing, so can be poured straight into freezerproof serving dishes.*

**SERVES SIX**

**INGREDIENTS**

15ml | 1 tbsp INSTANT COFFEE GRANULES

30ml | 2 tbsp BOILING WATER

7.5ml | 1½ tsp GROUND CINNAMON

4 EGG YOLKS

115g | 4oz | generous ½ cup GRANULATED (WHITE) SUGAR

120ml | 4fl oz | ½ cup COLD WATER

300ml | ½ pint | 1¼ cups DOUBLE (HEAVY) CREAM, lightly whipped

200g | 7oz | scant 1 cup CRÈME FRAÎCHE

extra GROUND CINNAMON to decorate

**2** Put the sugar in a small pan, add the cold water and heat gently, stirring occasionally, until the sugar has dissolved.

**3** Increase the heat and boil for 4–5 minutes without stirring until the syrup registers 115°C | 239°F on a sugar thermometer. Alternatively, test by dropping a little of the syrup into a cup of cold water. Pour the water away. If the syrup can be shaped to a soft ball, it is ready.

**4** Put the bowl of egg yolks over the pan of simmering water and whisk in the sugar syrup. Whisk until the mixture is very thick and then remove from the heat. Continue whisking until it is cool.

**5** Whisk the coffee and cinnamon into the yolk mixture, then fold in the cream. Pour into a tub or individual freezerproof glass dishes. Freeze for 4 hours or until firm. If frozen in a tub, scoop into bowls and decorate with a dusting of cinnamon.

**COOK'S TIP** *Test the syrup regularly. When it is nearly ready the syrup will fall slowly from the spoon. If the syrup fails to form a ball when tested in cold water, boil for a few minutes more; if the syrup forms strands that snap it is overdone and you must start again.*

**1** Spoon the coffee into a heatproof bowl, stir in the boiling water until dissolved, then stir in the cinnamon. Put the egg yolks in a large heatproof bowl and whisk them lightly until frothy. Bring a medium pan of water to the boil and lower the heat so that it simmers gently.

# Gingered Semi-freddo

*This Italian ice cream is rather like the original soft scoop ice cream. Made with a boiled sugar syrup rather than a traditional egg custard and generously speckled with chopped stem ginger this delicious ice cream will stay soft when frozen.*

**SERVES SIX**

**INGREDIENTS**

4 EGG YOLKS

115g | 4oz | generous ½ cup CASTER (SUPERFINE) SUGAR

120ml | 4fl oz | ½ cup COLD WATER

300ml | ½ pints | 1¼ cups DOUBLE (HEAVY) CREAM

115g | 4oz | ⅔ cup DRAINED PRESERVED STEM GINGER, finely chopped, plus extra slices, to decorate

45ml | 3 tbsp WHISKY (optional)

**1** Put the egg yolks in a large heatproof bowl and whisk until frothy. Bring a pan of water to the boil and simmer gently.

**2** Mix the sugar and measured cold water in a pan and heat gently, stirring occasionally, until the sugar has dissolved.

**3** Increase the heat and boil for 4–5 minutes without stirring until the syrup registers 115°C | 239°F on a sugar thermometer. Alternatively, test by dropping a little of the syrup into a cup of cold water. Pour the water away. You should be able to shape the syrup into a ball.

**4** Put the bowl of egg yolks over the pan of simmering water and whisk in the sugar syrup. Continue whisking until the mixture is very thick. Remove from the heat and whisk until cool.

**5** Whip the cream and lightly fold it into the yolk mixture, with the chopped ginger and whisky, if using. Pour into a plastic tub or similar freezerproof container and still freeze for 1 hour.

**6** Stir the semi-freddo to bring any ginger that has sunk to the bottom of the tub to the top, then return to the freezer for 5–6 hours until firm. Scoop into dishes or chocolate cases (see Cook's Tip). Decorate with slices of ginger.

**COOK'S TIP** *Semi-freddo looks wonderful in chocolate cases, made by spreading melted chocolate over squares of baking parchment and then draping them over upturned tumblers. Peel the paper off when the chocolate has set and turn the cases the right way up before filling.*

# Classic Dark Chocolate

*Rich, dark and wonderfully luxurious, this ice cream can be served solo or drizzled with warm chocolate sauce.*
*If you are making it in advance, don't forget to soften the ice cream before serving so that the*
*full flavour of the chocolate comes through.*

**SERVES FOUR TO SIX**

**INGREDIENTS**

4 EGG YOLKS

75g | 3oz | 6 tbsp CASTER
(SUPERFINE) SUGAR

5ml | 1 tsp CORNFLOUR
(CORNSTARCH)

300ml | ½ pint | 1¼ cups
SEMI-SKIMMED
(LOW-FAT) MILK

200g | 7oz DARK
(BITTERSWEET) CHOCOLATE

300ml | ½ pint | 1¼ cups
WHIPPING CREAM

SHAVED CHOCOLATE,
to decorate

**1** Whisk the egg yolks, sugar and cornflour in a bowl until thick and foamy. Pour the milk into a pan, bring it just to the boil, then gradually whisk it into the yolk mixture.

**2** Return the mixture to the pan and cook over a gentle heat, stirring constantly until the custard thickens and is smooth. Take the pan off the heat.

**3** Break the chocolate into small pieces and stir into the hot custard until it has melted. Leave to cool, then chill.

**4 BY HAND:** Whip the cream until it has thickened but still falls from a spoon. Fold into the custard then pour into a plastic tub or similar freezerproof container. Freeze for 6 hours or until firm enough to scoop, beating once or twice with a fork or in a food processor.

**USING AN ICE CREAM MAKER:** Mix the chocolate custard with the whipping cream. Churn until firm enough to scoop.

**5** Serve in scoops, decorated with chocolate shavings.

**COOK'S TIP** *For the best flavour use a good quality chocolate with at least 75% cocoa solids, such as top-of-the-range Belgian dark (bittersweet) chocolate or Continental-style dark cooking chocolate.*

# Chocolate Double Mint

*Full of body and flavour, this creamy, smooth ice cream combines the sophistication of dark chocolate with the satisfying coolness of fresh chopped mint. Crushed peppermints provide extra crunch.*

## SERVES FOUR

### INGREDIENTS

4 EGG YOLKS

75g|3oz|6 tbsp CASTER (SUPERFINE) SUGAR

5ml|1 tsp CORNFLOUR (CORNSTARCH)

300ml|½ pint|1¼ cups SEMI-SKIMMED (LOW-FAT) MILK

200g|7oz DARK (BITTERSWEET) CHOCOLATE, broken into squares

40g|1½oz|¼ cup PEPPERMINTS

60ml|4 tbsp CHOPPED FRESH MINT

300ml|½ pint|1¼ cups WHIPPING CREAM

sprigs of FRESH MINT dusted with ICING (CONFECTIONERS') SUGAR, to decorate

**1** Put the egg yolks, sugar and cornflour in a bowl and whisk until thick and foamy. Pour the milk into a heavy pan, bring to the boil, then gradually whisk into the yolk mixture.

**2** Scrape the mixture back into the pan and cook over a gentle heat, stirring constantly until the custard thickens and is smooth. Scrape it back into the bowl, add the chocolate, a little at a time, and stir until melted. Cool, then chill.

**3** Put the peppermints in a strong plastic bag and crush them with a rolling pin. Stir them into the custard with the chopped mint.

**4 BY HAND:** Whip the cream until it has thickened, but is still soft enough to fall from a spoon. Fold it into the custard, scrape the mixture into a plastic tub or similar freezerproof container and freeze for 6–7 hours, beating once or twice with a fork or electric whisk to break up the ice crystals.

**USING AN ICE CREAM MAKER:** Mix the custard and cream together and churn the mixture until firm enough to scoop.

**5** Serve the ice cream in scoops and then decorate with mint sprigs dusted with sifted icing sugar.

**COOK'S TIP** *If you freeze the ice cream in a tub, don't beat it in a food processor when breaking up the ice crystals or the crunchy texture of the crushed peppermints will be lost.*

# Dark Chocolate and Hazelnut Praline Ice Cream

*For nut lovers and chocoholics everywhere, this luxurious combination is the ultimate indulgence. For a change, you might like to try using other types of nuts for the praline instead.*

**SERVES FOUR TO SIX**

**INGREDIENTS**

4 EGG YOLKS

5ml|1 tsp CORNFLOUR (CORNSTARCH)

175g|6oz| scant 1 cup GRANULATED (WHITE) SUGAR

300ml|½ pint|1¼ cups SEMI-SKIMMED (LOW-FAT) MILK

150g|5oz DARK (BITTERSWEET) CHOCOLATE, broken into squares

115g|4oz|1 cup HAZELNUTS

60ml|4 tbsp WATER

300ml|½ pint|1¼ cups WHIPPING CREAM

**1** Put the egg yolks in a bowl and add the cornflour, with half the sugar. Whisk until thick and foamy. Bring the milk just to the boil in a heavy pan then gradually pour it on to the yolk mixture, whisking constantly. Scrape back into the pan and cook over a gentle heat, stirring constantly, until the custard has thickened and is smooth.

**2** Take the pan off the heat and stir the chocolate into the hot custard, a few squares at a time. Cool, then chill. Brush a baking sheet with oil and set it aside.

**3** Meanwhile put the hazelnuts, remaining sugar and measured water in a large, heavy frying pan. Place over a gentle heat and heat without stirring until the sugar has dissolved.

**4** Increase the heat slightly and cook until the syrup surrounding the nuts has turned pale golden. Quickly pour the mixture on to the oiled baking sheet and leave until the praline cools and hardens.

**5 BY HAND:** Whip the cream until it has thickened but still soft enough to fall from a spoon. Fold it into the custard and pour the mixture into a freezerproof container. Freeze for 4 hours, beating once with a fork or in a food processor to break up the ice crystals.

**USING AN ICE CREAM MAKER:** Pour the chocolate custard into the ice cream maker and add the cream. Churn for 25 minutes until thick and firm enough to scoop.

**6** Break the praline into pieces. Reserve a few pieces for decoration and finely chop the rest.

**7 BY HAND:** Beat it once more, then fold in the chopped praline. Freeze for 2–3 hours or until firm.

**USING AN ICE CREAM MAKER:** Scrape the ice cream into a tub and stir in the praline. Freeze for 2–3 hours or until firm enough to scoop.

**8** Scoop on to plates and decorate with the reserved praline.

# Triple Chocolate Terrine

*This variation on the popular Neapolitan layered ice cream is made with smooth, dark,*

*milk and white chocolate. Serve it in slices, sandwiched between rectangular wafer biscuits*

*or in a pool of warm dark chocolate sauce.*

**SERVES EIGHT TO TEN**

**INGREDIENTS**

6 EGG YOLKS

115g | 4oz | ½ cup CASTER
(SUPERFINE) SUGAR

5ml | 1 tsp CORNFLOUR
(CORNSTARCH)

450ml | ¾ pint | scant 2 cups
SEMI-SKIMMED (LOW-FAT) MILK

115g | 4oz DARK (BITTERSWEET)
CHOCOLATE, broken into squares

115g | 4oz MILK CHOCOLATE,
broken into squares

115g | 4oz WHITE CHOCOLATE,
broken into squares

2.5ml | ½ tsp NATURAL
VANILLA EXTRACT

450ml | ¾ pint | scant 2 cups
WHIPPING CREAM

**1** Whisk the egg yolks, sugar and cornflour in a bowl until thick and foamy. Pour the milk into a pan and bring it to the boil. Gradually pour it on to the yolk mixture, whisking constantly, then return the mixture to the pan and cook over a gentle heat, stirring until the custard thickens and is smooth.

**2** Divide the custard equally among three bowls of equal size. Add the dark chocolate to one bowl, the milk chocolate to another and the white chocolate and vanilla extract to the third.

**3** Stir with separate spoons until the chocolate has melted. Cool, then chill. Line a 25 x 7.5 x 7.5cm | 10 x 3 x 3in terrine or loaf tin (pan) with clear film (plastic wrap).

**4 BY HAND:** Whip the cream until it has just thickened but still falls from a spoon, divide among the bowls and fold into the custard. Pour each flavour into a separate tub or similar freezerproof container and freeze for 3–4 hours until thickened. Beat with a fork or electric mixer until smooth.

**USING AN ICE CREAM MAKER:** Stir a third of the cream into each bowl, then churn the milk chocolate custard mixture until thick. Return the bowls of flavoured custard and cream to the refrigerator.

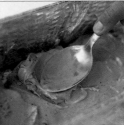

**5 BY HAND:** Spoon the milk chocolate ice cream into the lined pan, level the surface using the back of a spoon and freeze until firm. Spoon the white chocolate ice cream into the pan, level the surface and freeze until firm. Repeat the process with the dark chocolate ice cream, making sure the surface is smooth and level.

**USING AN ICE CREAM MAKER:** Churn the white chocolate ice cream until thick and smooth then spoon it into the pan. Level the surface and freeze until firm. Continue in the same way with the white chocolate and, finally, with the dark chocolate

**6** Cover the terrine with clear film, then freeze it overnight. To serve, remove the clear film cover, then invert on to a plate. Peel off the clear film and serve in slices.

**COOK'S TIP** *Make sure each layer of ice cream is firm before adding another or the layers may merge. If you have made the ice cream by hand, the dark (bittersweet) chocolate layer may need to be softened at room temperature before spreading.*

# Chunky Chocolate Ice Cream

*The three different chocolates in this decadent ice cream make it so delectable that it will rapidly disappear unless you hide it at the back of the freezer.*

**SERVES FOUR TO SIX**

**INGREDIENTS**

4 EGG YOLKS

75g | 3oz | 6 tbsp CASTER (SUPERFINE) SUGAR

5ml | 1 tsp CORNFLOUR (CORNSTARCH)

300ml | ½ pint | 1¼ cups SEMI-SKIMMED (LOW-FAT) MILK

200g | 7oz MILK CHOCOLATE

50g | 2oz DARK (BITTERSWEET) CHOCOLATE, plus extra, to decorate

50g | 2oz WHITE CHOCOLATE

300ml | ½ pint | 1¼ cups WHIPPING CREAM

**1** Whisk the egg yolks, caster sugar and cornflour in a bowl until the mixture is thick and foamy. Pour the milk into a large, heavy pan. Heat the milk and bring it just to the boil, then gradually pour it on to the egg yolk mixture, whisking constantly.

**2** Return the custard mixture to the pan and cook over a gentle heat, stirring constantly with a wooden spoon until the custard thickens and is smooth.

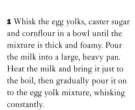

**3** Pour the custard back into the bowl. Break 150g | 5oz of the milk chocolate into squares, stir these into the hot custard, then cover closely. Leave to cool, then chill. Chop the remaining milk, dark and white chocolate finely and reserve to use as decoration.

**4 BY HAND:** Whip the cream until it has thickened but is still soft enough to fall from a spoon.

**USING AN ICE CREAM MAKER:** Mix the chocolate custard and the whipping cream and churn for 25–30 minutes until thick.

**5 BY HAND:** Fold the whipped cream into the custard, pour into a plastic tub or similar freezerproof container and freeze for 4 hours, beating once with a fork, electric whisk or in a food processor.

**USING AN ICE CREAM MAKER:** Scoop the churned ice cream out of the machine and into a plastic tub.

**6 BY HAND:** Beat the ice cream one more time. Fold in the pieces of chocolate and freeze for at least 2–3 hours, or until firm enough to scoop. Decorate with more pieces of chocolate.

**USING AN ICE CREAM MAKER:** Fold in the pieces of chocolate and freeze for 2–3 hours until firm enough to scoop. Decorate with more pieces of chocolate.

**COOK'S TIP** *For maximum flavour, use good quality Belgian chocolate or your favourite chocolate bar; avoid using dark (bittersweet), milk or white cake covering.*

# Chocolate Ripple Ice Cream

**SERVES FOUR TO SIX**

**INGREDIENTS**

4 EGG YOLKS

75g | 3oz | 6 tbsp CASTER
(SUPERFINE) SUGAR

5ml | 1 tsp CORNFLOUR
(CORNSTARCH)

300ml | ½ pint | 1¼ cups
SEMI-SKIMMED
(LOW-FAT) MILK

250g | 9oz DARK (BITTERSWEET)
CHOCOLATE, broken into squares

25g | 1oz | 2 tbsp BUTTER, diced

30ml | 2 tbsp GOLDEN
(LIGHT CORN) SYRUP

90ml | 6 tbsp SINGLE (LIGHT)
CREAM or CREAM and
MILK MIXED

300ml | ½ pint | 1¼ cups
WHIPPING CREAM

WAFER BISCUITS, to serve

*This creamy, dark chocolate ice cream, unevenly rippled with wonderful swirls of rich chocolate sauce, will stay deliciously soft even after freezing. Not that it will remain in the freezer for long!*

**1** Put the egg yolks, sugar and cornflour in a bowl and whisk until thick and foamy. Pour the milk into a pan, bring it just to the boil, then gradually pour it on to the yolk mixture, whisking constantly.

**2** Return the mixture to the pan and cook over a gentle heat, stirring until the custard thickens and is smooth. Pour it back into the bowl and stir in 150g | 5oz of the chocolate until melted. Cover and leave it to cool, then chill.

**3** Put the remaining chocolate into a pan and add the butter. Spoon in the golden syrup. Heat gently, stirring, until the chocolate and butter have melted.

**4** Stir in the single cream or cream and milk mixture. Heat gently, stirring, until smooth then leave the chocolate sauce to cool.

**5 BY HAND:** Whip the cream until it has thickened, but is still soft enough to fall from a spoon. Fold it into the custard, pour into a plastic tub or similar freezerproof container and freeze for 5 hours until thick, beating once with a fork or electric whisk or in a food processor. Beat the ice cream in the tub one more time.

**USING AN ICE CREAM MAKER:** Stir the cream into the custard and churn the mixture for 20–25 minutes until thick.

**6** Add alternate spoonfuls of ice cream and chocolate sauce to a 1.5 litre | 2½ pint | 6 cup plastic container. Freeze for 5–6 hours until firm. Serve with wafers.

# Chocolate and Brandy Parfait

*This parfait is traditionally made with a mixture of chocolate and coffee, but here it is blended with cocoa powder for extra strength. Melted Belgian chocolate and a generous tot of brandy are the secret of its superb flavour.*

**SERVES SIX**

**INGREDIENTS**

45ml | 3 tbsp UNSWEETENED COCOA POWDER

60ml | 4 tbsp BOILING WATER

150g | 5oz DARK (BITTERSWEET) CHOCOLATE, broken into squares

4 EGG YOLKS

115g | 4oz | ½ cup CASTER (SUPERFINE) SUGAR

120ml | 4fl oz | ½ cup WATER

300ml | ½ pint | 1¼ cups DOUBLE (HEAVY) CREAM

60–75ml | 4–5 tbsp BRANDY

drizzled WHITE CHOCOLATE RINGS, to decorate

**1** Mix the cocoa to a paste with the boiling water. Put the chocolate into a heatproof bowl. Bring a pan of water to the boil, remove from the heat and place the bowl on top until the chocolate melts. In a separate bowl, whisk the yolks until frothy.

**2** Heat the sugar and measured water gently in a pan, stirring occasionally, until dissolved, then boil for 4–5 minutes, without stirring, until it registers 115°C | 239°F on a sugar thermometer. You can also test by dropping a little syrup into cold water. The syrup should make a soft ball.

**3** Quickly whisk the syrup into the yolks. Lift the bowl of chocolate off the pan and bring the water to a simmer. Place the bowl with the yolk mixture on top and whisk until very thick. Lift it off the pan and continue whisking until cool.

**4** Whisk in the cocoa mixture, then fold in the melted chocolate. Whip the cream lightly and fold it in, with the brandy. Pour the mixture into 6–8 freezerproof serving dishes, then freeze for 4 hours or until firm. Decorate with white chocolate rings, made by drizzling melted white chocolate on baking parchment and leaving it to set.

**COOK'S TIP** *If you are not sure whether the syrup is ready it is better to use it sooner rather than later. If it is overboiled it will set like a rock when added to the cool yolks.*

# Double White Chocolate Ice Cream

*Crunchy chunks of white chocolate are a bonus in this delicious ice cream. Serve it scooped in waffle cones dipped in dark chocolate, for a sensational treat.*

**SERVES EIGHT**

**INGREDIENTS**

4 EGG YOLKS

75g | 3oz | 6 tbsp CASTER (SUPERFINE) SUGAR

5ml | 1 tsp CORNFLOUR (CORNSTARCH)

300ml | ½ pint | 1¼ cups SEMI-SKIMMED (LOW-FAT) MILK

250g | 9oz WHITE CHOCOLATE

10ml | 2 tsp VANILLA EXTRACT

300ml | ½ pint | 1¼ cups WHIPPING CREAM

8 CHOCOLATE DIPPED CONES, to serve

**1** Whisk the egg yolks, sugar and cornflour in a bowl until the mixture is thick and foamy. Pour the milk into a heavy pan, bring it to the boil, then gradually pour it on to the yolk mixture, whisking constantly.

**2** Return the custard mixture to the pan and cook over a gentle heat, stirring constantly until the custard thickens and is smooth. Pour the hot custard back into the same bowl.

**3** Chop the white chocolate and add 150g | 5oz of the chopped white chocolate to the hot custard, with the vanilla extract. Gently stir until the chocolate has melted, leave to cool, then chill.

**4 BY HAND:** Whip the cream until it has thickened but still falls from a spoon. Fold it into the custard and pour into a plastic tub or similar freezerproof container. Freeze for 4 hours, beating once with a fork or electric whisk or in a food processor. Beat the ice cream again, then stir in the remaining chocolate and return to the freezer for 2 hours.

**USING AN ICE CREAM MAKER:** Stir the cream into the custard, then churn the mixture until thick. Add the remaining chocolate and churn for 5–10 minutes until firm. Serve in chocolate dipped cones.

**VARIATION** *If you prefer, scoop the ice cream into glass dishes and decorate with white chocolate curls or extra diced chocolate. Ice cream served this way won't go quite as far, so will only serve 4–6.*

# C 'n' C Sherbet

*This dark chocolate sherbet is a cross between a water ice and a light cream-free ice cream, and is ideal for chocoholics who are trying to count calories.*

**SERVES FOUR TO SIX**

**INGREDIENTS**

600ml | 1 pint | 2½ cups
SEMI-SKIMMED (LOW-FAT) MILK

40g | 1½oz | ⅓ cup GOOD QUALITY
UNSWEETENED COCOA POWDER
(such as VAN HOUTEN)

115g | 4oz | ½ cup CASTER
(SUPERFINE) SUGAR

5ml | 1 tsp INSTANT COFFEE GRANULES

CHOCOLATE-COVERED RAISINS,
to decorate

**1** Heat the milk in a pan. Meanwhile, put the cocoa in a bowl. Add a little of the hot milk to the cocoa and mix to a paste.

**2** Add the remaining milk to the cocoa mixture, stirring all the time, then pour the chocolate milk back into the pan. Bring to the boil, stirring continuously.

**3** Take the pan off the heat and stir in the sugar and the coffee granules. Pour into a jug (pitcher), leave to cool, then chill well.

**4 BY HAND:** Pour the mixture into a plastic tub or similar freezerproof container and freeze for 6 hours until firm, beating once or twice with a fork, electric mixer or in a food processor to break up the ice crystals. Allow to soften slightly before scooping into dishes. Sprinkle each portion with a few chocolate-covered raisins.

**ICE CREAM MAKER:** Churn the chilled mixture until very thick. Scoop into dishes. Sprinkle each portion with a few chocolate-covered raisins.

**COOK'S TIP** *Use good quality cocoa and don't overheat the milk mixture or the finished ice may taste bitter. If there are any lumps of cocoa in the milk, beat the mixture with a balloon whisk to remove them.*

# Iced Tiramisu

*This favourite Italian combination is not usually served as a frozen dessert, but it does make a marvellous ice cream. Like the more traditional version, it tastes very rich, despite the fact that virtually fat-free fromage frais is a major ingredient.*

**SERVES FOUR**

**INGREDIENTS**

150g | 5oz | ¾ cup CASTER (SUPERFINE) SUGAR

150ml | ¼ pint | ⅔ cup WATER

250g | 9oz | generous 1 cup MASCARPONE

200g | 7oz | scant 1 cup VIRTUALLY FAT-FREE FROMAGE FRAIS or CRÈME FRAÎCHE

5ml | 1 tsp NATURAL VANILLA EXTRACT

10ml | 2 tsp INSTANT COFFEE, dissolved in 30ml | 2 tbsp BOILING WATER

30ml | 2 tbsp COFFEE LIQUEUR or BRANDY

75g | 3oz SPONGE FINGER BISCUITS (COOKIES)

UNSWEETENED COCOA POWDER, for dusting

CHOCOLATE CURLS, to decorate

**1** Put 115g | 4oz | ½ cup of the sugar into a small pan. Add the water and bring to the boil, stirring until the sugar has dissolved. Leave the syrup to cool, then chill it.

**2** Put the mascarpone into a bowl. Beat it with a spoon until it is soft, then stir in the fromage frais or crème fraîche. Add the chilled sugar syrup, a little at a time, then stir in the vanilla extract.

**3 BY HAND:** Spoon the mixture into a plastic tub or similar freezerproof container and freeze for 4 hours, beating once with a fork, electric mixer or in a food processor to break up the ice crystals.

**USING AN ICE CREAM MAKER:** Churn the mascarpone mixture until it is thick but too soft to scoop.

**4** Meanwhile, put the instant coffee mixture in a small bowl, sweeten with the remaining sugar, then add the liqueur or brandy. Stir well and leave to cool.

**5** Crumble the biscuits into small pieces and toss them in the coffee mixture. If you have made the ice cream by hand, beat it again.

**6** Spoon a third of the ice cream into a 900ml | 1½ pint | 3¾ cup plastic container, spoon over half the biscuits then top with half the remaining ice cream.

**7** Sprinkle over the last of the coffee-soaked biscuits, then cover with the remaining ice cream. Freeze for 2–3 hours until firm enough to scoop. Dust with cocoa powder and spoon into glass dishes. Decorate with chocolate curls, and serve.

# Classic Coffee Ice Cream

*This bittersweet blend is a must for those who like their coffee strong and dark with just a hint of cream. When serving, decorate with the chocolate-covered coffee beans that are available from some larger supermarkets and high-class confectioners.*

**4 BY HAND:** Whip the cream until it has thickened but still falls from a spoon. Fold into the custard, add the coffee, then pour into a plastic tub or similar freezerproof container. Freeze for 6 hours until firm, beating once or twice with a fork, electric mixer or in a food processor to break up the crystals.

**ICE CREAM MAKER:** Mix the coffee and cream with the chilled custard, then churn the mixture until firm enough to scoop.

**5** Scoop the ice cream into glass dishes, sprinkle with chocolate-covered coffee beans and serve.

**SERVES FOUR TO SIX**

**INGREDIENTS**

90ml | 6 tbsp FINE FILTER COFFEE

250ml | 8fl oz | 1 cup
BOILING WATER

4 EGG YOLKS

75g | 3oz | 6 tbsp CASTER
(SUPERFINE) SUGAR

5ml | 1 tsp CORNFLOUR
(CORNSTARCH)

300ml | ½ pint | 1¼ cups
SEMI-SKIMMED (LOW-FAT) MILK

150ml | ¼ pint | ⅔ cup
DOUBLE (HEAVY) CREAM

CHOCOLATE-COVERED
COFFEE BEANS, to decorate

**1** Put the coffee in a cafetière (press pot) or jug (pitcher) and pour on the boiling water. Leave to cool, then strain and chill until required.

**2** Whisk the egg yolks, caster sugar and cornflour in a bowl until the mixture is thick and foamy. Pour the milk into a heavy pan, bring to the boil, then gradually pour on to the yolk mixture, whisking constantly.

**3** Return the mixture to the pan and cook over a gentle heat, stirring all the time until the custard thickens and is smooth. Pour it back into the bowl and cover closely with clear film (plastic wrap). Cool, then chill.

**COOK'S TIP** *If you only have coffee beans, put 50g | 2oz | ¼ cup in a mortar and crush with a pestle. Bring 300ml | ½ pint | 1¼ cups semi-skimmed (low-fat) milk to the boil, and infuse crushed beans for 15 minutes. Strain and use the flavoured milk to make the custard.*

# Coffee Toffee Swirl

*A wonderful combination of creamy vanilla, marbled with coffee-flavoured toffee. Serve on its own or as a sundae with classic coffee and chocolate ice cream.*

**SERVES FOUR TO SIX**

**INGREDIENTS**

**For the toffee sauce**

10ml/2 tsp CORNFLOUR (CORNSTARCH)

170g | 5¾oz can EVAPORATED MILK

75g | 3oz | 6 tbsp MUSCOVADO (MOLASSES) SUGAR

20ml | 4 tsp INSTANT COFFEE GRANULES

15ml | 1tbsp BOILING WATER

**For the ice cream**

4 EGG YOLKS

75g | 3oz | 6 tbsp CASTER (SUPERFINE) SUGAR

5ml | 1 tsp CORNFLOUR (CORNSTARCH)

300ml | ½ pint | 1¼ cups SEMI-SKIMMED (LOW-FAT) MILK

5ml | 1tsp VANILLA EXTRACT

300ml | ½ pint | 1¼ cups WHIPPING CREAM

**COOK'S TIP** *If the sauce is too thick to drizzle, gently warm the base of the pan for a few seconds, stirring well.*

**VARIATION** *The sauce is also delicious drizzled over plain vanilla ice cream.*

**1** To make the sauce, put cornflour and a little evaporated milk in a small, heavy pan and mix to a smooth paste. Add the sugar and remaining evaporated milk. Cook over a gentle heat, stirring until sugar has dissolved, then increase the heat and cook, stirring continuously, until slightly thickened and just beginning to darken in colour.

**2** Take the pan off the heat. Mix the coffee with the boiling water and stir into the sauce. Cool the sauce quickly by plunging the base of the pan into cold water.

**3** Whisk the egg yolks, sugar and cornflour together until thick and foaming. Bring milk just to the boil in a heavy pan then gradually whisk into the yolk mixture. Return to the pan and cook over a gentle heat, stirring continuously until thickened and smooth. Pour back into the bowl, stir in vanilla and leave to cool.

**4 BY HAND:** Whip the cream until thickened but still soft enough to fall from a spoon. Fold into custard then pour into a plastic container and freeze for 4 hours, beating once, halfway through, with a fork, electric whisk or food processor.

**USING AN ICE CREAM MAKER:** Mix the custard and cream together and churn until thick but not firm enough to scoop.

**5 BY HAND:** Beat the ice cream again to break up any ice crystals.

**USING AN ICE CREAM MAKER:** Transfer the semi-frozen churned ice cream to a plastic container.

**6** Beat the toffee sauce well and drizzle it thickly over the ice cream. Marble together by roughly running a knife through the mixture. Cover and freeze the ice cream for 4-5 hours until it is firm enough to scoop. Serve in scoops in bowls or plates.

# classic fruit & nut ice creams

From classic fruit-flavoured ice creams to those speckled with chopped toasted nuts, this chapter imaginatively introduces the most widely used ice cream flavours. Fresh fruit purées, liqueured dried fruits and satisfying nuts transform a basic ice cream into something very special.

# Simple Strawberry Ice Cream

*Capture the essence of childhood summers with this easy-to-make ice cream.*
*Whipping cream is better than double cream for this recipe as*
*it doesn't overwhelm the taste of the fresh fruit.*

### SERVES FOUR TO SIX

### INGREDIENTS

500g | 1¼lb | 4 cups
STRAWBERRIES, hulled

50g | 2oz | ½ cup ICING
(CONFECTIONERS') SUGAR

juice of ½ LEMON

300ml | ½ pint | 1¼ cups
WHIPPING CREAM

extra STRAWBERRIES,
to decorate

**1** Purée the strawberries in a food processor or blender until smooth then add the icing sugar and lemon juice and process again to mix. Strain the purée into a bowl. Chill until very cold.

**2 BY HAND:** Whip the cream until it is just thickened but still falls from a spoon. Fold into the purée, then pour into a plastic tub or similar freezerproof container. Freeze for 6 hours until firm, beating twice with a fork, electric whisk or in a food processor to break up the ice crystals.

**USING AN ICE CREAM MAKER:**
Churn the purée until mushy, then pour in the cream and churn until thick enough to scoop. Scoop into dishes and decorate with a few extra strawberries.

**COOK'S TIP** *If possible, taste the strawberries before buying them. Halve large strawberries for decoration.*

**VARIATION** *Raspberry or any other berry fruit can be used to make this ice cream, in the same way as strawberry.*

# Gooseberry and Clotted Cream Ice Cream

*Often a rather neglected fruit, conjuring up images of the tired-looking crumble that used to be served at school or in the works canteen. This indulgent ice cream puts gooseberries in a totally different class. Its delicious, slightly tart flavour goes particularly well with tiny, melt-in-the-mouth meringues.*

## SERVES FOUR TO SIX

### INGREDIENTS

500g | 1¼lb | 4 cups GOOSEBERRIES, topped and tailed

60ml | 4 tbsp WATER

75g | 3oz | 6 tbsp CASTER (SUPERFINE) SUGAR

150ml | ¼ pint | ⅔ cup WHIPPING CREAM

a few drops of GREEN FOOD COLOURING (optional)

120ml | 4fl oz | ½ cup CLOTTED CREAM

FRESH MINT SPRIGS, to decorate

MERINGUES, to serve

**1** Put the gooseberries in a large pan and add the water and sugar. Cover and simmer for 10 minutes or until soft. Transfer the mixture into a food processor or blender and process to a smooth purée. Strain the purée over a bowl. Cool, then chill.

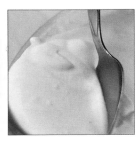

**2 BY HAND:** Chill the purée in a plastic tub or similar container. Whip the cream until it is thick but still falls from a spoon. Fold into the purée with the green food colouring, if using. Freeze for 2 hours, then beat with a fork, electric mixer or in a food processor, to break up. Return to the freezer for 2 hours.

**3 BY HAND:** Beat the ice cream again, then fold in the clotted cream. Freeze for 2–3 hours.

**USING AN ICE CREAM MAKER:** Mix the chilled purée with the whipping cream, add a few drops of green food colouring if using and churn until thickened and semi-frozen. Add the clotted cream and continue to churn until thick enough to scoop.

**4** To serve, scoop the ice cream into dishes or small plates, decorate with fresh mint sprigs and add a few small meringues to each serving.

**COOK'S TIP** *Just a small amount of clotted cream adds a surprising richness to this simple ice cream. If the gooseberry purée is very tart, you can add extra sugar when mixing in the whipping cream.*

# Blackberry Ice Cream

*There could scarcely be fewer ingredients in this delicious, vibrant ice cream. If you make the ice cream in a machine, don't be tempted to add the cream with the fruit or the mixture will become buttery by the time it has been churned and is stiff enough to scoop.*

**SERVES FOUR TO SIX**

**INGREDIENTS**

500g | 1¼lb | 5 cups BLACKBERRIES, hulled, plus extra, to decorate

75g | 3oz | 6 tbsp CASTER (SUPERFINE) SUGAR

30ml | 2 tbsp WATER

300ml | ½ pint | 1¼ cups WHIPPING CREAM

CRISP DESSERT BISCUITS (COOKIES), to serve

**1** Put the blackberries into a pan, and add the sugar and water. Cover and simmer for 5 minutes until just soft.

**2** Strain the fruit over a bowl and press it through the mesh, using the back of a wooden spoon. Leave to cool, then chill.

**3** BY HAND: Whip the cream until it is just thick but still soft enough to fall from a spoon, then mix it with the chilled fruit purée. Pour the mixture into a plastic tub or similar freezerproof container and freeze for 2 hours.

**USING AN ICE CREAM MAKER:**
Churn the chilled purée for 10–15 minutes until it is thick, then gradually pour in the cream. There is no need to whip the cream first.

**4** BY HAND: Mash the mixture with a fork, or beat it in a food processor to break up the ice crystals. Return it to the freezer for 4 hours more, beating the mixture again after 2 hours.

**USING AN ICE CREAM MAKER:**
Continue to churn the ice cream until it is firm enough to scoop.

**5** Scoop into dishes and decorate with extra blackberries. Serve with crisp dessert biscuits.

**VARIATION** *Frozen blackberries can be used for the purée. You will need to increase the cooking time to 10 minutes and stir occasionally. Blackcurrants can be used instead of blackberries. A combination of blackberries and peeled and sliced cooking apples also works well.*

# Banana and Toffee Ice Cream

*The addition of sweetened condensed milk helps to bring out the natural flavour of the bananas and, surprisingly, the ice cream is not excessively sweet.*

**SERVES FOUR TO SIX**

**INGREDIENTS**

3 RIPE BANANAS

juice of 1 LEMON

370g | 12½oz can SWEETENED CONDENSED MILK

150ml | ¼ pint | ⅔ cup WHIPPING CREAM

150g | 5oz TOFFEES

chopped TOFFEES, to decorate

**1** Process the bananas to a purée in a food processor or blender, then add the lemon juice and process briefly to mix. Scrape the purée into a plastic tub or similar freezerproof container.

**2** Pour in the condensed milk, stirring with a metal spoon, then add the cream. Mix well, cover and freeze for 4 hours or until mushy.

**3** Unwrap the toffees and chop them finely, using a sharp knife. If this proves difficult, put them in a double plastic bag and hit them with a rolling pin.

**4** Beat the semi-frozen ice cream with a fork or electric mixer to break up the ice crystals, then stir in the toffees. Return the ice cream to the freezer for 3–5 hours or until firm. Scoop on to a plate or into a bowl and decorate with chopped toffees. Serve at once.

**COOK'S TIP** *Because of the consistency of the sweetened condensed milk this ice cream takes a long time to freeze and is best made by hand rather than by machine. To reduce the initial freezing time, start chilling the mixture in a stainless steel roasting pan, transferring to a plastic tub only after adding the toffees. If you are making this ice cream for small children, you may prefer to leave the toffees out or use chopped chocolate instead.*

# Apricot and Amaretti Ice Cream

*Prolong the very short season of fresh apricots by transforming them into this superb ice cream with crushed amaretti biscuits and whipped cream.*

**SERVES FOUR TO SIX**

**INGREDIENTS**

500g | 1¼lb FRESH APRICOTS, halved and stoned

juice of 1 ORANGE

50g | 2oz | ¼ cup CASTER (SUPERFINE) SUGAR

300ml | ½ pint | 1¼ cups WHIPPING CREAM

50g | 2oz AMARETTI BISCUITS (COOKIES)

**1** Put the apricots, orange juice and sugar in a pan. Cover and simmer for 5 minutes until the fruit is tender. Leave to cool.

**2** Lift out one third of the fruit and set it aside on a plate. Transfer the remaining contents of the pan into a food processor or blender and process to a smooth purée.

**3 BY HAND:** Whip the cream until it is just thick but still soft enough to fall from a spoon. Gradually add the fruit purée, folding it into the mixture. Pour into a plastic tub or similar freezerproof container and freeze for 4 hours, beating once with a fork, electric mixer or in a food processor.

**USING AN ICE CREAM MAKER:** Churn the apricot purée until it is slushy, then gradually add the cream. Continue to churn until the ice cream is thick, but not firm enough to scoop.

**4 BY HAND:** Beat for a second time. Crumble in the amaretti biscuits.

**USING AN ICE CREAM MAKER:** Scrape the ice cream into a tub. Crumble in the amaretti biscuits.

**5** Add the reserved apricots and gently fold these ingredients into the ice cream. Freeze for 2–3 hours or until firm enough to scoop.

**COOK'S TIP** *Chill the fruit purée if you have time; this will speed up the churning or freezing process. If you have some amaretto liqueur, fold in 45ml/3 tbsp with the biscuits.*

# Peach and Cardamom Yogurt Ice

**SERVES FOUR**

**INGREDIENTS**

8 CARDAMOM PODS

6 PEACHES,
total weight about 500g | 1¼lb,
halved, and stoned (pitted)

75g | 3oz | 6 tbsp CASTER
(SUPERFINE) SUGAR

30ml | 2 tbsp WATER

200ml | 7fl oz | scant 1 cup
BIO NATURAL (PLAIN) YOGURT

*The velvety texture of this smooth peach ice cream spiced with cardamom suggests it is made with cream, but the secret ingredient is actually natural yogurt; great for those watching their waistline.*

**1** Put the cardamom pods on a board and crush them with the bottom of a ramekin, or in a pestle and mortar.

**2** Chop the peaches roughly and put them in a pan. Add the crushed cardamom pods, with their black seeds, and the sugar and water. Cover and simmer for 10 minutes or until the fruit is tender. Leave to cool.

**3** Transfer the peach mixture into a food processor or blender, process until smooth, then strain the mixture over a bowl.

**4 BY HAND:** Add the yogurt to the strained purée and mix together in the bowl.

**5 BY HAND:** Pour into a plastic tub and freeze for 5–6 hours until firm, beating once or twice with a fork, electric whisk or in a processor to break up the ice crystals.

**USING AN ICE CREAM MAKER:** Churn the purée until thick, then scrape it into a plastic tub or similar container. Stir in the yogurt and freeze until firm enough to hold a scoop shape.

**6** Scoop the ice cream on to a large platter, and serve at once.

**COOK'S TIP** *Use bio natural (plain) yogurt for its extra mild taste. Greek (US strained plain) yogurt or ordinary natural yogurt are both sharper and more acidic and tend to overwhelm the delicate taste of the peaches. Use a melon baller to make miniature scoops in individual dishes.*

# Apricot Parfait

*Pots of creamy, delicately flavoured French-style ice cream conceal a hidden layer of poached apricots. If you don't have time to make the caramel, top each dessert with a spoonful of extra thick double cream and some thin strips of extra apricot.*

**SERVES SIX**

**INGREDIENTS**

200g | 7oz | scant 1 cup
DRIED APRICOTS

300ml | ½ pint | 1¼ cups APPLE JUICE

75g | 3oz | 6 tbsp
DEMERARA (RAW) SUGAR

4 EGG YOLKS

115g | 4oz | generous ½ cup CASTER
(SUPERFINE) SUGAR

120ml | 4fl oz | ½ cup WATER

150ml | ¼ pint | ⅔ cup
WHIPPING CREAM

grated rind and juice of ½ LEMON

**1** Put the apricots in a pan. Pour over the apple juice and soak for 3–4 hours. Meanwhile, line a baking sheet with foil. Using an inverted ramekin as a guide, draw six circles on the foil. Brush with a little oil.

**2** Preheat the grill (broiler) to its lowest setting. Sprinkle the demerara sugar into the marked circles. Place under the grill, on its lowest shelf setting and leave for 3–4 minutes until the sugar has dissolved and caramelized. Leave to cool and harden.

**3** Simmer the soaked apricots for 10 minutes until they are soft and plump. Leave to cool, then lift out nine apricots with a slotted spoon.

**4** Chop these apricots roughly and divide them among six freezerproof ramekins. Purée the remaining apricots and juice until smooth.

**5** Whisk the egg yolks in a large, heatproof bowl until frothy. Put the caster sugar and water in a pan, heat gently until the sugar has dissolved, then boil for 4–5 minutes, until the syrup registers 115°C | 239°F on a sugar thermometer. Alternatively, test by dropping a little of the syrup into a cup of cold water. Pour the water away. The syrup should shape into a soft ball.

**6** Quickly whisk the hot syrup into the egg yolks. Put the bowl over a large pan of simmering water and whisk the mixture until it is thick.

**7** Lift the bowl off the pan and continue whisking the mixture until it is cool and the whisk leaves a trail when lifted.

**8** Whip the cream lightly, fold it into the yolk mixture, then gently fold in the apricot purée, with the lemon rind and juice.

**9** Pour the parfait mixture into the six ramekins and freeze for 4 hours until firm. When ready to serve, roughly break the caramelized sugar into chunky pieces and use to decorate the ices.

# Rum and Raisin Ice Cream

*An old favourite with fathers and grandfathers. For children this ice cream always seemed so much more sophisticated than mere vanilla. The longer you can leave the raisins to soak in the rum the stronger the flavour will be.*

**SERVES FOUR TO SIX**

**INGREDIENTS**

150g | 5oz | scant 1 cup
LARGE RAISINS

60ml | 4 tbsp DARK RUM

4 EGG YOLKS

75g | 3oz | 6 tbsp LIGHT
MUSCOVADO (BROWN) SUGAR

5ml | 1 tsp CORNFLOUR
(CORNSTARCH)

300ml | ½ pint | 1¼ cups
SEMI-SKIMMED (LOW-FAT) MILK

300ml | ½ pint | 1¼ cups
WHIPPING CREAM

DESSERT BISCUITS (COOKIES) or
ICE CREAM CONES, to serve

**4 BY HAND:** Whip the cream until it is just thick but still falls from a spoon. Fold it into the custard and pour the mixture into a plastic tub or similar freezerproof container. Freeze for 4 hours, beating once with a fork, electric mixer or in a food processor. Then beat again.

**USING AN ICE CREAM MAKER:** Pour the cream into the custard, then churn until thick. Transfer to a plastic container.

**1** Put the raisins in a bowl, add the rum and mix well. Cover and leave to soak for 3–4 hours or overnight if possible.

**2** Whisk the egg yolks, muscovado sugar and cornflour in a large bowl until the mixture is thick and foamy. Pour the milk into a heavy pan, and bring it to just below boiling point.

**3** Gradually whisk the milk into the eggs, then pour the mixture back into the pan. Cook over a gentle heat, stirring constantly until the custard thickens and is smooth. Take off the heat and leave to cool.

**5** Fold the soaked raisins into the ice cream, cover and freeze for 2–3 hours or until firm enough to scoop. Serve in bowls or tall glasses with dessert biscuits, or serve simply in ice cream cones.

**COOK'S TIP** *If you scoop it into cones, the ice cream will serve 6–8 people. If you haven't any dark rum, white rum, brandy or even whisky can be used instead.*

# Rhubarb and Ginger Ice Cream

*A fruit so highly favoured by Queen Victoria; two varieties of rhubarb were grown and named after her and her consort Prince Albert. The classic combination of gently poached rhubarb and chopped ginger is brought up to date by blending it with mascarpone to make this pretty blush-pink ice cream.*

### SERVES FOUR TO SIX

#### INGREDIENTS

5 pieces of PRESERVED
STEM GINGER

450g | 1lb trimmed
RHUBARB, sliced

115g | 4oz | ½ cup CASTER
(SUPERFINE) SUGAR

30ml | 2 tbsp WATER

150g | 5oz | ⅔ cup MASCARPONE

150ml | ¼ pint | ⅔ cup
WHIPPING CREAM

WAFER CUPS,
to serve (optional)

**1** Using a sharp knife, roughly chop the stem ginger and set it aside. Put the rhubarb slices into a pan and add the sugar and water. Cover and simmer for 5 minutes until the rhubarb is just tender and still bright pink.

**2** Transfer the mixture into a food processor or blender, process until smooth, then leave to cool. Chill if time permits.

**3 BY HAND:** Mix together the mascarpone, cream and ginger with the rhubarb purée.

**USING AN ICE CREAM MAKER:** Churn the rhubarb purée for 15–20 minutes until it is thick.

**4 BY HAND:** Pour the mixture into a plastic tub or similar freezerproof container and freeze for 6 hours or until firm, beating once or twice during the freezing time to break up the ice crystals.

**USNG AN ICE CREAM MAKER:** Put the mascarpone into a bowl, soften it with a wooden spoon, then gradually beat in the cream. Add the chopped ginger, then transfer to the ice cream maker and churn until the ice cream is firm. Serve as scoops in bowls or wafer baskets.

# Nougat Ice Cream

*Taking its inspiration from the delicious sweetmeats served in France as one of the 13 traditional Christmas desserts, this is a superb ice cream, especially when served with iced liqueurs as iced petits fours.*

**SERVES SIX TO EIGHT**

**INGREDIENTS**

50g | 2oz | ½ cup HAZELNUTS

50g | 2oz | ½ cup PISTACHIO NUTS

50g | 2oz | ⅓ cup CANDIED PEEL, in large pieces

6–8 sheets RICE PAPER

3 EGG WHITES

150g | 5oz | 1¼ cups ICING (CONFECTIONERS') SUGAR, sifted

300ml | ½ pint | 1¼ cups DOUBLE (HEAVY) CREAM

10ml | 2 tsp ORANGE FLOWER WATER

**1** Spread out the hazelnuts on a baking sheet and brown them lightly under a hot grill (broiler). Mix them with the pistachios and chop all the nuts roughly. Slice the candied peel into bitesize slivers.

**2** Line the base and sides of a 28 x 18 x 4cm | 11 x 7 x 1½in cake tin (pan) with clear film (plastic wrap), then with four of the pieces of rice paper, folding the paper into the corners and overlapping the sheets slightly.

**3** Put the egg whites and icing sugar into a large, heatproof bowl. Place it over a pan of simmering water and whisk for 5 minutes or until the meringue is very thick.

**4** Take off the heat and continue whisking until soft peaks form. In a separate bowl, whip the cream and orange flower water lightly, then fold in the meringue.

**5** Spoon half the meringue mixture into the lined cake tin, easing it into the corners.

**6** Sprinkle the meringue with half the nuts and candied peel. Cover with the remaining meringue mixture.

**7** Sprinkle with the remaining nuts and fruit. Cover with two more sheets of rice paper and freeze for at least 6 hours or overnight until completely firm.

**8** Carefully turn the ice cream out of the tin and peel off the clear film. If the base of the ice cream is soft, cover it with the remaining two sheets of rice paper, pressing it on to the ice cream so that it sticks. Cut into small squares or triangles, arrange on individual plates and serve.

**VARIATION** *Use toasted blanched almonds instead of pistachios if you prefer. The meringue can be flavoured with rose water or grated lemon rind instead of orange flower water.*

# Maple and Pecan Nut Ice Cream

*This all-American ice cream is even more delicious when it is served with*
*extra maple syrup and topped with whole pecan nuts.*

**SERVES FOUR TO SIX**

**INGREDIENTS**

115g|4oz|1 cup PECAN NUTS

4 EGG YOLKS

50g|2oz|¼ cup CASTER
(SUPERFINE) SUGAR

5ml|1 tsp CORNFLOUR
(CORNSTARCH)

300ml|½ pint|1¼ cups
SEMI-SKIMMED (LOW-FAT) MILK

60ml|4 tbsp MAPLE SYRUP

300ml|½ pint|1¼ cups
WHIPPING CREAM

extra MAPLE SYRUP AND PECAN
NUTS, to serve

**1** Cut the pecan nuts in half lengthways, spread them out on a baking sheet and grill (broil) them under medium heat for 2–3 minutes until lightly browned. Remove from the heat and leave to cool.

**2** Place the egg yolks, sugar and cornflour into a bowl and whisk until thick and foamy. Pour the milk into a heavy pan, bring to the boil, then gradually whisk it into the yolk mixture.

**3** Return the mixture to the pan and cook over a gentle heat, stirring constantly until the custard thickens and is smooth.

**4** Pour the custard back into the bowl, and stir in the maple syrup. Leave to cool, then chill.

**5 BY HAND:** Whip the cream until it is thick but still falls from a spoon. Fold it into the custard and pour into a plastic tub or similar freezerproof container. Freeze for 4 hours, beating once with a fork, electric mixer or in a food processor to break up the ice crystals. After this time, beat it again.

**USING AN ICE CREAM MAKER:** Stir the cream into the custard, then churn the mixture until thick. Scrape into a plastic container.

**6** Fold in the nuts. Freeze for 2–3 hours until firm enough to scoop into dishes. Pour extra maple syrup over each portion and top with extra pecan nuts.

**COOK'S TIP** *Avoid "maple-flavoured" syrup, the flavour is harsher and tends to taste rather synthetic. Look out for "pure maple syrup" on the label.*

# Rocky Road Ice Cream

*This American classic ice cream is a mouthwatering combination of roughly crushed praline, rich vanilla custard and whipping cream.*

**SERVES FOUR TO SIX**

**INGREDIENTS**

4 EGG YOLKS

5ml | 1 tsp CORNFLOUR (CORNSTARCH)

225g | 8oz | generous 1 cup GRANULATED (WHITE) SUGAR

300ml | ½ pint | 1¼ cups SEMI-SKIMMED (LOW-FAT) MILK

10ml | 2 tsp NATURAL VANILLA EXTRACT

OIL, for greasing

50g | 2oz | ½ cup MACADAMIA NUTS

50g | 2oz | ½ cup HAZELNUTS

50g | 2oz | ½ cup FLAKED (SLICED) ALMONDS

60ml | 4 tbsp WATER

300ml | ½ pint | 1¼ cups WHIPPING CREAM

**1** Put the egg yolks in a bowl and stir in the cornflour, with 75g | 3oz | 6 tbsp of the sugar. Whisk until the mixture has turned thick and foamy. Pour the milk into a heavy pan, bring it to the boil, then gradually whisk it into the yolk mixture in the bowl.

**2** Return the mixture to the pan. Cook over a gentle heat, stirring constantly until the custard thickens and is smooth. Pour it back into the bowl and stir in the natural vanilla extract. Leave to cool, then chill.

**3** Grease a large baking sheet with oil. Put the remaining sugar in a large, heavy frying pan, sprinkle the nuts on top and pour over the water. Heat gently, without stirring, until the sugar has dissolved completely, then boil the syrup for 3–5 minutes until it is just beginning to turn golden.

**4** Quickly pour the nut mixture on to the oiled baking sheet and leave to cool and harden.

**5 BY HAND:** Whip the cream until it is thick but still falls from a spoon. Fold it into the custard and pour into a plastic tub or similar freezerproof container. Freeze for 4 hours, beating once with a fork, electric mixer or in a food processor and then beat it again.

**USING AN ICE CREAM MAKER:** Stir the cream into the custard and churn until stiff but too soft to scoop. Scrape into a tub.

**6** Smash the praline with a rolling pin to break off about a third. Reserve this for the decoration. Put the rest of the praline into a strong plastic bag and hit it several times with a rolling pin until it breaks into bitesize pieces.

**7** Fold the crushed praline into the ice cream and freeze it for 2–3 hours until firm. Scoop into glasses and decorate with the reserved praline, broken into large pieces.

**COOK'S TIP** *If you can't locate macadamia nuts, use extra hazelnuts. If the nuts fail to brown evenly when you are making the praline in the frying pan, don't stir the syrup. Instead, tilt the pan first one way then the other.*

# Cashew and Orange Flower Ice Cream

*Delicately perfumed with orange flower water and a little orange rind, this nutty, lightly sweetened ice cream evokes images of puddings that are popular in the Middle East.*

**SERVES FOUR TO SIX**

**INGREDIENTS**

4 EGG YOLKS

75g | 3oz | 6 tbsp CASTER (SUPERFINE) SUGAR

5ml | 1 tsp CORNFLOUR (CORNSTARCH)

300ml | ½ pint | 1¼ cups SEMI-SKIMMED (LOW-FAT) MILK

300ml | ½ pint | 1¼ cups WHIPPING CREAM

150g | 5oz | 1¼ cups CASHEW NUTS, finely chopped

15ml | 1 tbsp ORANGE FLOWER WATER

grated rind of ½ ORANGE, plus CURLS OF THINLY PARED ORANGE RIND, to decorate

**1** Whisk the egg yolks, caster sugar and cornflour in a bowl until thick and foamy. Pour the semi-skimmed milk into a heavy pan, gently bring it to the boil, then gradually whisk it into the egg yolk mixture.

**2** Return to the pan and cook over a gentle heat, stirring constantly until smooth. Pour back into the bowl. Cool, then chill.

**3** Heat the cream in a pan. When it boils, stir in the chopped cashew nuts. Leave to cool.

**4** Stir the orange flower water and grated orange rind into the chilled custard. Process the nut cream in a food processor or blender until it forms a fine paste, then stir it into the custard mixture.

**5 BY HAND:** Pour the mixture into a plastic tub or similar freezerproof container and freeze for 6 hours, beating twice with a fork or whisk with an electric mixer to break up the ice crystals.

**USING AN ICE CREAM MAKER:** Churn the mixture until it is firm enough to scoop.

**6** To serve, scoop the ice cream into dishes and decorate each portion with an orange rind curl.

**COOK'S TIP** *For a more intense flavour, roast the cashew nuts before chopping them. Thinly pare the orange rind, then wrap each strip in turn around a cocktail stick and leave it for a minute or two.*

# Pistachio Ice Cream

*This continental favourite owes its enduring popularity to its delicate pale green colour and distinctive yet subtle flavour. Buy the pistachio nuts as you need them as they quickly go stale if left in the cupboard.*

**SERVES FOUR TO SIX**

**INGREDIENTS**

4 EGG YOLKS

75g | 3oz | 6 tbsp CASTER (SUPERFINE) SUGAR

5ml | 1 tsp CORNFLOUR (CORNSTARCH)

300ml | ½ pint | 1¼ cups SEMI-SKIMMED (LOW-FAT) MILK

115g | 4oz | 1 cup PISTACHIOS, plus a few extra, to decorate

300ml | ½ pint | 1¼ cups WHIPPING CREAM

a little GREEN FOOD COLOURING

CHOCOLATE DIPPED WAFFLE CONES, to serve (optional)

**1** Place the egg yolks, sugar and cornflour in a bowl and whisk until the mixture is thick and foamy.

**2** Pour the milk into a pan, gently bring it to the boil, then gradually whisk it into the bowl containing the egg yolk mixture.

**3** Return the mixture to the pan and cook it over a gentle heat, stirring constantly until the custard thickens and is smooth. Pour it back into the bowl, set aside to cool, then chill in the refrigerator until required.

**4** Shell the pistachios and put them in a food processor or blender. Add 30ml | 2 tbsp of the cream and grind the mixture to a coarse paste.

**5** Pour the rest of the cream into a small pan. Bring it to the boil, stir in the coarsely ground pistachios, then leave to cool.

**6** Mix the chilled custard and pistachio cream together and tint the mixture delicately with a few drops of food colouring.

**7 BY HAND:** Pour the tinted custard and pistachio mixture into a plastic tub or similar freezerproof container. Freeze for 6 hours, beating once or twice with a fork or in an electric mixer to break up the ice crystals. Scoop the ice cream into cones or dishes to serve and sprinkle each portion with a few extra pistachios.

**USING AN ICE CREAM MAKER:** Churn the mixture until firm enough to scoop. Serve in cones or dishes, sprinkled with extra pistachios.

**COOK'S TIP** *If you make the ice cream by hand, it is important not to beat the frozen mixture in a food processor or the pistachios will become too finely ground. Bought waffle cones can be decorated by dipping them in melted chocolate and sprinkling them with extra chopped pistachios.*

# cream-free
# & low-fat ices

Whether for dietary reasons or simply through choice, many people do not like to indulge in rich traditional ice creams. On the following pages are some intensely flavoured desserts using low-fat and dairy-free ingredients. With recipes that range from a smooth creamy coconut ice to a refreshing orange and yogurt ice cream, there is an iced dessert to suit everyone.

# Kulfi

*This famous Indian ice cream is traditionally made by slowly boiling milk until it has reduced to about one third of the original quantity. Although you can save time by using condensed milk, nothing beats this delicious ice cream when made in the authentic manner.*

**SERVES FOUR**

**INGREDIENTS**

1.5 litres | 2½ pints | 6¼ cups
FULL-FAT (WHOLE) MILK

3 CARDAMOM PODS

25g | 1oz | 2 tbsp CASTER
(SUPERFINE) SUGAR

50g | 2oz | ½ cup PISTACHIOS,
skinned plus a few to decorate

a few PINK ROSE PETALS,
to decorate

**1** Pour the milk into a large, heavy pan. Bring to the boil, lower the heat and simmer gently for 1 hour, stirring occasionally.

**2** Put the cardamom pods in a mortar and crush them with a pestle. Add the pods and the seeds to the milk and continue to simmer for 1–1½ hours or until the milk has reduced to about 475ml | 16fl oz | 2 cups.

**3** Strain the milk into a jug (pitcher), stir in the sugar and leave to cool.

**4** Grind half the pistachios to a smooth powder in a blender, nut grinder or cleaned coffee grinder. Cut the remaining pistachios into thin slivers and set them aside for decoration. Stir the ground nuts into the milk mixture.

**5** Pour the milk and pistachio mixture into four kulfi moulds. Freeze overnight until firm.

**6** To unmould the kulfi, half fill a plastic container or bowl with very hot water, stand the moulds in the water and count to ten. Immediately lift out the moulds and invert them on a baking sheet.

**7** Transfer the ice creams to a platter or individual plates. To decorate, scatter sliced pistachios over the ice creams and then the rose petals. Serve at once.

**COOK'S TIP** *Stay in the kitchen while the milk is simmering, so that you can control the heat to keep the milk gently bubbling without boiling over. If you don't have any kulfi moulds, use lolly moulds without the tops or even disposable plastic cups. If the ices won't turn out, dip a cloth in very hot water, wring it out and place it on the tops of the moulds to soften the ice cream, or plunge the moulds back into hot water for a few more seconds.*

# Dondurma Kaymalki

*This sweet, pure white ice cream comes from the Middle East, where it is traditionally thickened with sahlab and flavoured with orange flower water and mastic, a resin used in chewing gum. As sahlab and mastic are both difficult to obtain in the West, cornflour and condensed milk have been used in their place.*

**SERVES FOUR TO SIX**

**INGREDIENTS**

45ml | 3 tbsp CORNFLOUR (CORNSTARCH)

600ml | 1 pint | 2½ cups FULL-FAT (WHOLE) MILK

213g | 7½oz can SWEETENED CONDENSED MILK

15ml | 1 tbsp CLEAR HONEY

10ml | 2 tsp ORANGE FLOWER WATER

a few SUGARED ALMONDS, to serve

**1** Put the cornflour in a pan and mix to a smooth paste with a little of the milk. Stir in the remaining milk and the condensed milk and bring the mixture to the boil, stirring until it is thick and smooth. Pour the mixture into a bowl.

**2** Stir in the honey and orange flower water. Cover with a plate to prevent the formation of a skin, leave to cool, then chill.

**3 BY HAND:** Pour the mixture into a plastic tub or similar freezerproof container and freeze for 6–8 hours, beating twice with a fork, electric mixer or in a food processor to break up the ice crystals.

**USING AN ICE CREAM MAKER:** Churn until firm enough to scoop.

**4** To serve, scoop into dishes and serve with a few sugared almonds.

**VARIATION** *Rose water can be used instead of orange flower water. If you have made the ice cream by hand, remember to transfer it to the refrigerator about half an hour before you are ready to scoop.*

# Date and Tofu Ice

*All you sceptics who claim to hate tofu, prepare to be converted by this creamy date and apple ice cream.*
*Generously spiced with cinnamon, it not only tastes good but is packed with soya protein,*
*contains no added sugar, is low in fat and free from all dairy products.*

**SERVES FOUR**

**INGREDIENTS**

250g | 9oz | 1½ cups STONED
(PITTED) DATES

600ml | 1 pint | 2½ cups APPLE JUICE

5ml | 1 tsp GROUND CINNAMON

285g | 10½oz pack CHILLED TOFU,
drained and cubed

150ml | ¼ pint | ⅔ cup
UNSWEETENED SOYA MILK

**1** Put the dates in a pan. Pour in
300ml | ½ pint | 1¼ cups of the
apple juice and leave to soak for
2 hours. Simmer for 10 minutes,
then leave to cool. Using a slotted
spoon, lift out one-quarter of the
dates, chop roughly and set aside.

**2** Purée the remaining dates in a
food processor or blender. Add the
cinnamon and process with
enough of the remaining apple
juice to make a smooth paste.

**3** Add the cubes of tofu, a few at a
time, processing after each addition.
Finally, add the remaining apple
juice and the soya milk.

**4 BY HAND:** Pour the mixture into
a plastic tub or similar freezerproof
container and freeze for 4 hours,
beating once with a fork, electric
mixer or in a food processor to
break up the ice crystals. After this
time, beat again with a fork to
ensure a smooth texture.

**USING AN ICE CREAM MAKER:** Churn
the mixture until very thick, but not
thick enough to scoop. Scrape into a
plastic tub.

**5** Stir in most of the chopped dates
and freeze for 2–3 hours until firm.

**6** Scoop into dessert glasses and
decorate with the remaining
chopped dates.

**COOK'S TIP** *As tofu is a non-dairy
product it will not blend completely, so
don't be concerned if the mixture
contains tiny flecks of tofu.*

# Coconut Ice

*Despite its creamy taste, this ice cream contains neither cream nor egg and is very refreshing. Serve it with scoops of Red Berry Sorbet.*

**SERVES FOUR TO SIX**

**INGREDIENTS**

150ml | ¼ pint | ⅔ cup WATER

115g | 4oz | ½ cup CASTER (SUPERFINE) SUGAR

2 LIMES

400ml | 14fl oz can COCONUT MILK

TOASTED COCONUT SHAVINGS, to decorate (see Cook's Tip)

**1** Put the water in a small pan. Tip in the caster sugar and bring to the boil, stirring constantly until the sugar has all dissolved. Remove the pan from the heat and leave the syrup to cool, then chill well.

**2** Grate the limes finely, taking care to avoid the bitter pith. Squeeze them and pour the juice and rind into the pan of syrup. Add the coconut milk.

**3 BY HAND:** Pour the mixture into a plastic tub or similar freezerproof container and freeze for 5–6 hours until firm, beating twice with a fork, electric whisk or in a food processor to break up the crystals. Scoop into dishes and decorate with toasted coconut shavings.

**ICE CREAM MAKER:** Churn the mixture until firm enough to scoop. Serve in dishes, decorated with the toasted coconut shavings.

**COOK'S TIP** *Use the flesh from a coconut to make a pretty decoration. Having rinsed the flesh with cold water, cut off thin slices using a swivel-bladed vegetable peeler. Toast the slices under a moderate grill (broiler) until the coconut has curled and the edges have turned golden. Cool slightly, then sprinkle the shavings over the coconut ice.*

# Banana Gelato

*This mild, creamy banana ice cream is made with soya milk, making it good for children who are lactose intolerant or allergic to dairy products.*

**SERVES FOUR TO SIX**

**INGREDIENTS**

115g | 4oz | ½ cup CASTER (SUPERFINE) SUGAR

150ml | ¼ pint | ⅔ cup WATER

1 LEMON

3 RIPE BANANAS

300ml | ½ pint | 1¼ cups UHT VANILLA-FLAVOURED SOYA DESSERT

**1** Put the sugar and water in a pan and bring to the boil, stirring until the sugar has dissolved. Set the syrup aside to cool.

**2** Squeeze the lemon. Put the bananas in a bowl and mash with a fork. Slowly add the lemon juice.

**3 BY HAND:** Stir in the cooled sugar syrup and the vanilla-flavoured soya dessert. Pour the mixture into a large plastic container and freeze for 6–7 hours until firm, beating twice during that time with a fork, electric mixer or in a food processor to break up the ice crystals. Scoop into dishes and serve.

**USING AN ICE CREAM MAKER:** Stir in the cooled sugar syrup and the soya dessert. Churn the mixture until thick, then scrape it into a freezerproof container and freeze for 3–4 hours until firm. Scoop into dishes and serve.

**COOK'S TIP** *This recipe makes 1 litre | 1¾ pints | 4 cups of frozen gelato, so if you are using an ice cream maker with only a small capacity it may be wise to churn the mixture in two batches. Check your manufacturer's handbook.*

# Honeyed Goat's Milk Gelato

*Goat's milk is more widely available than it used to be and is more easily tolerated by some individuals than cow's milk. It makes a surprisingly rich iced dessert.*

**SERVES FOUR**

**INGREDIENTS**

6 EGG YOLKS

50g | 2oz | ¼ cup CASTER (SUPERFINE) SUGAR

10ml | 2 tsp CORNFLOUR (CORNSTARCH)

600ml | 1 pint | 2½ cups GOAT'S MILK

60ml | 4 tbsp CLEAR HONEY

POMEGRANATE SEEDS, to decorate

**1** Whisk the egg yolks, sugar and cornflour in a bowl until pale and thick. Pour the goat's milk into a heavy pan, bring it to the boil, and then gradually whisk it into the bowl containing the yolk mixture.

**2** Return the custard mixture to the pan and cook over a gentle heat, stirring constantly until the custard thickens and is smooth. Pour it back into the clean bowl.

**3** Stir the honey into the milk mixture. Leave to cool, then chill.

**4 BY HAND:** Pour the mixture into a plastic tub or similar freezerproof container and freeze for 6 hours until firm enough to scoop, beating twice with a fork, electric whisk or in a food processor to break up the ice crystals.

**USING AN ICE CREAM MAKER:** Churn the chilled mixture until thick enough to scoop.

**5** To serve, scoop into dessert glasses and decorate with a few pomegranate seeds.

**COOK'S TIP** *Make sure the spoon measures are level or the honey flavour will be too dominant.*

**VARIATION** *This ice cream is also delicious with a little ginger; stir in 40g | 1½oz | ¼ cup finely chopped preserved stem ginger when the ice cream is partially frozen.*

# Raspberry Sherbet

*Traditional sherbets are made in much the same way as sorbets but with added milk. This modern low fat version is made from raspberry purée blended with sugar syrup and virtually fat free fromage frais, then flecked with crushed raspberries.*

**SERVES SIX**

**INGREDIENTS**

175g | 6oz | ¾ cup CASTER (SUPERFINE) SUGAR

150ml | ¼ pint | ⅔ cup WATER

500g | 1¼lb | 3½ cups RASPBERRIES, plus extra, to serve

500ml | 17fl oz | generous 2 cups VIRTUALLY FAT-FREE FROMAGE FRAIS or CRÈME FRAÎCHE

**1** Put the sugar and water in a small pan and bring to the boil, stirring until the sugar has dissolved. Pour into a jug (pitcher) and cool.

**2** Put 350g | 12oz | 2½ cups of the raspberries in a food processor or blender. Process to a purée, then strain over a large bowl to remove the seeds. Stir the sugar syrup into the raspberry purée and chill the mixture until it is very cold.

**3** Add the fromage frais to the purée and whisk until smooth.

**4 BY HAND:** Pour the mixture into a plastic tub or similar freezerproof container and freeze for 4 hours, beating once with a fork, electric whisk or in a food processor to break up the ice crystals. After this time, beat it again.

**USING AN ICE CREAM MAKER:** Churn the mixture until it is thick but too soft to scoop. Scrape into a freezerproof container.

**5** Crush the remaining raspberries between your fingers and add them to the partially frozen ice cream. Mix lightly then freeze for 2–3 hours until firm. Scoop the ice cream into dishes and serve with extra raspberries.

**COOK'S TIP** *If you intend to make this in an ice cream maker, check your handbook before you begin churning as this recipes makes 900ml | 1½ pints | 3¾ cups of mixture. If this is too large a quantity for your machine, make it in two batches or by hand.*

# Orange and Yogurt Ice

*Serve this refreshing low-fat yogurt ice simply, in cones, or scoop it into bought meringue baskets and decorate it with blueberries and mint for a more sophisticated treat.*

**3 BY HAND:** Spoon the yogurt into a bowl, gradually add the chilled orange juice and syrup mixture and mix well. Pour the mixture into a plastic tub. Freeze for 6 hours or until firm, beating twice with a fork or in a food processor to break up the ice crystals.

**USING AN ICE CREAM MAKER:** Churn the orange mixture until thick, but not thick enough to scoop. Switch off the machine, remove the paddle, if necessary, add the yogurt and mix well. Replace the paddle and continue to churn the ice cream for 15–20 minutes until thick. Scrape it into a plastic tub or similar freezerproof container and freeze until firm.

**4** Scoop the yogurt ice into cones or meringue nests and decorate with blueberries and mint.

**SERVES SIX**

**INGREDIENTS**

90ml | 6 tbsp WATER

10ml | 2 tsp POWDERED GELATINE

115g | 4oz | ½ cup CASTER (SUPERFINE) SUGAR

250ml | 8fl oz | 1 cup "FRESHLY SQUEEZED" ORANGE JUICE from a carton or bottle

500ml | 17fl oz | generous 2 cups BIO (PLAIN) YOGURT

CONES or MERINGUE NESTS, BLUEBERRIES and FRESH MINT SPRIGS, to serve

**1** Put 30ml | 2 tbsp of the water in a small bowl and sprinkle the powdered gelatine over the top. Set aside until spongy. Meanwhile, put the sugar in a small pan, add the remaining water and heat through gently until the sugar has dissolved completely.

**2** Take off the heat, add the gelatine and stir until dissolved. Cool, stir in the orange juice and chill for 15–30 minutes.

**COOK'S TIP** *Meringue nests are not difficult to make, but if you do not have the time, bought ones are a perfectly acceptable alternative.*

# bombes & terrines

Layered, marbled or speckled with fruit and nuts, bombes and terrines make stunning iced desserts that reveal a feast of colour and texture when cut into. Uncomplicated to assemble, but requiring plenty of freezing time, they're best made several days in advance, ready and waiting for that special occasion.

# Tropical Fruit and Ginger Bombes

*A very simple iced dessert, shaped like miniature Christmas puddings in squares of muslin. Serve with fresh tropical fruit, passion fruit sauce, or compote.*

**SERVES SIX**

**INGREDIENTS**

75g | 3oz | ½ cup DRIED MANGO, finely chopped

75g | 3oz | ½ cup DRIED PAWPAW, finely chopped

75g | 3oz | ½ cup DRIED PINEAPPLE, finely chopped

30ml | 2 tbsp GLACÉ (CANDIED) GINGER, or PRESERVED STEM GINGER, finely chopped

60ml | 4 tbsp COINTREAU or other ORANGE-FLAVOURED LIQUEUR

250g | 9oz | generous 1 cup RICOTTA CHEESE

250g | 9oz | generous 1 cup MASCARPONE CHEESE

45ml | 3 tbsp DOUBLE (HEAVY) CREAM

15ml | 1 tbsp ICING (CONFECTIONERS') SUGAR

**1** Cut six 23cm | 9in squares of muslin and set them aside. Mix the dried fruit and ginger in a bowl. Add the liqueur and leave to stand for 1–2 hours.

**2** Lightly mix the ricotta and mascarpone in a bowl until evenly mixed but not runny.

**3** Add the steeped fruits and ginger, with any remaining liqueur, to the mixture, then stir in the cream and icing sugar. Spoon one-sixth of the mixture into the middle of each muslin square.

**4** Bring the edges of the muslin up around the filling squeezing fairly tightly to form a ball. Secure with string. Make five more bombes in the same way. Freeze for at least 3 hours.

**5** To serve, place the bombes on plates and remove the muslin.

# Raspberry Cranachan Bombe

**SERVES EIGHT**

**INGREDIENTS**

750ml | 1¼ pints | 3 cups RASPBERRY SORBET

550ml | 18fl oz | 2½ cups DOUBLE (HEAVY) CREAM

60ml | 4 tbsp CLEAR HONEY

75ml | 5 tbsp WHISKY

50g | 2oz | ½ cup MEDIUM OATMEAL, toasted

**1** Soften the sorbet by letting it stand at room temperature for about 20 minutes. Meanwhile, chill a 1.5 litre | 2½ pint | 6¼ cup bombe mould or pudding (dessert) basin.

**2** Using a large spoon, evenly pack the sorbet on to the base and up the sides of the mould. If this proves difficult and the sorbet starts to slide around, freeze it for about 10 minutes before continuing. Return the bombe mould to the freezer.

*The flavours in this recipe stem from a traditional Scottish dessert comprising a whisky and honey flavoured cream with toasted oatmeal and raspberries.*

**3** Whip the cream with the honey and whisky until it forms soft peaks, then fold in the oatmeal. Spoon into the sorbet-lined mould and level the surface. Cover with clear film (plastic wrap) and freeze overnight.

**4** To serve, loosen the edges of the mould with a knife. Dip the mould very briefly in hot water then invert on to a serving plate. Serve in wedges.

**VARIATION** *Cointreau or another orange-flavoured liqueur could be used instead of whisky. If preferred, 75g | 3oz | ¼ cup finely chopped and toasted hazelnuts could be substituted for the oatmeal.*

# Layered Chocolate and Chestnut Bombes

*These delicious little bombes look especially effective if they are served on plates that have been drizzled with melted plain chocolate, but if you're short of time you can create a very decorative effect simply by dusting the plates with cocoa powder or scattering the bombes with grated chocolate.*

**SERVES SIX**

**INGREDIENTS**

3 EGG YOLKS

75g | 3oz | 6 tbsp CASTER (SUPERFINE) SUGAR

10ml | 2 tsp CORNFLOUR (CORNSTARCH)

300ml | ½ pint | 1¼ cups MILK

115g | 4oz PLAIN (SEMISWEET) CHOCOLATE, broken into pieces, plus 50g | 2oz, to decorate

150g | 5oz | ½ cup SWEETENED CHESTNUT PURÉE

30ml | 2 tbsp BRANDY or COINTREAU

130g | 4½oz | generous ½ cup MASCARPONE CHEESE

5ml | 1 tsp VANILLA EXTRACT

450ml | ¾ pint | scant 2 cups DOUBLE (HEAVY) CREAM

**1** Whisk the egg yolks in a bowl with the sugar, cornflour and a little of the milk. Bring the remaining milk to the boil in a heavy pan. Pour the milk over the egg mixture, whisking well. Return to the pan and cook over a very gentle heat, stirring, until thickened. Do not boil the custard or it may curdle. Divide the custard equally among three bowls.

**2** Add 115g | 4oz of the chocolate to one bowl and leave until melted, stirring frequently until smooth. If the chocolate fails to melt completely, and the bowl is suitable, microwave very briefly.

**3** If the chestnut purée is firm, beat it until softened, then stir it into the second bowl, with the brandy or Cointreau. Add the mascarpone and the vanilla essence to the third bowl of custard. Cover each custard closely with a circle of baking parchment and leave to cool.

**4** Whip the cream until it forms soft peaks. Fold a third of it into each of the cooled custard mixtures. Spoon the chestnut mixture into six 150ml | ¼ pint | ⅔ cup plain or fluted individual moulds and level the surface.

**5** Spoon the chocolate mixture over the chestnut mixture in the moulds and level the surface. Spoon the vanilla mixture over the chocolate. Cover and freeze for 6 hours or overnight.

**6** To serve, melt the chocolate for decoration in a heatproof bowl set over a pan of gently simmering water. Transfer to a paper piping bag and snip off the tip. Alternatively use a piping bag fitted with a writing nozzle.

**7** Scribble lines of the melted chocolate over the serving plates to decorate. Loosen the edge of each mould with a knife. Dip each mould very briefly in hot water then invert on to a flat surface. Using a palette knife, carefully transfer the moulds to the serving plates. Leave to stand for 10 minutes at room temperature to allow the ice cream to soften before serving.

**VARIATION** *If you can't get sweetened chestnut purée use the same quantity of unsweetened purée and add an extra 30ml | 2 tbsp caster (superfine) sugar.*

# Caramel and Pecan Terrine

*The combination of caramel and nuts in this dessert is really delicious. Take care that the syrup does not become too dark or the ice cream will taste bitter.*

**SERVES SIX**

**INGREDIENTS**

115g | 4oz | generous ½ cup
GRANULATED (WHITE) SUGAR

75ml | 5 tbsp WATER

450ml | ¾ pint | scant 2 cups
DOUBLE (HEAVY) CREAM

30ml | 2 tbsp ICING
(CONFECTIONERS') SUGAR

75g | 3oz | ¾ cup PECAN NUTS,
toasted

**1** Heat the sugar and water in a small, heavy pan until the sugar dissolves. Boil rapidly until the sugar has turned pale golden. Remove from the heat and leave to stand until the syrup develops a rich brown colour.

**2** Pour 90ml | 6 tbsp of the cream over the caramel. Heat to make a smooth sauce. Leave to cool.

**3** Dampen a 450g | 1lb loaf tin (pan), then line the base and sides with clear film (plastic wrap). Whip a further 150ml | ¼ pint | ⅔ cup of the cream with the icing sugar until it forms soft peaks. Then whip the remaining cream in a separate bowl and stir in the caramel sauce and pecan nuts.

**4** Spoon a third of the caramel cream into the prepared tin and spread with half the plain whipped cream. Spread half of the remaining caramel cream over the top, then top with the last of the plain cream. Finally add the remaining caramel cream and level the surface. Freeze for 6 hours.

**5** To serve, dip the tin in very hot water for 2 seconds, invert on to a serving plate and peel away the film. Serve sliced.

**COOK'S TIP** *Watch the caramel syrup closely after removing it from the heat. If it starts to turn too dark, dip the base of the pan in cold water to arrest the cooking. If the syrup remains very pale, return the pan to the heat and cook the syrup for a little longer.*

# Marzipan and Kumquat Terrine

*Tangy poached kumquats make a perfect contrast to the sweet almond paste in this frozen terrine. Any leftover kumquats keep well in the refrigerator for a week, making a lovely topping for vanilla ice cream.*

**SERVES SIX**

**INGREDIENTS**

350g | 12oz | 3 cups KUMQUATS

115g | 4oz | generous ½ cup CASTER (SUPERFINE) SUGAR

150ml | ¼ pint | ⅔ cup WATER

2 EGG YOLKS

10ml | 2 tsp CORNFLOUR (CORNSTARCH)

300ml | ½ pint | 1¼ cups FULL-CREAM (WHOLE) MILK

200g | 7oz GOLDEN MARZIPAN, grated

2.5ml | ½ tsp ALMOND EXTRACT

300ml | ½ pint | 1¼ cups WHIPPING CREAM

**1** Cut the kumquats in half and scoop out the seeds with the tip of a knife. Heat the sugar and water gently in a heavy pan until the sugar dissolves. Add the kumquats and cook gently for about 10 minutes until tender. Leave the syrup to cool.

**2** Whisk the egg yolks in a bowl with the cornflour and 60ml | 4 tbsp of the syrup until smooth. In a heavy pan, bring the milk just to the boil, then gradually pour it over the egg yolk mixture, whisking constantly.

**3** Return to the pan and cook over a gentle heat for 2 minutes, stirring constantly, until the custard has thickened. Do not let it boil or the custard may curdle. Transfer the custard to a bowl and stir in the marzipan and almond extract. Cover the surface closely with greaseproof paper to prevent the formation of a skin on the surface and leave until cold.

**4** Line a small terrine or loaf tin (pan) with clear film (plastic wrap) and set aside. Put a generous third of the kumquats into a food processor. Pour in a further 60ml | 4 tbsp of the kumquat syrup and blend until smooth and pulpy.

**5 BY HAND:** Whip the cream until thickened and fold into the custard with the kumquat pulp. Pour into the lined tin and freeze overnight.

**USING AN ICE CREAM MAKER:** Stir the cream and pulp into the custard and churn until thick. Pour into the tin and freeze for 4 hours.

**6** Transfer the tin to the refrigerator about 1 hour before serving to allow it to soften slightly. Invert onto a plate and remove the tin. Peel away the film and serve the ice cream topped with the remaining kumquats.

# Spicy Pumpkin and Orange Bombe

*Pumpkin has a subtle flavour that is truly transformed with the addition of*

*citrus fruits and spices. Here, the delicious mixture is encased in syrupy sponge*

*and served with an orange and whole spice syrup.*

**SERVES EIGHT**

**INGREDIENTS**

**For the sponge**

115g | 4oz | ½ cup UNSALTED (SWEET) BUTTER, softened

115g | 4oz | ½ cup CASTER (SUPERFINE) SUGAR

115g | 4oz | 1 cup SELF-RAISING (SELF-RISING) FLOUR

2.5ml | ½ tsp BAKING POWDER

2 EGGS

**For the ice cream**

1 ORANGE

300g | 11oz | scant 1½ cups GOLDEN GRANULATED (WHITE) SUGAR

300ml | ½ pint | 1¼ cups WATER

2 CINNAMON STICKS, halved

10ml | 2 tsp WHOLE CLOVES

30ml | 2 tbsp ORANGE FLOWER WATER

400g | 14oz can UNSWEETENED PUMPKIN PURÉE

300ml | ½ pint | 1¼ cups EXTRA THICK DOUBLE (HEAVY) CREAM

2 pieces PRESERVED STEM GINGER, grated

ICING (CONFECTIONERS') SUGAR, for dusting

**1** Preheat the oven to 180°C | 350°F | Gas 4. Grease and line a 450g | 1lb loaf tin (pan). Beat the softened butter, caster sugar, flour, baking powder and eggs in a bowl until creamy.

**2** Scrape the mixture into the prepared tin, level the surface and bake for 30–35 minutes until firm in the middle. Leave to cool.

**3** Make the ice cream. Pare thin strips of rind from the orange, scrape off any white pith, then cut the strips into very fine shreds. Squeeze the orange and set the juice aside. Heat the sugar and water in a small, heavy pan until the sugar dissolves. Bring to the boil and boil rapidly without stirring for 3 minutes.

**4** Stir in the orange shreds, juice, cinnamon and cloves and heat gently for 5 minutes. Strain the syrup, reserving the orange shreds and spices. Measure 300ml | ½ pint | 1¼ cups of the syrup and reserve. Return the spices to the remaining syrup and stir in the orange flower water. Pour into a jug (pitcher) and set aside to cool.

**5** Beat the pumpkin purée with 175ml | 6fl oz | ¾ cup of the measured strained syrup until evenly combined. Stir in the cream and ginger. Cut the cake into 1cm | ½in slices. Dampen a 1.5 litre | 2½ pint | 6¼ cup pudding or dessert basin and line it with clear film (plastic wrap). Pour the remaining strained syrup into a shallow dish.

**6** Dip the cake slices briefly in the syrup and use to line the prepared basin, placing the syrupy coated sides against the bowl. Trim the pieces to fit where necessary, so that the lining is even and any gaps are filled. Chill.

**7 BY HAND:** Pour the pumpkin mixture into a shallow container and freeze until firm. Scrape the ice cream into the sponge-lined basin, level the surface and freeze until firm, preferably overnight.

**USING AN ICE CREAM MAKER:** Churn the pumpkin mixture until very thick, then scrape it into the sponge-lined basin. Level the surface and freeze until firm, preferably overnight.

**8** To serve, invert the ice cream on to a serving plate. Lift off the bowl and peel away the clear film. Dust with the icing sugar and serve in wedges with the spiced syrup spooned over.

**COOK'S TIP** *If you prefer a smooth syrup, strain to remove the cinnamon sticks and cloves before spooning it over the bombe.*

# Coconut and Lemon Grass Ice Cream

*Lemon grass adds an exotic fragrance to ice creams and sorbets. If you can't get fresh, use the dried stalks or preserved stalks in jars.*

**SERVES FIVE TO SIX**

**INGREDIENTS**

4 LEMON GRASS STALKS

400ml | 14fl oz | 1⅔ cups
COCONUT MILK

3 EGG YOLKS

90g | 3½oz | ½ cup CASTER
(SUPERFINE) SUGAR

10ml | 2 tsp CORNFLOUR
(CORNSTARCH)

150ml | ¼ pint | ⅔ cup
WHIPPING CREAM

finely grated rind of 1 LIME

**For the lime syrup**

75g | 3oz | 6 tbsp CASTER
(SUPERFINE) SUGAR

75ml | 5 tbsp WATER

1 LIME, very thinly sliced,
plus 30ml | 2 tbsp LIME JUICE

**1** Cut the lemon grass stalks in half lengthways and bruise the stalks with a rolling pin. Put them in a heavy pan, add the coconut milk and bring to just below boiling point. Remove from the heat and leave to infuse for 30 minutes, remove the lemon grass.

**2** Whisk the egg yolks in a bowl with the sugar and cornflour until smooth. Gradually add the coconut milk, whisking constantly.

**3** Return to the pan and heat gently, stirring until the custard thickens. Remove from the heat and strain into a clean bowl. Cover with baking parchment and chill.

**4 BY HAND:** Lightly whip the cream, add the grated lime rind and fold into the custard. Pour into a container and freeze for 3–4 hours, beating twice as it thickens. Spoon into dariole moulds and return to the freezer for 3 hours.

**USING AN ICE CREAM MAKER:** Stir the cream and lime rind into the custard. Churn until thick, then spoon into 5–6 dariole moulds. Freeze for at least 3 hours.

**5** Heat the sugar and water in a heavy pan until the sugar dissolves. Boil for 5 minutes without stirring. Reduce the heat, add the lime slices and juice and simmer for 5 minutes more. Cool.

**6** To turn out, loosen with a knife and briefly dip in very hot water. Serve with syrup and lime slices.

# Walnut Castles

*This recipe is loosely based on a classic Indian Kulfi, using finely chopped walnuts instead of the more familiar pistachios.*

**SERVES SIX**

**INGREDIENTS**

2 litres | 3½ pints | 9 cups
FULL-CREAM (WHOLE) MILK

15 whole CARDAMOM PODS

75g | 3oz | 6 tbsp CASTER
(SUPERFINE) SUGAR

115g | 4oz | 1 cup WALNUTS,
finely chopped

30ml | 2 tbsp ROSEWATER

15ml | 1 tbsp LEMON JUICE

CHOPPED WALNUTS,
to decorate

**1** Put the milk and cardamom pods in a large, heavy pan. Bring to the boil, then simmer vigorously without boiling over. Continue until reduced to about 750ml | 1¼ pints | 3 cups.

**2** Strain the milk into a bowl, discarding the cardamom pods. Add the caster sugar, chopped walnuts and rosewater and leave to cool then stir in the lemon juice.

**BY HAND:** Pour the mixture into a shallow container and freeze until thickened and firm.

**USING AN ICE CREAM MAKER:** Churn the mixture until thick. Spoon into six 120ml | 4fl oz | ½ cup dariole moulds or plastic cups and freeze overnight.

**3** To serve, briefly dip the moulds in very hot water, then turn out on to individual dessert plates. Serve scattered with chopped walnuts.

# tortes & gâteaux

Iced tortes and gâteaux make an impressive finale to any dinner gathering, yet they're so convenient for the cook. Encased or layered with sponge, meringue or crisp biscuit, these delicious recipes provide an extensive collection of both classic and modern flavours.

# Zabaglione Ice Cream Torte

*For anyone who likes zabaglione, the famous, whisked Italian dessert, this simple iced version is an absolute must! Its taste and texture are just as good, and there's no last-minute whisking to worry about.*

**SERVES TEN**

**INGREDIENTS**

175g | 6oz AMARETTI BISCUITS (COOKIES)

115g | 4oz | ½ cup READY-TO-EAT DRIED APRICOTS, finely chopped

65g | 2½oz | 5 tbsp UNSALTED (SWEET) BUTTER, melted

**For the ice cream**

65g | 2½oz | 5 tbsp LIGHT MUSCOVADO (BROWN) SUGAR

75ml | 5 tbsp WATER

5 EGG YOLKS

250ml | 8fl oz | 1 cup DOUBLE (HEAVY) CREAM

75ml | 5 tbsp MADEIRA or CREAM SHERRY

**For the apricot compote**

150g | 5oz | generous ½ cup READY-TO-EAT DRIED APRICOTS

25g | 1oz | 2 tbsp LIGHT MUSCOVADO (BROWN) SUGAR

150ml | ¼ pint | ⅔ cup WATER

**1** Put the biscuits in a strong plastic bag and crush finely with a rolling pin. Tip into a bowl and stir in the apricots and melted butter until evenly combined.

**2** Using a dampened dessertspoon, pack the mixture evenly on to the bottom and up the sides of a 24cm | 9½in loose-based flan tin (pan) about 4cm | 1½in deep. Chill.

**3** Make the ice cream. Put the sugar and water in a small, heavy pan and heat, stirring, until the sugar has dissolved. Bring to the boil and boil for 2 minutes without stirring. Meanwhile bring a large pan of water to simmering point. Put the yolks in a heatproof bowl to fit over the pan without touching the water.

**4** Off the heat, whisk the egg yolks until pale, then gradually whisk in the sugar syrup. Put the bowl over the pan of simmering water and continue to whisk for about 10 minutes or until the mixture leaves a trail when the whisk is lifted.

**5** Remove the bowl from the heat and carry on whisking for a further 5 minutes or until the mixture is cold. In a separate bowl, whip the cream with the Madeira or sherry until it stands in peaks.

**6** Using a large metal spoon, fold the cream into the whisked mixture. Spoon it into the biscuit case, level the surface, cover and freeze overnight.

**7** To make the compote, simmer the apricots and sugar in the water until the apricots are plump and the juices are syrupy, adding a little more water if necessary. Leave to cool.

**8** Serve the torte in slices with a little of the compote spooned over each portion.

# Chocolate and Brandied Fig Torte

*A seriously rich torte for chocolate lovers. If you are not keen on figs, use dried prunes, dates or apricots.*

**SERVES EIGHT**

**INGREDIENTS**

250g | 9oz | 1½ cups DRIED FIGS

60ml | 4 tbsp BRANDY

200g | 7oz GINGERSNAP BISCUITS (COOKIES)

175g | 6oz | ¾ cup UNSALTED (SWEET) BUTTER, softened

150ml | ¼ pint | ⅔ cup MILK

250g | 9oz PLAIN (SEMISWEET) CHOCOLATE, broken into pieces

45ml | 3 tbsp CASTER (SUPERFINE) SUGAR

UNSWEETENED COCOA POWDER, for dusting

LIGHTLY WHIPPED CREAM or CRÈME FRAÎCHE, to serve

**1** Chop the figs and put them into a bowl, pour over the brandy and leave for 2–3 hours until most of the brandy has been absorbed. Break the biscuits into large chunks, put them in a strong plastic bag and crush them with a rolling pin.

**2** Melt half the butter and stir in the biscuit crumbs until combined. Pack on to the bottom and up the sides of a 20cm | 8in loose-based flan tin (pan), which is about 3cm | 1¼in deep. Chill.

**3** Pour the milk into a pan, add the chocolate pieces and heat gently until the chocolate has melted and the mixture is smooth, stirring frequently. Pour the chocolate mixture into a bowl and leave to cool.

**4** In a separate bowl, beat the remaining butter with the caster sugar until the mixture is pale and creamy.

**5** Add the chocolate mixture, whisking until it is well mixed. Fold in the figs, and any remaining brandy, and spoon the mixture into the biscuit case. Level the surface, cover and freeze overnight.

**6** Transfer the torte to the refrigerator about 30 minutes before serving so that the filling softens slightly. Dust lightly with cocoa powder and serve in slices, with lightly whipped cream or crème fraîche.

# Rhubarb and Ginger Wine Torte

*Rhubarb is not often used in iced desserts, but this luxurious torte uses it in a classic partnership with ginger. The result is a refreshingly tart flavour, making it the perfect choice for those who prefer less sweet desserts.*

**SERVES EIGHT**

**INGREDIENTS**

500g | 1¼lb RHUBARB, trimmed

115g | 4oz | ½ cup CASTER (SUPERFINE) SUGAR

30ml | 2 tbsp WATER

200g | 7oz | scant 1 cup CREAM CHEESE

150ml | ¼ pint | ⅔ cups DOUBLE (HEAVY) CREAM

40g | 1½oz | ¼ cup PRESERVED STEM GINGER, finely chopped

a few drops of PINK FOOD COLOURING (optional)

250ml | 8fl oz | 1 cup GINGER WINE

175g | 6oz SPONGE FINGERS

FRESH MINT or LEMON BALM SPRIGS, dusted with icing (confectioners') sugar, to decorate

**1** Chop the rhubarb roughly and put it in a pan with the sugar and water. Cover and cook very gently for 5–8 minutes until the rhubarb is just tender. Process in a food processor or blender until smooth, then leave to cool.

**2** Beat the cream cheese in a bowl until softened. Stir in the cream, rhubarb purée and ginger, then a little food colouring, if you like. Line a 900g/2lb/6–8 cup loaf tin (pan) with clear film (plastic wrap).

**3 BY HAND:** Pour the mixture into a shallow container and freeze until firm.

**USING AN ICE CREAM MAKER:**
Churn in an ice cream maker until firm.

**4** Pour the ginger wine into a shallow dish. Spoon a thin layer of ice cream over the bottom of the tin. Working quickly, dip the sponge fingers in the ginger wine, then lay them lengthways over the ice cream in a single layer (*left*). Trim the sponge fingers to fit.

**5** Spread another layer of ice cream over the biscuits. Repeat the process, adding two to three more layers and finishing with ice cream. Cover and freeze overnight.

**6** Transfer to the refrigerator 30 minutes before serving, to soften slightly. Briefly dip in very hot water then invert it on to a flat dish. Peel off the clear film and decorate.

**COOK'S TIP** *Taste the rhubarb mixture just before churning it and add a little icing (confectioners') sugar if you find the flavour too tart.*

# Iced Christmas Torte

*Not everyone likes traditional Christmas pudding. This makes an exciting alternative but don't feel that you have to limit it to the festive season. Packed with dried fruit and nuts, it is perfect for any special occasion and looks and tastes sensational.*

**SERVES EIGHT TO TEN**

**INGREDIENTS**

75g | 3oz | ¼ cup
DRIED CRANBERRIES

75g | 3oz | scant ½ cup
PITTED PRUNES

50g | 2oz | ⅓ cup SULTANAS
(GOLDEN RAISINS)

175ml | 6fl oz | ¾ cup PORT

2 pieces PRESERVED STEM
GINGER, finely chopped

25g | 1oz | 2 tbsp
UNSALTED (SWEET) BUTTER

45ml | 3 tbsp LIGHT
MUSCOVADO (BROWN) SUGAR

90g | 3½oz | scant 2 cups
FRESH WHITE BREADCRUMBS

600ml | 1 pint | 2½ cups
DOUBLE (HEAVY) CREAM

30ml | 2 tbsp ICING
(CONFECTIONERS') SUGAR

5ml | 1 tsp MIXED SPICE

75g | 3oz | ¾ cup BRAZIL NUTS,
finely chopped

SUGARED BAY LEAVES
(see Cook's Tip) and FRESH
CHERRIES, to decorate

**1** Put the cranberries, prunes and sultanas in a food processor and process briefly. Transfer them into a bowl and add the port and ginger. Leave for 2 hours.

**2** Melt the butter in a frying pan. Add the sugar and heat gently until dissolved. Tip in the breadcrumbs, then fry over low heat for 5 minutes until lightly coloured and crisp. Leave to cool.

**3** Transfer the breadcrumbs into a food processor or blender and process to finer crumbs. Sprinkle a third into an 18cm/7in loose-based springform tin (pan) and freeze.

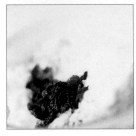

**4** Whip the cream with the icing sugar and mixed spice until the mixture is thick but not yet standing in peaks. Fold in the brazil nuts with the dried fruit mixture and any port that has not been absorbed.

**5** Spread a third of the mixture over the breadcrumb base in the tin, taking care not to dislodge the crumbs. Sprinkle with another layer of the breadcrumbs. Repeat the layering, finishing with a layer of the cream mixture. Freeze the torte overnight.

**6** Make the sugared bay leaves. Chill the torte for about 1 hour before serving, decorated with sugared bay leaves and fresh cherries.

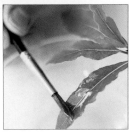

**COOK'S TIP** *To make the sugared bay leaves wash and dry the leaves, then paint both sides with beaten egg white. Sprinkle with caster (superfine) sugar. Leave to dry on baking parchment for 2–3 hours.*

# Pistachio and Nougat Torte

*Pistachios, nougat, honey and rose water make a perfect blend of flavours in this quick and easy torte. Transfer to the refrigerator about an hour before serving.*

**SERVES EIGHT**

**INGREDIENTS**

75g | 3oz | ¼ cup
PISTACHIOS

150g | 5oz NOUGAT

300ml | ½ pint | 1¼ cups
WHIPPING CREAM

90ml | 6 tbsp CLEAR HONEY

30ml | 2 tbsp ROSEWATER

250g | 9oz | generous 1 cup
FROMAGE FRAIS or
CRÈME FRAÎCHE

8 TRIFLE SPONGES

ICING (CONFECTIONERS')
SUGAR, for dusting

FRESH RASPBERRIES,
POACHED APRICOTS or
CHERRIES, to serve (optional)

**1** Soak the pistachios in boiling water for 2 minutes. Drain them thoroughly, then rub them between pieces of kitchen paper to remove the skins. Peel off any skins that remain, then chop them roughly.

**2** Using a small sharp knife or scissors cut the nougat into small pieces. Pour the cream into a bowl, add the honey and rose water and whip until it is just beginning to hold its shape.

**3** Stir in the fromage frais or crème fraîche, chopped pistachios and nougat, and mix well. Slice the trifle sponges horizontally into three very thin layers.

**4** Line a 15–17cm | 6–6½in square loose-based cake tin (pan) with baking parchment. Arrange a layer of sponges on the bottom, trimming the pieces to fit.

**5** Pack the prepared filling into the tin and level the surface. Cover with the remaining sponges, then cover and freeze overnight.

**6** To serve, invert the torte on to a serving plate and dust with icing sugar. Serve with raspberries, poached apricots or cherries, if you like.

# White Chocolate and Brownie Torte

*This is a deliciously easy dessert, guaranteed to appeal to just about everyone! If you can't buy good-quality brownies, use a moist chocolate sponge.*

**SERVES TEN**

**INGREDIENTS**

300g/11oz
WHITE CHOCOLATE,
broken into pieces

600ml/1 pint/2½ cups
DOUBLE (HEAVY) CREAM

250g/9oz
RICH CHOCOLATE BROWNIES

UNSWEETENED COCOA
POWDER, for dusting

**1** Dampen the sides of a 20cm | 8in springform tin (pan) and line with a strip of baking parchment. Put the chocolate in a small pan. Add 150ml | ¼ pint | ⅔ cup of the cream and heat very gently until the chocolate has melted. Stir until smooth, then pour into a bowl and leave to cool.

**2** Break the chocolate brownies into chunky pieces and scatter these on the bottom of the tin. Pack them down lightly to make a fairly dense base.

**3** Whip the remaining cream until it forms peaks, then fold in the white chocolate mixture. Spoon into the tin to cover the layer of brownies, then tap the tin gently on the work surface to level the chocolate mixture. Cover and freeze overnight.

**4** Transfer the torte to the refrigerator about 45 minutes before serving. Decorate with a light dusting of cocoa powder before serving.

# Iced Strawberry and Lemon Curd Gâteau

*Layer two favourite flavours in this fresh fruit gâteau, which is perfect for summer entertaining and takes only minutes to assemble.*

**4** Fit the cake in the tin, cut-side down. Freeze the cake for 10 minutes, then spread the strawberry ice cream evenly over the sponge and freeze until firm.

## SERVES EIGHT

## INGREDIENTS

115g | 4oz | ½ cup UNSALTED (SWEET) BUTTER, softened

115g | 4oz | generous ½ cup CASTER (SUPERFINE) SUGAR

2 EGGS

115g | 4oz | 1 cup SELF-RAISING (SELF-RISING) FLOUR

2.5ml | ½ tsp BAKING POWDER

**3** Line the sides of the clean cake tin with a strip of baking parchment. Using a sharp knife, carefully slice off the top of the cake where it has formed a crust. Save this for another purpose.

**5** Pour the cream into a bowl, whip it until it forms soft peaks, then fold in the lemon curd and lemon juice. Spoon the mixture over the strawberry ice cream. Cover and freeze overnight.

**6** About 45 minutes before you intend to serve the dessert, decorate it and make the sauce. Cut half the strawberries into thin slices. Put the rest in a food processor or blender and add the sugar and liqueur. Purée the mixture to make a sauce.

**7** Arrange the sliced strawberries over the frozen gâteau. Serve with the sauce spooned over.

## To finish

500ml | 17fl oz | 2¼ cups STRAWBERRY ICE CREAM

300ml | ½ pint | 1¼ cups DOUBLE (HEAVY) CREAM

200g | 7oz | scant 1 cup GOOD QUALITY LEMON CURD

30ml | 2 tbsp LEMON JUICE

500g | 1¼lb | 5 cups STRAWBERRIES, hulled

25g | 1oz | 2 tbsp CASTER (SUPERFINE) SUGAR

45ml | 3 tbsp COINTREAU or other ORANGE-FLAVOURED LIQUEUR

**1** Preheat the oven to 180°C | 350°F | Gas 4. Grease and line a 23cm | 9in round springform cake tin (pan). In a mixing bowl, beat the butter with the sugar, eggs, flour and baking powder until creamy.

**2** Spoon the mixture into the prepared tin and bake for about 20 minutes or until just firm. Leave to cool for 5 minutes, then turn the cake out on a wire rack. Cool completely. Wash and dry the cake tin, ready to use again.

# Zucotto

*An Italian-style dessert with a rich ricotta, fruit, chocolate and nut filling, zucotto is encased in a moist, chocolate and liqueur-flavoured sponge.*

**SERVES EIGHT**

**INGREDIENTS**

3 EGGS

75g | 3oz | 6 tbsp CASTER (SUPERFINE) SUGAR

75g | 3oz | ⅔ cup PLAIN (ALL-PURPOSE) FLOUR

25g | 1oz | ¼ cup UNSWEETENED COCOA POWDER

90ml | 6 tbsp KIRSCH

250g | 9oz | generous 1 cup RICOTTA CHEESE

50g | 2oz | ½ cup ICING (CONFECTIONERS') SUGAR

50g | 2oz PLAIN (SEMISWEET) CHOCOLATE, finely chopped

50g | 2oz | ½ cup BLANCHED ALMONDS, chopped and toasted

75g | 3oz | scant ½ cup GLACÉ (CANDIED) CHERRIES, quartered

2 pieces PRESERVED STEM GINGER, finely chopped

150ml | ¼ pint | ⅔ cup DOUBLE (HEAVY) CREAM

UNSWEETENED COCOA POWDER, for dusting

**1** Preheat the oven to 180°C | 350°F | Gas 4. Grease and line a 23cm | 9in cake tin (pan). Whisk the eggs and sugar in a heatproof bowl over a pan of simmering water until the whisk leaves a trail. Remove from the heat and continue to whisk for 2 minutes.

**2** Sift the flour and cocoa into the bowl and fold it into the mixture. Transfer to the prepared tin and bake for about 20 minutes until just firm. Leave to cool.

**3** Cut the cake horizontally into three layers. Set aside 30ml | 2 tbsp of the kirsch. Drizzle the remaining kirsch over the layers.

**4** Beat the ricotta in a bowl until softened, then beat in the icing sugar, chocolate, almonds, cherries, ginger and reserved kirsch.

**5** Pour the cream into a separate bowl and whip it lightly. Using a large metal spoon, fold the cream into the ricotta mixture. Chill. Cut a 20cm | 8in circle from one sponge layer, using a plate as a guide, and set it aside.

**6** Use the remaining sponge to make the case for the zucotto. Cut the cake to fit the bottom of a 2.8–3.4 litre | 5–6 pint | 12½–15 cup freezerproof mixing bowl. Cut more sponge for the sides of the bowl, fitting the pieces together and taking them about one third of the way up.

**7** Spoon the ricotta filling into the bowl up to the height of the sponge, and level the surface.

**8** Fit the reserved circle of sponge on top of the filling. Trim off the excess sponge around the edges. Cover and freeze overnight.

**9** Transfer the zucotto to the refrigerator 45 minutes before serving, so that the filling softens slightly. Invert it on to a serving plate. Dust with cocoa powder and serve in slices.

# Raspberry Mousse Gâteau

*A lavish quantity of raspberries gives this gâteau its vibrant colour and full flavour. Make it at the height of summer, when raspberries are plentiful and full of flavour.*

**3** Leave to cool, then remove the cake from the tin and place it on a wire rack. Wash and dry the tin.

**4** Line the sides of the clean tin with a strip of baking parchment and carefully lower the cake back into it. Freeze until the raspberry filling is ready.

**5** Set aside 200g | 7oz | generous 1 cup of the raspberries. Put the remainder in a clean bowl, stir in the icing sugar, process to a purée in a food processor or blender. Sieve the purée into a bowl, then stir in the whisky, if using.

**SERVES EIGHT TO TEN**

**INGREDIENTS**

2 EGGS

50g | 2oz | ¼ cup CASTER (SUPERFINE) SUGAR

50g | 2oz | ½ cup PLAIN (ALL-PURPOSE) FLOUR

30ml | 2 tbsp UNSWEETENED COCOA POWDER

600g | 1lb 5oz | 3½ cups RASPBERRIES

115g | 4oz | 1 cup ICING (CONFECTIONERS') SUGAR

60ml | 4 tbsp WHISKY (optional)

300ml | ½ pint | 1¼ cups WHIPPING CREAM

2 EGG WHITES

**1** Preheat the oven to 180°C | 350°F | Gas 4. Grease and line a 23cm | 9in springform cake tin (pan). Whisk the eggs and sugar in a heatproof bowl set over a pan of gently simmering water until the whisk leaves a trail when lifted. Remove the bowl from the heat and continue to whisk the mixture for 2 minutes.

**2** Sift the flour and cocoa powder over the mixture and fold it in with a large metal spoon. Spoon the mixture into the tin and spread it gently to the edges. Bake for 12–15 minutes until just firm.

**6** Whip the cream to form soft peaks. Whisk the egg whites until they are stiff. Using a large metal spoon, fold the cream, then the egg whites into the raspberry purée.

**7** Spread half the raspberry mixture over the cake. Scatter with the reserved raspberries. Spread the remaining raspberry mixture on top and level the surface. Cover and freeze the gâteau overnight.

**8** Transfer the gâteau to the refrigerator 1 hour before serving. Remove it from the tin, place on a serving plate and serve in slices.

# Rich Chocolate Mousse Gâteau

*Because this gâteau is heavily laced with liqueur, you can easily get away with a bought sponge. The mousse is rich, so serve small portions.*

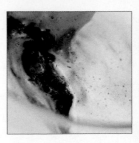

**SERVES TWELVE**

**INGREDIENTS**

400g | 14oz MOIST CHOCOLATE SPONGE CAKE

75ml | 5 tbsp COINTREAU or other ORANGE-FLAVOURED LIQUEUR

finely grated rind and juice of 1 ORANGE

300g | 11oz PLAIN (SEMISWEET) CHOCOLATE, broken into pieces

25g | 1oz | ¼ cup UNSWEETENED COCOA POWDER

45ml | 3 tbsp GOLDEN (LIGHT CORN) SYRUP

3 EGGS

300ml | ½ pint | 1¼ cups WHIPPING CREAM

150ml | ¼ pint | ⅔ cup DOUBLE (HEAVY) CREAM, lightly whipped

UNSWEETENED COCOA POWDER, for dusting

**1** Cut the cake into 5mm | ¼in thick slices. Set a third aside, and use the remainder to make a case for the mousse. Line the bottom of a 23cm | 9in springform or loose-based cake tin (pan) with cake, trimming to fit neatly, then use more for the sides, making a case about 4cm | 1½ in deep.

**2** Mix 30ml | 2 tbsp of the liqueur with the orange juice and drizzle over the sponge case.

**3** Put the chocolate in a heatproof bowl. Add the cocoa powder, syrup and remaining liqueur and place the bowl over a pan of gently simmering water. Leave until the chocolate has melted, then remove from the heat. Stir until smooth.

**4** Whisk the eggs with the orange rind in a mixing bowl until they are thick and pale. Whip the whipping cream until it forms soft peaks.

**5** Fold the chocolate mixture into the whisked eggs, using a large metal spoon, then fold in the cream. Scrape the mixture into the sponge case and level the surface.

**6** Cover with the reserved chocolate cake, trimming the pieces to fit. Cover and freeze overnight.

**7** Transfer to the refrigerator 30 minutes before serving. Invert on to a plate, spread with the double cream and dust with cocoa powder.

# Maple and Walnut Meringue Gâteau

*This simple dessert makes a feast for all meringue lovers. Before serving, let it thaw slightly in the refrigerator to enjoy the full flavour.*

**SERVES TEN TO TWELVE**

**INGREDIENTS**

4 EGG WHITES

200g | 7oz | scant 1 cup LIGHT MUSCOVADO (BROWN) SUGAR

150g | 5oz | 1¼ cups WALNUT PIECES

600ml | 1 pint | 2½ cups DOUBLE (HEAVY) CREAM

150ml | ¼ pint | ⅔ cup MAPLE SYRUP, plus extra, to serve

**1** Preheat the oven to 140°C | 275°F | Gas 1. Draw three 23cm | 9in circles on separate sheets of baking parchment. Invert the sheets on three baking sheets. Whisk the egg whites in a bowl until stiff.

**2** Whisk in the sugar, about 15ml | 1 tbsp at a time, whisking well after each addition until the meringue is stiff and glossy. Spread to within 1cm | ½in of the edge of each marked circle. Bake for about 1 hour or until crisp, swapping the baking sheets around halfway through cooking. Leave to cool.

**3** Set aside 45ml | 3 tbsp of the walnuts. Finely chop the remainder. Whip the cream with the maple syrup until it forms soft peaks. Fold in the chopped walnuts. Use about a third of the mixture to sandwich the meringues together on a flat, freezerproof serving plate.

**4** Spread the remaining cream mixture over the top and sides of the gâteau. Sprinkle with the reserved walnuts and freeze overnight.

**5** Transfer the gâteau to the refrigerator about 1 hour before serving to soften slightly. Drizzle over the top a little of the extra maple syrup just before serving. Serve in slices.

# Soft Fruit and Crushed Meringue Gâteau

*This recipe takes five minutes to make but looks and tastes as though a lot of preparation went into it. Use really good vanilla ice cream.*

**SERVES SIX**

**INGREDIENTS**

400g | 14oz | 3½ cups MIXED SMALL STRAWBERRIES, RASPBERRIES or REDCURRANTS

30ml | 2 tbsp ICING (CONFECTIONERS') SUGAR

750ml | 1¼ pints | 3 cups CLASSIC VANILLA ICE CREAM

6 MERINGUE NESTS

**1** Dampen a 900g | 2lb loaf tin (pan) and line it with clear film (plastic wrap). If using strawberries, chop them into small pieces. Put them in a bowl and add the raspberries or redcurrants and icing sugar. Toss until the fruit is beginning to break up but do not let it become mushy.

**2** Put the ice cream in a bowl and break it up with a fork. Crumble the meringues into the bowl and add the soft fruit mixture.

**3** Fold all the ingredients together until evenly combined and lightly marbled. Pack into the prepared tin and press down gently to level. Cover and freeze overnight. To serve, invert on to a plate and peel away the clear film. Serve in slices.

# Brandied Apple Charlotte

*Loosely based on a traditional Apple Charlotte, this iced version combines
brandy-steeped dried apple with a spicy ricotta cream
to make an unusual and very tasty dessert.*

**SERVES EIGHT TO TEN**

**INGREDIENTS**

130g | 4½oz | ¾ cup
DRIED APPLES

75ml | 5 tbsp BRANDY

50g | 2oz | ¼ cup
UNSALTED (SWEET) BUTTER

115g | 4oz | ½ cup
LIGHT MUSCOVADO
(BROWN) SUGAR

2.5ml | ½ tsp MIXED SPICE

60ml | 4 tbsp WATER

75g | 3oz | ½ cup SULTANAS
(GOLDEN RAISINS)

300g | 11oz MADEIRA CAKE,
cut into 1cm | ½in slices

250g | 9oz | generous 1 cup
RICOTTA CHEESE

30ml | 2 tbsp LEMON JUICE

150ml | ¼ pint | ⅔ cup
DOUBLE (HEAVY) or
WHIPPING CREAM

ICING (CONFECTIONERS')
SUGAR and FRESH MINT
SPRIGS, to decorate

**1** Roughly chop the dried apples, then transfer them to a clean bowl. Pour over the brandy and set aside for about 1 hour until most of the brandy has been absorbed.

**2** Melt the butter in a frying pan. Add the sugar and stir over a low heat for 1 minute. Add the ground mixed spice, water and soaked apples, with any remaining brandy. Cook gently for 5 minutes or until the apples are tender. Stir in the sultanas and leave to cool.

**3** Use the Madeira slices to line the sides of a 20cm | 8in square or round springform or loose-based cake tin (pan). Place in the freezer while you make the filling.

**4** Beat the ricotta in a bowl until it has softened, then stir in the apple mixture and lemon juice. Whip the cream in a separate bowl and fold it in. Spoon the mixture into the lined tin and level the surface. Cover and freeze overnight.

**5** Transfer the charlotte to the refrigerator 1 hour before serving. Invert it on to a plate, dust with sugar, and decorate with mint sprigs.

# Chocolate, Rum and Raisin Roulade

**SERVES SIX**

**INGREDIENTS**

*This richly flavoured dessert can be assembled and frozen a week or two in advance. Use vanilla, chocolate or coffee ice cream if you prefer, though all versions will be just as enjoyably indulgent.*

**For the roulade**

115g | 4oz PLAIN (SEMISWEET) CHOCOLATE, broken into pieces

4 EGGS, separated

115g | 4oz | generous ½ cup CASTER (SUPERFINE) SUGAR

UNSWEETENED COCOA POWDER and ICING (CONFECTIONERS') SUGAR, for dusting

**For the filling**

150ml | ¼ pint | ⅔ cup DOUBLE (HEAVY) CREAM

15ml | 1 tbsp ICING (CONFECTIONERS') SUGAR

30ml | 2 tbsp RUM

300ml | ½ pint | 1¼ cups RUM AND RAISIN ICE CREAM

**1** Make the roulade. Preheat the oven to 180°C | 350°F | Gas 4. Grease a 33 x 23cm | 13 x 9in Swiss roll tin (pan) and line with baking parchment. Grease the parchment. Melt the chocolate in a heatproof bowl set over a pan of simmering water. In a separate bowl, whisk the egg yolks with the caster sugar until thick and pale.

**2** Stir the melted chocolate into the yolk mixture. Whisk the egg whites in a grease-free bowl until stiff. Stir a quarter of the whites into the yolk mixture to lighten it, then fold in the remainder.

**3** Pour the mixture into the prepared tin and spread it gently into the corners. Bake for about 20 minutes until the cake has risen and is just firm. Turn it out on to a sheet of baking parchment which has been supported on a baking sheet and generously dusted with caster sugar. Leave to cool, then peel away the lining paper.

**4** Make the filling. Whip the cream with the icing sugar and rum until it forms soft peaks, then spread the mixture to within 1cm | ½in of the edges of the sponge. Freeze for 1 hour.

**5** Using a dessertspoon, scoop up long curls of the ice cream and lay an even layer over the cream.

**6** Starting from a narrow end carefully roll up the sponge, using the paper to help. Slide the roulade off the paper-lined baking sheet and on to a long plate that is freezerproof. Cover and freeze overnight. Transfer to the refrigerator 30 minutes before serving. Serve dusted with cocoa powder and icing sugar.

# Iced Lime Cheesecake

*This cheesecake has a deliciously tangy, sweet flavour, but needs no gelatine to set the filling, unlike most unbaked cheesecakes. It is not difficult to prepare and looks pleasantly summery with its citrus decoration.*

**SERVES TEN**

**INGREDIENTS**

175g | 6oz ALMOND BISCUITS (COOKIES)

65g | 2½oz | 5 tbsp UNSALTED (SWEET) BUTTER

8 LIMES

115g | 4oz | ½ cup CASTER (SUPERFINE) SUGAR

90ml | 6 tbsp WATER

200g | 7oz | scant 1 cup COTTAGE CHEESE

250g | 9oz | generous 1 cup MASCARPONE CHEESE

300ml | ½ pint | 1¼ cups DOUBLE (HEAVY) CREAM

**1** Lightly grease the sides of a 20cm | 8in springform tin (pan) and line with a strip of baking parchment. Break up the almond biscuits slightly, put them in a strong plastic bag and crush them with a rolling pin.

**2** Melt the butter in a small pan and stir in the biscuit crumbs until evenly combined. Spoon the mixture into the tin and pack it down with the back of a spoon. Freeze the biscuit mixture while you make the filling.

**3** Finely grate the rind and squeeze the juice from five of the limes. Heat the sugar and water in a small pan, stirring until the sugar dissolves. Bring to the boil and boil for 2 minutes without stirring, then remove the syrup from the heat, stir in the lime juice and rind and leave to cool.

**4** Press the cottage cheese through a sieve (strainer) into a bowl. Beat in the mascarpone, then the lime syrup.

**BY HAND:** Lightly whip the cream and fold into the cheese mixture. Pour into a shallow container and freeze until thick.

**USING AN ICE CREAM MAKER:** Add the cream and churn in an ice cream maker until thick.

**5** Meanwhile, cut a slice off either end of each of the remaining limes, stand them on a board and slice off the skins. Cut them into very thin slices.

**6** Arrange the lime slices around the sides of the tin, pressing them against the paper.

**7** Pour the cheese mixture over the biscuit base in the tin and level the surface. Cover and freeze the cheesecake overnight.

**8** About 1 hour before you are going to serve the cheesecake, carefully transfer it to a serving plate and put it in the refrigerator to soften slightly.

# Iced Butterscotch Tart

*Dark muscovado sugar gives this dessert its deliciously smooth butterscotch flavour. Remember to chill the*

*evaporated milk for a couple of hours before you are ready to make the filling.*

*This will ensure that it whisks well.*

**SERVES EIGHT**

**INGREDIENTS**

**For the case**

90g | 3½oz GINGERSNAP
BISCUITS (COOKIES)

75g | 3oz | ¾ cup GROUND
HAZELNUTS, toasted

50g | 2oz | ¼ cup UNSALTED
(SWEET) BUTTER, melted

**For the filling**

300ml | ½ pint | 1¼ cups
EVAPORATED MILK, chilled

150g | 5oz | ⅔ cup
DARK MUSCOVADO
(MOLASSES) SUGAR

1 EGG WHITE

150ml | ¼ pint | ⅔ cup
DOUBLE (HEAVY) CREAM

CHOPPED TOASTED
HAZELNUTS and DEMERARA
(RAW) SUGAR, to decorate

**1** Break up the biscuits slightly, put them in a strong plastic bag and crush them with a rolling pin. Tip them into a bowl and add the toasted nuts and the butter. Mix until evenly combined.

**2** Press on to the bottom and slightly up the sides of a 24cm | 9½in loose-based flan tin (pan) or freezerproof pie dish that is about 4cm | 1½in deep.

**3** Whisk the evaporated milk and sugar in a large bowl until the mixture is pale and thick and leaves a thick trail when the whisk is lifted.

**4** In a separate grease-free bowl, whisk the egg white until stiff. Whip the double cream separately until it forms soft peaks.

**5** Using a large metal spoon, fold first the cream and then the egg white into the whisked evaporated milk and sugar. Pour the mixture into the biscuit case. Cover and freeze overnight.

**6** To serve, sprinkle the tart with hazelnuts and demerara sugar and cut in thin wedges.

**COOK'S TIP** *Ground and chopped pecans, walnuts or almonds can be used instead of the hazelnuts.*

# hot
## ice cream
## puddings

There's nothing to beat the soft, melting texture of ice cream as it seeps into a deliciously warm pastry or mingles with the juices of a hot fruit compote, bringing out the flavour of both. The following chapter combines quick-and-easy puddings with make-ahead desserts. Serve immediately to enjoy the lingering warmth.

# Baby Alaskas with Liqueured Apricots

*Just as effective as a traditional baked Alaska, these individual ices are concealed under their own little meringue mountains.*

**SERVES SIX**

**INGREDIENTS**

40g | 1½oz | 3 tbsp CASTER (SUPERFINE) SUGAR

60ml | 4 tbsp WATER

150g | 5oz | generous ½ cup READY-TO-EAT APRICOTS, roughly chopped

30ml | 2 tbsp COINTREAU or other ORANGE-FLAVOURED LIQUEUR

500ml | 17fl oz | 2¼ cups VANILLA, HONEY or any NUT-FLAVOURED ICE CREAM

6 LARGE ALMOND or GINGER BISCUITS (COOKIES)

3 EGG WHITES

175g | 6oz | scant 1 cup CASTER (SUPERFINE) SUGAR

**1** Heat the sugar and water in a small, heavy pan, stirring occasionally, until the sugar has dissolved. Add the apricots and simmer gently for 5 minutes until they have absorbed most of the syrup. Stir in the liqueur and leave to chill.

**2** Freeze six small dariole moulds or metal pudding moulds for 15 minutes. At the same time, remove the ice cream from the freezer and leave for 15 minutes to soften slightly.

**VARIATION** *Feel free to experiment and substitute your favourite liqueur for the orange one recommended here. You can also use any other dried fruits instead of the apricots, if you prefer.*

**3** Using a dessertspoon, pack most of the ice cream into the moulds, leaving a deep cavity in the middle of each. Return each mould to the freezer once completed.

**4** When all the moulds have been lined with ice cream, remove them from the freezer again and fill the middles with the apricots. Cover the apricots with more ice cream and freeze until firm.

**5** Dip each mould in very hot water for 1–2 seconds, then invert. Slide a biscuit under each ice cream and transfer to a baking sheet. Place in the freezer.

**6** Whisk the egg whites in a grease-free bowl until they are stiff. Gradually whisk in the caster sugar, a tablespoonful at a time, whisking well after each addition until the mixture has become stiff and glossy.

**7** Using a metal spatula spread a thick layer of the meringue over each ice cream, making sure the meringue meets the biscuits and seals in the ice cream. Swirl the surface decoratively. Return the covered ice creams to the freezer.

**8** About 15 minutes before serving, preheat the oven to 230°C | 450°F | Gas 8. Bake the Alaskas for about 2 minutes until the meringue is pale golden. Serve immediately.

# Coconut and Passion Fruit Alaska

*A really classic ice cream extravaganza, baked Alaska lends itself to many variations on the basic theme.*
*This version comprises a passion-fruit-steeped coconut sponge, topped with tropical fruit ice*
*cream and smothered in a delicious coconut-flavoured meringue.*

### SERVES EIGHT

### INGREDIENTS

#### For the sponge

115g | 4oz | ½ cup UNSALTED (SWEET) BUTTER, softened

115g | 4oz | generous ½ cup CASTER (SUPERFINE) SUGAR

2 EGGS

115g | 4oz | 1 cup SELF-RAISING (SELF-RISING) FLOUR

2.5ml | ½ tsp BAKING POWDER

5ml | 1 tsp ALMOND EXTRACT

40g | 1½oz | ½ cup DESICCATED (DRY UNSWEETENED) COCONUT

15ml | 1 tbsp MILK

#### To finish

1 litre | 1¾ pints | 4 cups PASSION FRUIT, MANGO or TROPICAL FRUIT ICE CREAM

60ml | 4 tbsp KIRSCH

3 PASSION FRUIT

3 EGG WHITES

115g | 4oz | generous ½ cup CASTER (SUPERFINE) SUGAR

50g | 2oz | ½ cup CREAMED COCONUT, grated or 120ml | 4fl oz | ½ cup COCONUT CREAM

**1** Preheat the oven to 180°C | 350°F | Gas 4. Grease and line an 18cm | 7in round cake tin (pan). Put all the sponge ingredients in a bowl and whisk until smooth. Spoon into the prepared tin and bake for 35 minutes until the sponge is just firm. Leave to cool on a wire rack.

**2** Dampen a 1.2 litre | 2 pint | 5 cup pudding basin and line it with clear film (plastic wrap). Remove the ice cream from the freezer for 15 minutes to soften slightly.

**3** Pack the ice cream into the lined bowl and return it to the freezer for 1 hour. Place the sponge on a small baking sheet or ovenproof plate and drizzle the surface with kirsch. Remove the pulp from the fruit and scoop over the sponge.

**4** Dip the bowl containing the ice cream into very hot water for about 2 seconds to loosen the shaped ice cream. Invert it on to the sponge. Peel away the clear film and put the cake and ice cream in the freezer.

**5** To make the meringue, whisk the egg whites in a clean bowl until stiff. Gradually add the sugar, a tablespoon at a time, whisking well after each addition, until the meringue is thick and glossy. Fold in the coconut.

**6** Using a metal spatula, spread the meringue over the ice cream and sponge to cover both completely. Return to the freezer.

**7** About 15 minutes before serving, preheat the oven to 220°C | 425°F | Gas 7. Bake for 4–5 minutes, watching closely, until the peaks are golden. Serve immediately.

# Ice Cream Croissants with Chocolate Sauce

**MAKES FOUR**

**INGREDIENTS**

75g | 3oz PLAIN (SEMISWEET)
CHOCOLATE, broken into pieces

15g | ½oz | 1 tbsp UNSALTED
(SWEET) BUTTER

30ml | 2 tbsp GOLDEN (LIGHT
CORN) SYRUP

4 CROISSANTS

90ml | 6 tbsp
GOOD QUALITY READY-MADE
VANILLA CUSTARD

4 large scoops of
CLASSIC VANILLA ICE CREAM

ICING (CONFECTIONERS')
SUGAR, for dusting

**1** Preheat the oven to 180°C |
350°F | Gas 4. Put the chocolate in
a small, heavy pan. Add the butter
and syrup and heat very gently
until smooth, stirring the mixture
frequently.

**2** Split the croissants in half
horizontally and place the bases on
a baking sheet. Spoon the custard
over the bases, cover with the lids
and bake for 5 minutes until
warmed through.

**3** Remove the lids and place a
scoop of ice cream in each
croissant. Spoon half the sauce
over the ice cream and press the
lids down gently. Bake the
croissants for 1 minute more.

**4** Dust the filled croissants with
icing sugar, spoon over the
remaining chocolate sauce and
serve immediately.

*A deliciously easy croissant "sandwich" with a filling
of vanilla custard, ice cream and chocolate sauce
melting inside the warmed bread.*

# Baked Bananas with Ice Cream

*Baked bananas make the perfect partners for delicious vanilla ice cream topped with a toasted
hazelnut sauce. A quick and easy dessert that looks as good as it tastes.*

**SERVES FOUR**

**INGREDIENTS**

4 LARGE BANANAS

15ml | 1 tbsp LEMON JUICE

4 large scoops of
CLASSIC VANILLA ICE CREAM

**For the sauce**

25g | 1oz | 2 tbsp UNSALTED
(SWEET) BUTTER

50g | 2oz | ½ cup HAZELNUTS

45ml | 3 tbsp GOLDEN (LIGHT
CORN) SYRUP

30ml | 2 tbsp LEMON JUICE

**1** Preheat the oven to 180°C |
350°F | Gas 4. Place the unpeeled
bananas on a baking sheet and
brush them with the lemon juice.
Bake for about 20 minutes until
the skins are turning black and the
flesh gives a little when the
bananas are gently squeezed.

**COOK'S TIP** *Bake the bananas over the
dying coals of a barbecue, if you like.
Put them on the rack as soon as you
have removed all the main course items.*

**2** Meanwhile, make the sauce.
Melt the butter in a small pan.
Chop the hazelnuts and add to the
pan. Cook gently for 1 minute.
Add the syrup and lemon juice and
heat, stirring, for 1 minute more.

**3** To serve, slit each banana open
with a knife and open out the
skins. Transfer to serving plates
and serve with scoops of ice
cream. Pour the sauce over.

# Toasted Marzipan Parcels with Plums

*Melting ice cream, encased in lightly toasted marzipan, makes an irresistible dessert for anyone who likes the flavour of almonds. Lightly poached apricots, cherries, apples or pears can be used instead of the plums.*

**SERVES FOUR**

**INGREDIENTS**

400g | 14oz GOLDEN MARZIPAN

ICING (CONFECTIONERS')
SUGAR, for dusting

250ml | 8fl oz | 1 cup ALMOND,
GINGER or VANILLA ICE CREAM

**For the plum compote**

3 RED PLUMS, about 250g | 9oz

25g | 1oz | 2 tbsp CASTER
(SUPERFINE) SUGAR

75ml | 5 tbsp WATER

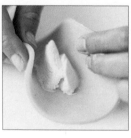

**1** Roll out the marzipan on a surface lightly dusted with icing sugar to a 45 x 23cm | 18 x 9in rectangle. Stamp out eight rounds using a 12cm | 4½in cookie cutter.

**2** Place a spoonful of the ice cream in each circle. Bring the marzipan up over the ice cream and press the edges together to completely encase.

**3** Crimp the edges with your fingers. Transfer to a small baking sheet and freeze. Fill and shape the remaining parcels in the same way and freeze overnight.

**4** Make the plum compote. Cut the plums in half, remove the stones (pits), then cut each half into two wedges. Heat the sugar and water in a heavy pan, stirring occasionally, until the sugar has completely dissolved.

**5** Add the plums and cook very gently for 5 minutes or until they have softened but retain their shape. Test with the tip of a sharp knife – the flesh of the plums should be just tender.

**6** Preheat the grill (broiler) to high. Place the marzipan parcels on the grill rack and cook for 1–2 minutes, watching closely, until the crimped edge of the marzipan is lightly browned. Transfer the parcels to serving plates and serve with the warm plum compote.

**COOK'S TIP** *Don't let the parcels become too brown under the grill (broiler) or the ice cream will quickly seep out. Use a firm-textured ice cream and make sure the parcels are frozen solid before grilling (broiling) them.*

# Hot Ice Cream Fritters

*Deep-fried ice cream may seem a contradiction in terms, but once you've made these crisp fritters, you'll be converted! The secret is to encase the ice cream thoroughly in two layers of sweet biscuit crumb. This will turn crisp and golden during frying, and the ice cream inside will only melt slightly.*

**SERVES FOUR**

**INGREDIENTS**

750ml | 1¼ pints | 3 cups
FIRM VANILLA ICE CREAM

115g | 4oz AMARETTI or
RATAFIA BISCUITS (COOKIES)

115g | 4oz | 2 cups FRESH BROWN
BREADCRUMBS

1 EGG

45g | 1¾oz | 3 tbsp PLAIN
(ALL-PURPOSE) FLOUR

OIL, for deep frying

**For the caramel sauce**

115g | 4oz | generous ½ cup CASTER
(SUPERFINE) SUGAR

150ml | ¼ pint | ⅔ cup WATER

150ml | ¼ pint | ⅔ cup DOUBLE
(HEAVY) CREAM

**1** Line a baking sheet with baking parchment and put it in the freezer for 15 minutes, at the same time removing the ice cream from the freezer to soften slightly. Scoop about 12 balls of ice cream, making them as round as possible and place them on the lined baking sheet. Freeze for at least 1 hour until firm.

**2** Meanwhile, put the amaretti or ratafia biscuits in a strong plastic bag and crush them with a rolling pin. Tip into a bowl and add the breadcrumbs. Mix well, and then transfer half the mixture to a plate. Beat the egg in a shallow dish. Sprinkle the flour on to a second plate.

**3** Using cool hands, and working very quickly, roll each ice cream ball in the flour, then dip in the beaten egg until coated. Roll the balls in the mixed crumbs until completely covered. Return the coated ice cream balls to the baking sheet and freeze for at least 1 hour more.

**4** Repeat the process, using the remaining flour, egg and breadcrumbs, so that each ball has an additional coating. Return the ice cream balls to the freezer for at least 4 hours, preferably overnight.

**5** Make the sauce. Heat the sugar and water in a small, heavy pan, stirring occasionally, until the sugar has dissolved. Bring to the boil and boil the syrup for about 10 minutes without stirring until deep golden. Immediately immerse the base of the pan in a bowl of cold water to prevent the syrup from cooking any more.

**6** Pour the cream into the syrup and return the pan to the heat. Stir until the sauce is smooth. Set aside while you fry the ice cream.

**7** Pour oil into a heavy pan to a depth of 7.5cm | 3in. Heat to 185°C | 365°F or until a cube of bread added to the oil browns in 30 seconds. Add several of the ice cream balls and fry for about 1 minute until the coating on each is golden. Drain on kitchen paper and quickly cook the remainder in the same way. Serve the fritters with the caramel sauce.

**COOK'S TIP** *If the ice cream scoops are irregularly shaped, form into neat balls after coating in the first layer.*

# Filo, Ice Cream and Mincemeat Parcels

**MAKES TWELVE**

*Looking rather like crispy fried pancakes, these golden parcels reveal hot chunky mincemeat and melting vanilla ice cream when cut open. They can be assembled days in advance, ready for easy, last-minute frying.*

**INGREDIENTS**

1 FIRM PEAR

225g | 8oz | 1 cup MINCEMEAT

finely grated rind of 1 LEMON

12 sheets of FILO PASTRY,
thawed if frozen

a little beaten EGG

250ml | 8 fl oz | 1 cup
CLASSIC VANILLA ICE CREAM

OIL, for deep frying

CASTER (SUPERFINE) SUGAR
for dusting

**1** Peel, core and chop the pear. Put it in a small bowl and then stir in the mincemeat and lemon rind.

**2** Lay one filo sheet on the work surface and cut it into two 20cm | 8in squares. Brush one square lightly with beaten egg then cover with the second square.

**3** Lay 10ml | 2 tsp mincemeat on the filo, placing it 2.5cm | 1in away from one edge and spreading it slightly to cover a 7.5cm | 3in area. Lay 10ml | 2 tsp of the ice cream over the mincemeat. Brush all around the edges of the filo with beaten egg.

**4** Fold over the two opposite sides of the pastry to cover the filling. Roll up the strip, starting from the filled end. Transfer to a baking sheet and freeze. Make 11 more rolls in the same way.

**5** When you are ready to serve, pour oil into a heavy pan to a depth of 7.5cm | 3in. Heat it to 185°C | 365°F or until a cube of bread added to the oil browns in 30 seconds.

**6** Fry several parcels at a time for 1–2 minutes until pale golden, turning them over during cooking. Drain on kitchen paper while frying the remainder. Dust with caster sugar and serve immediately.

**COOK'S TIP** *Filo pastry sheets vary considerably in size. Don't worry if you can't get two 20cm | 8in squares from each slice. It won't matter if the squares are slightly smaller or even rectangular as long as they can be rolled to enclose the filling.*

# Walnut and Vanilla Ice Palmiers

*These walnut pastries can be served freshly baked, but for convenience, make them ahead and reheat them in a moderate oven for 5 minutes.*

**MAKES SIX**

**INGREDIENTS**

75g | 3oz | ¾ cup WALNUT PIECES

350g | 12oz PUFF PASTRY,
thawed if frozen

beaten EGG, to glaze

45ml | 3 tbsp CASTER
(SUPERFINE) SUGAR

about 200ml | 7fl oz | scant 1 cup
CLASSIC VANILLA ICE CREAM

**1** Preheat the oven to 200°C | 400°F | Gas 6. Lightly grease a large baking sheet with butter. Chop the walnuts finely. On a lightly floured surface roll the pastry to a thin rectangle 30 x 20cm | 12 x 8in.

**2** Trim the edges of the pastry then brush with the egg. Sprinkle all but 45ml | 3 tbsp of the walnuts and 30ml | 2 tbsp of the sugar. Run the rolling pin over the walnuts to press them into the pastry.

**3** Roll up the pastry from one short side to the middle, then roll up the other side until the two rolls meet. Brush the points where the rolls meet with a little beaten egg. Using a sharp knife, cut the pastry into slices 1cm | ½in thick.

**4** Lay the slices on the work surface and flatten them with a rolling pin. Transfer to the baking sheet. Brush with more of the beaten egg and sprinkle with the reserved walnuts and sugar.

**5** Bake for about 15 minutes until pale golden. Serve warm, in pairs, sandwiched with ice cream.

# Peach, Blackberry and Ice Cream Gratin

*A wonderfully easy dessert in which the flavours of the peaches, blackberries, ice cream and muscovado mingle together as they grill. Use large, ripe peaches with enough space for the filling.*

**2** Brush the cut surfaces with lemon juice and transfer to a shallow flameproof dish. Grill (broil) for 2 minutes. Remove from the heat, but leave the grill on to maintain the temperature.

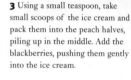

**3** Using a small teaspoon, take small scoops of the ice cream and pack them into the peach halves, piling up in the middle. Add the blackberries, pushing them gently into the ice cream.

**4** Sprinkle the filled peaches with the muscovado sugar and replace under the hot grill (broiler) for 1–2 minutes until the sugar has dissolved and the ice cream is beginning to melt. Serve.

**SERVES FOUR**

**INGREDIENTS**

4 LARGE PEACHES

15ml | 1 tbsp LEMON JUICE

120ml | 4fl oz | ½ cup CLASSIC VANILLA ICE CREAM

115g | 4oz | 1 cup SMALL BLACKBERRIES

40g | 1½oz | 3 tbsp LIGHT MUSCOVADO (BROWN) SUGAR

**1** Preheat the grill (broiler). Cut the peaches in half and remove the stones (pits). Cut a thin slice off the rounded side of each peach so that they sit flat on the surface.

**COOK'S TIP** *Other berries, such as fresh blueberries, can be used instead of blackberries, if you prefer.*

*Don't take the ice cream out of the freezer until just before you are ready to fill the peaches, and then work quickly. The ice cream must still be solid or it will melt too quickly when the dessert is under the hot grill (broiler).*

# Apple Ice Cream with Cinnamon Bread

*Cooking the apples with butter, lemon and spice accentuates their flavour and makes a marvellous ice cream. It is good over apple pies and other pastries, but even better with crisp fried sugared bread.*

**SERVES SIX**

**INGREDIENTS**

675g | 1½lb COOKING APPLES

50g | 2oz | ¼ cup
UNSALTED (SWEET) BUTTER

1.5ml | ¼ tsp MIXED SPICE

finely grated rind and juice
of 1 LEMON

90g | 3½oz | scant ½ cup
CREAM CHEESE

2 EGG WHITES, beaten

150ml | ¼ pint | ⅔ cup
DOUBLE (HEAVY) CREAM

MINT SPRIGS, to decorate

**For the cinnamon bread**

6 thick slices of WHITE BREAD

1 EGG, beaten

1 EGG YOLK

2.5ml | ½ tsp NATURAL
VANILLA EXTRACT

150ml | ¼ pint | ⅔ cup
SINGLE (LIGHT) CREAM

65g | 2½oz | 5 tbsp CASTER
(SUPERFINE) SUGAR

2.5ml | ½ tsp GROUND CINNAMON

25g | 1oz | 2 tbsp UNSALTED
(SWEET) BUTTER

45ml | 3 tbsp OIL

**1** Peel, core and slice the apples. Melt the butter in a pan. Add the apple slices, mixed spice and lemon rind. Cover and cook very gently for 10 minutes until the apple slices are soft. Leave to cool.

**2** Tip the apples and juices into a food processor then the lemon juice and cream cheese. Blend until smooth. In separate bowls, whisk the egg whites until stiff and the cream until it forms soft peaks.

**3** Scrape the purée into a bowl. Fold in the cream, then the egg whites. Spoon into a plastic tub and freeze overnight.

**4** Make the cinnamon bread about 20 minutes before serving. Cut the crusts off the bread slices, then cut each slice diagonally in half. Beat together the egg, egg yolk, vanilla extract, cream and 15ml | 1 tbsp of the sugar.

**5** Arrange the bread triangles in a single layer on a large, shallow plate or tray. Pour the cream mixture over the bread triangles and leave for about 10 minutes until the mixture has been thoroughly absorbed.

**6** Mix the remaining sugar with the cinnamon on a plate. Melt the butter in the oil in a large frying pan. When it is hot, add half the bread and fry until golden underneath. Turn the slices with a metal spatula and fry the other side.

**7** Drain the slices lightly on kitchen paper, then coat them on both sides in the cinnamon sugar and keep them hot. Cook the remaining slices in the same way. Serve at once, topped with scoops of the apple ice cream. Decorate with the mint sprigs.

# Ice Cream with Hot Cherry Sauce

*Hot cherry sauce makes a classic yet really simple accompaniment to ice cream for serving on any occasion. Use only good-quality chocolate and vanilla.*

**SERVES FOUR**

**INGREDIENTS**

425g | 15oz can PITTED BLACK CHERRIES

10ml | 2 tsp CORNFLOUR (CORNSTARCH)

finely grated rind of 1 LEMON, plus 10ml | 2 tsp JUICE

15ml | 1 tbsp CASTER (SUPERFINE) SUGAR

2.5ml | ½ tsp GROUND CINNAMON

30ml | 2 tbsp BRANDY or KIRSCH (optional)

400ml | 14fl oz | 1⅔ cups DARK (BITTERSWEET) CHOCOLATE ICE CREAM

400ml | 14fl oz | 1⅔ cups CLASSIC VANILLA ICE CREAM

DRINKING CHOCOLATE POWDER, for dusting

**1** Drain the cherries, reserving the canning juices. Spoon the cornflour into a small pan and blend to a paste with a little of the reserved juice.

**2** Stir in the remaining canning juice with the lemon rind and juice, sugar and cinnamon. Bring to the boil, stirring, until smooth and glossy.

**3** Add the cherries, with the brandy or kirsch, if using. Stir gently, then cook for 1 minute. Scoop the ice cream into shallow dishes. Spoon the sauce around, dust with chocolate powder and serve.

# Syrupy Brioche Slices with Vanilla Ice Cream

*Keep a few individual brioche buns in the freezer to make this fabulous five-minute pudding. For a slightly tarter taste, use lemon instead of orange rind.*

**SERVES FOUR**

**INGREDIENTS**

grated rind and juice of 1 ORANGE

50g | 2oz | ¼ cup CASTER (SUPERFINE) SUGAR

90ml | 6 tbsp WATER

1.5ml | ¼ tsp GROUND CINNAMON

4 BRIOCHE BUNS

15ml | 1 tbsp ICING (CONFECTIONERS') SUGAR

400ml | 14fl oz | 1⅔ cups CLASSIC VANILLA ICE CREAM

**1** Lightly grease a gratin dish and set aside. Put the orange rind and juice, sugar, water and cinnamon in a heavy pan. Heat gently, stirring, until the sugar has dissolved, then boil for 2 minutes without stirring.

**2** Remove the syrup from the heat and pour it into a shallow heatproof dish. Preheat the grill (broiler). Cut each brioche vertically into three thick slices. Dip one side of each slice in the hot syrup and arrange in the gratin dish, syrupy sides down. Reserve the remaining syrup. Grill (broil) the brioche until lightly toasted.

**3** Turn over and dust with icing sugar. Grill for 2–3 minutes more until they begin to caramelize around the edges.

**4** Transfer to serving plates and top with scoops of ice cream. Spoon over the remaining syrup and serve immediately.

# Blueberry and Vanilla Crumble Torte

*In this heavenly pudding, vanilla ice cream is packed into a buttery crumble case and baked until the ice cream starts to melt over the crumble. Remember that you need to start making this the day before you intend to serve it.*

**SERVES EIGHT**

**INGREDIENTS**

225g | 8oz | 2 cups PLAIN (ALL-PURPOSE) FLOUR

5ml | 1 tsp BAKING POWDER

175g | 6oz | ¾ cup UNSALTED (SWEET) BUTTER, diced

150g | 5oz | ¾ cup CASTER (SUPERFINE) SUGAR

1 EGG

75g | 3oz | ¾ cup GROUND ALMONDS

10ml | 2 tsp natural VANILLA EXTRACT

5ml | 1 tsp MIXED SPICE

500ml | 17fl oz | 2¼ cups CLASSIC VANILLA ICE CREAM

175g | 6oz | 1½ cups BLUEBERRIES

ICING (CONFECTIONERS') SUGAR, for dusting

**1** Preheat the oven to 180°C | 350°F | Gas 4. Put the flour and baking powder in a food processor. Add the butter and process briefly to mix. Add the sugar and process briefly again until the mixture is crumbly. Remove about 175g | 6oz | 1½ cups of the crumble mixture and set this aside.

**2** Add the egg, ground almonds, vanilla extract and mixed spice to the remaining crumble mixture and blend to a paste.

**3** Scrape the paste into a 20cm | 8in springform tin (pan). Press it on to the base and halfway up the sides to make an even case. Line the pastry case with baking parchment and fill with baking beans.

**4** Sprinkle the crumble mixture on to a baking sheet. Bake the crumble for 20 minutes and the case for about 30 minutes until pale golden. Remove the baking parchment and beans from the case and bake it for 5 minutes more. Leave to cool.

**5** Pack the ice cream into the almond pastry case and level the surface. Scatter with the blueberries and then the baked crumble mixture. Freeze overnight.

**6** About 25 minutes before serving, preheat the oven to 180°C | 350°F | Gas 4. Bake the torte for 10–15 minutes, until the ice cream has started to soften. Dust with icing sugar and serve in wedges.

**COOK'S TIP** *The crumble mixture can be made without a food processor if you do not have one. Simply rub the butter into the flour and baking powder, then stir in the sugar. To make the paste, simply stir the additional ingredients into the remaining crumble mixture.*

# Orange Crêpes with Mascarpone Cream

*Baking these delicate crêpes does not actually make them hot when served. Quite simply, the sorbet and mascarpone start to melt together in their crisp pancake cases to make a delicious dessert that is neither too rich nor too sweet.*

**SERVES EIGHT**

**INGREDIENTS**

**For the crêpes**

115g | 4oz | 1 cup PLAIN (ALL-PURPOSE) FLOUR

300ml | ½ pint | 1¼ cups MILK

1 EGG, plus 1 EGG YOLK

finely grated rind of 1 ORANGE

30ml | 2 tbsp CASTER (SUPERFINE) SUGAR

OIL, for frying

**To finish**

250g | 9oz | generous 1 cup MASCARPONE CHEESE

15ml | 1 tbsp ICING (CONFECTIONERS') SUGAR

90ml | 6 tbsp SINGLE (LIGHT) CREAM

45ml | 3 tbsp COINTREAU or ORANGE JUICE

500ml | 17fl oz | 2¼ cups ORANGE SORBET

ICING (CONFECTIONERS') SUGAR, for dusting

**1** Make the crêpes. Put the flour, milk, egg, egg yolk, orange rind and sugar in a food processor and blend until smooth. Pour the batter into a jug (pitcher) and leave to stand for 30 minutes.

**2** Heat a little of the oil in a medium frying pan or crêpe pan until very hot. Drain off the excess. Pour a little of the batter into the pan, tilting the pan so that the batter coats the base thinly. Pour any excess back into the jug.

**3** Cook the crêpe until the underside is golden, then flip it over with a palette knife or metal spatula and cook the other side. Slide the crêpe on to a plate and cook seven more crêpes, lightly oiling the pan each time and stacking the cooked ones.

**4** Preheat the oven to 200°C | 400°F | Gas 6. In a bowl, beat the mascarpone with the icing sugar, cream and liqueur or orange juice until smooth. Spread the mixture on the crêpes, taking it almost to the edges.

**5** Using a teaspoon, scoop shavings of sorbet and arrange them to one side of each topped crêpe. Fold the crêpes in half and dust with icing sugar. Fold again into quarters and dust with more icing sugar. Lay the crêpes in a large shallow baking dish and bake for 2 minutes until the sorbet starts to melt. Serve immediately.

# elegant iced
## desserts

Presentation plays just as important a role
with ice creams as it does with any other
dessert. Whether scooped into glasses and
bathed in a sweet glossy sauce, or cleverly
contained in a chocolate case, there is a
dessert here to suit the mood
of any occasion.

# Iced Vanilla Brûlées

*Freeze these little desserts in ramekins. Just before serving, sprinkle them with sugar and pop them under the grill to caramelize the topping.*

**SERVES SIX**

**INGREDIENTS**

1 VANILLA POD (BEAN)

600ml | 1 pint | 2½ cups FULL CREAM (WHOLE) MILK

50g | 2oz | ¼ cup FLAKED RICE

finely grated rind of 2 LEMONS

150g | 5oz | ¾ cup CASTER (SUPERFINE) SUGAR

300ml | ½ pint | 1¼ cups WHIPPING CREAM

sugared STRAWBERRIES, to serve

**1** Split the vanilla pod lengthways with a knife and put it in a pan. Pour in the milk and add the rice. Simmer for 8–10 minutes until the rice is turning pulpy.

**2** Remove the vanilla pod and scrape out the seeds. Return them to the pan and stir in the lemon rind and 75g | 3oz | 6 tbsp of the sugar. Leave to cool.

**3** Stir in the cream and churn the mixture in an ice cream maker. Divide among six 150ml | ¼ pint | ⅔ cup ramekins or heatproof dishes, and freeze for at least 3 hours or until firm. Preheat the grill (broiler). Sprinkle each dish with a layer of the remaining sugar.

**4** Cook under the preheated grill for about 5 minutes until the sugar has caramelized. Serve with the sugared strawberries.

**COOK'S TIP** *If you haven't got a vanilla pod (bean), use 5ml | 1 tsp natural vanilla extract instead.*

# Miniature Choc-ices

*For summer entertaining, these little chocolate-coated ice creams make a fun alternative to the more familiar after-dinner chocolates.*

**MAKES ABOUT 25**

**INGREDIENTS**

750ml | 1¼ pints | 3 cups CLASSIC VANILLA, CLASSIC DARK (BITTERSWEET) CHOCOLATE or CLASSIC COFFEE ICE CREAM

200g | 7oz PLAIN (SEMISWEET) CHOCOLATE, broken into pieces

25g | 1oz MILK CHOCOLATE, broken into pieces

25g | 1oz | ¼ cup chopped HAZELNUTS, lightly toasted

**1** Put a large baking sheet in the freezer for 10 minutes. Using a melon baller, scoop balls of the ice cream and place these on the baking sheet. Freeze for at least 1 hour until firm.

**2** Line a second baking sheet with baking parchment and place in the freezer for 15 minutes. Melt the plain chocolate in a heatproof bowl set over a pan of gently simmering water. Melt the milk chocolate in a separate bowl.

**3** Using a metal spatula, transfer the ice cream scoops to the baking parchment-lined sheet. Spoon a little plain chocolate over one scoop so that most of it is coated.

**4** Scatter immediately with chopped nuts, before the chocolate sets. Coat half the remaining scoops in the same way, scattering each one with nuts before the chocolate sets. Spoon the remaining plain chocolate over all the remaining scoops.

**5** Using a teaspoon, drizzle the milk chocolate over the choc-ices which are not topped with nuts. Freeze again until ready to serve.

**COOK'S TIP** *If the melted milk chocolate is very runny leave it for a few minutes to thicken up slightly before spooning it over the ice cream scoops. The milk chocolate can be piped on the choc-ices, using a piping bag fitted with a writing nozzle.*

# Chocolate Teardrops with Cherry Sauce

*These sensational chocolate cases are surprisingly easy to make. Once filled, they freeze well, making them the perfect choice for a special occasion dessert.*

**4** Put the amaretti biscuits in a plastic bag and crush them with a rolling pin. Pour the cream into a bowl, add the almond extract and icing sugar and whip until thick but still soft. Fold in the biscuits.

**6** Tap the baking sheet gently on the work surface so the filling becomes level. Freeze the filled chocolate cases for at least 3 hours or overnight.

**7** Make the sauce. Put the cornflour in a small pan and stir in a little of the water to make a paste. Stir in the remaining water, with the cherries, sugar and lemon juice. Bring just to the boil, stirring until thickened. Remove from the heat and leave to cool. Stir in the gin.

**8** To serve, remove the paper clips from the chocolate shapes, then carefully peel away the perspex. Transfer the shapes to individual dessert plates. Spoon a little sauce on to each plate and decorate with the pairs of cherries.

### SERVES SIX

### INGREDIENTS

90g | 3½oz PLAIN (SEMISWEET) CHOCOLATE, broken into pieces

115g | 4oz AMARETTI BISCUITS (COOKIES)

300ml | ½ pint | 1¼ cups WHIPPING CREAM

2.5ml | ½ tsp ALMOND EXTRACT

30ml | 2 tbsp ICING (CONFECTIONERS') SUGAR

6 pairs of FRESH CHERRIES, to decorate

### For the sauce

2.5ml | ½ tsp CORNFLOUR (CORNSTARCH)

75ml | 5 tbsp WATER

225g | 8oz | 2 cups FRESH CHERRIES, stoned (pitted) and halved

45ml | 3 tbsp CASTER (SUPERFINE) SUGAR

10ml | 2 tsp LEMON JUICE

45ml | 3 tbsp GIN

**3** Bring the ends of the strip together so that the coated side is on the inside. Hold the ends with a paper clip, then put on the baking sheet to set. Make five more shapes in the same way. Chill until set.

**5** Spoon the mixture carefully into the chocolate cases, making sure that the chocolate shape is filled with ice cream up to the rim.

**1** Cut out six perspex strips, each measuring 27 x 3cm | 10½ x 1¼in. Put the chocolate in a heatproof bowl over a pan of simmering water until melted. Remove from the heat and leave for 5 minutes. Line a baking sheet with baking parchment.

**2** Coat the underside of a perspex strip in the chocolate, apart from 1cm | ½in at each end. Try to keep the other side uncoated.

# Chocolate Millefeuille Slice

*Although this stunning dessert takes a little time to prepare, the good news is that it can be assembled days in advance, ready to impress dinner guests. Simply transfer it to the refrigerator about 30 minutes before serving so that it becomes easier to slice.*

**SERVES EIGHT**

**INGREDIENTS**

4 EGG YOLKS

10ml | 2 tsp CORNFLOUR (CORNSTARCH)

300ml | ½ pint | 1¼ cups MILK

175ml | 6fl oz | ¾ cup MAPLE SYRUP

250ml | 8fl oz | 1 cup CRÈME FRAÎCHE

115g | 4oz | 1 cup PECAN NUTS, chopped

**To finish**

200g | 7oz PLAIN (SEMISWEET) CHOCOLATE

300ml | ½ pint | 1¼ cups DOUBLE (HEAVY) CREAM

45ml | 3 tbsp ICING (CONFECTONERS') SUGAR

30ml | 2 tbsp BRANDY (optional)

lightly toasted PECAN NUTS

**1** Whisk the egg yolks in a bowl with the cornflour and a little of the milk until smooth. Pour the remaining milk into a pan, bring to the boil, then pour over the yolk mixture, stirring.

**2** Return the mixture to the pan and stir in the maple syrup. Cook gently, stirring until thick and smooth. Do not boil. Pour into a bowl and cover with backing parchment. Leave to cool.

**3 BY HAND:** Stir the crème fraîche into the cold custard and pour into a shallow container. Freeze for 3–4 hours, beating twice as it thickens, add the chopped pecan nuts and freeze again overnight.

**USING AN ICE CREAM MAKER:** Churn until thick and creamy, then add the chopped pecan nuts. Scrape into a freezerproof container and freeze overnight.

**4** Break 150g | 5oz of the chocolate into pieces and melt in a bowl over a pan of simmering water. On baking parchment draw four rectangles, each measuring 19 x 12cm | 7½ x 4⅔in. Spoon a quarter of the melted chocolate on to each rectangle and spread to the edges. Leave to set.

**5** Pare thin curls from the remaining chocolate using a potato peeler. Then whip the cream with the icing sugar and brandy if using, until it forms soft peaks. Carefully peel away the paper from a chocolate rectangle and place it on a flat freezer proof serving plate. Spread a third of the whipped cream on the chocolate, taking it almost to the edges.

**6** Using a teaspoon, shape small scoops of the ice cream and lay these over the cream. Cover with a second chocolate rectangle. Repeat the layering, finishing with chocolate. Scatter with the toasted pecan nuts and chocolate curls. Freeze overnight until firm. If freezing the slice for longer, cover it loosely with foil once it is frozen solid.

**7** Transfer the frozen slice to the refrigerator 30 minutes before serving to soften. Serve in slices.

**COOK'S TIP** *It is a good idea to assemble the millefeuille on the upside-down lid of a rectangular freezer tub. The cover can then be fitted and the dessert frozen. Carefully slide the dessert on to a rectangular plate to serve.*

# Hazelnut Cones with Vanilla Ice Cream and Hazelnut Caramel Sauce

*Unlike bought ice cream cones, these hazelnut biscuit cones not only fulfil a function but taste delicious too!*

*They keep well in an airtight container for several days, but should they start to soften, pop*

*them into a moderate oven for a minute or two.*

**SERVES EIGHT**

**INGREDIENTS**

90g | 3½oz | scant 1 cup
GROUND HAZELNUTS

50g | 2oz | ½ cup PLAIN
(ALL-PURPOSE) FLOUR

50g | 2oz | ¼ cup CASTER
(SUPERFINE) SUGAR

2 EGGS, lightly beaten

5ml | 1 tsp NATURAL
VANILLA EXTRACT

15ml | 1 tbsp MILK

**For the sauce**

75g | 3oz | 6 tbsp CASTER
(SUPERFINE) SUGAR

60ml | 4 tbsp WATER

50g | 2oz | ½ cup HAZELNUTS,
lightly toasted and roughly chopped

15ml | 1 tbsp LEMON JUICE

25g | 1oz | 2 tbsp
UNSALTED (SWEET) BUTTER

about 500ml | 17fl oz | 2¼ cups
VANILLA ICE CREAM

**1** Preheat the oven to 180°C | 350°F | Gas 4. Line a baking sheet with baking parchment. Mix the ground hazelnuts, flour and sugar in a bowl. Add the eggs, vanilla extract and milk to the bowl and mix to a smooth paste.

**2** Scoop up a shallow tablespoonful of the mixture and spoon it on to one end of the baking sheet. Add a second spoonful at the opposite end. Using a palette knife or metal spatula spread each spoonful to a circle about 13cm | 5in in diameter, making sure the paste is spread to an even thickness. Bake the biscuits for about 5 minutes until they start to turn pale gold around the edges.

**3** Working quickly, lift a biscuit from the paper and turn it over. Wrap it around a cream horn mould to make a cone shape. Repeat with the other biscuit. As soon as the biscuits become brittle, gently ease the cones away from the moulds. Repeat with the remaining mixture to make eight cones in all.

**4** Make the sauce. Heat the sugar and water in a small, heavy pan until the sugar has dissolved. Bring to the boil and boil rapidly, without stirring, until the caramel is a deep golden colour. Immediately immerse the base of the pan in cold water to prevent the caramel from further cooking. Protecting your hand with an oven glove, add 60ml | 4 tbsp water, standing back in case the syrup splutters.

**5** Add the hazelnuts, lemon juice and butter to the pan and cook gently until the sauce is smooth and glossy. Pour it into a small jug (pitcher).

**6** Scoop the vanilla ice cream into the hazelnut cones. Pour over a little sauce and serve immediately.

**COOK'S TIP** *Getting the biscuits to the right thickness is quite tricky, so treat the first batch as a trial run. If the mixture is spread too thickly the biscuits will be rather soft; if too thin, they will crack when moulded around the moulds.*

# Chocolate Ice Cream with Lime Sabayon

*Sabayon sauce has a light, foamy texture that perfectly complements the rich, smooth flavour of ice cream.*

*This tangy lime version is delicious with chocolate ice cream but can also be served*

*with tropical fruit, soft fruit or vanilla ice cream.*

**SERVES FOUR**

**INGREDIENTS**

2 EGG YOLKS

65g | 2½oz | 5 tbsp CASTER (SUPERFINE) SUGAR

finely grated rind and juice of 2 LIMES

60ml | 4 tbsp WHITE WINE or APPLE JUICE

45ml | 3 tbsp SINGLE (LIGHT) CREAM

500ml | 17fl oz | 2¼ cups CHOCOLATE CHIP or CLASSIC DARK (BITTERSWEET) CHOCOLATE ICE CREAM

pared strips of LIME RIND, to decorate

**1** Put the egg yolks and sugar in a heatproof bowl and beat until combined. Beat in the lime rind and juice, then the white wine or apple juice.

**2** Whisk the mixture over a pan of gently simmering water until the sabayon is smooth and thick, and the mixture leaves a trail when the whisk is lifted from the bowl. Lightly whisk in the cream. Remove the bowl from the pan and cover with a lid or plate.

**3** Working quickly, scoop the ice cream into four glasses. Spoon the sabayon sauce over the ice cream, decorate with the strips of lime rind and serve immediately.

# Ice Cream with Sweet Pine Nut Sauce

**SERVES FOUR**

**INGREDIENTS**

75g | 2½oz | 5 tbsp PINE NUTS

25g | 1oz | 2tbsp UNSALTED (SWEET) BUTTER

30ml | 2 tbsp CLEAR HONEY

30ml | 2 tbsp LIGHT MUSCOVADO (BROWN) SUGAR

pared rind and juice of 1 LEMON

250ml | 8 fl oz | 1 cup LEMON SORBET

250ml | 8 fl oz | 1 cup VANILLA ICE CREAM

**1** Toast the pine nuts lightly, then chop them roughly. Melt the butter in a small, heavy pan with the honey and sugar. Remove from the heat and stir in the lemon rind and juice.

*The delicious combination of lightly toasted pine nuts, tangy lemon and butter makes an easy sauce, perfect for enlivening vanilla ice cream and lemon sorbet.*

**2** Stir in the chopped pine nuts. Pour the sauce into a small jug (pitcher). Leave to cool until ready to serve.

**3** To serve, alternate small scoops of the lemon sorbet and the vanilla ice cream in four tall serving glasses. Generously spoon the pine nut sauce over the ices and serve immediately.

**COOK'S TIP** *The sauce will be very thin while it is still warm, but it becomes thicker as it cools. Best served before it is quite cold.*

# Iced Coffee Cups

*Small, sturdy coffee cups make attractive containers for this richly flavoured ice cream. Alternatively use ramekins or other small freezerproof dishes.*

**3** Spoon the cornflour into a small, heavy pan. Stir in a little of the hot coffee, then add the remaining coffee with the egg yolks and sugar. Cook over a gentle heat, stirring constantly until thickened. Do not boil or the mixture may curdle. Scrape into a bowl, cover closely with baking parchment and leave to cool.

**4** Whip the cream with the liqueur and cooled coffee mixture until it forms soft peaks.

**5** Spoon the mixture into the coffee cups, tapping them gently to level the surface. Freeze for at least 3 hours.

**6** Transfer the coffee cups to the refrigerator about 30 minutes before serving. Top with swirls of lightly whipped cream and dust with drinking chocolate powder.

**COOK'S TIP** *The number of people this will serve depends on the size of the cups. If they are very small, this quantity will serve at least eight.*

**SERVES SIX TO EIGHT**

**INGREDIENTS**

150ml | ¼ pint | ⅔ cup WATER

75ml | 5 tbsp GROUND ESPRESSO COFFEE

5ml | 1 tsp CORNFLOUR (CORNSTARCH)

4 EGG YOLKS

65g | 2½oz | 5 tbsp LIGHT MUSCOVADO (BROWN) SUGAR

300ml | ½ pint | 1¼ cups WHIPPING CREAM

30ml | 2 tbsp TIA MARIA or KAHLÚA LIQUEUR

lightly whipped CREAM and DRINKING CHOCOLATE POWDER, to decorate

**1** Pour the water into a small pan and stir in the coffee powder. Bring to the boil, remove from the heat and leave to infuse for 15 minutes.

**2** Strain through a muslin- (cheesecloth-) lined sieve (strainer).

# Chocolate Ice Cream in Florentine Baskets

*A similar mixture to that used when making florentines is perfect for shaping fluted baskets for holding scoops of ice cream. For convenience, make the baskets a couple of days in advance, but dip the edges in chocolate on the day you serve them.*

### SERVES EIGHT

### INGREDIENTS

115g | 4oz | ½ cup UNSALTED (SWEET) BUTTER, plus extra for greasing

50g | 2oz | ¼ cup CASTER (SUPERFINE) SUGAR

90ml | 6 tbsp GOLDEN (LIGHT CORN) SYRUP

90g | 3½oz | scant 1 cup PLAIN (ALL-PURPOSE) FLOUR

50g | 2oz | ½ cup FLAKED (SLICED) ALMONDS

50g | 2oz | ¼ cup GLACÉ (CANDIED) CHERRIES, finely chopped

25g | 1oz | 3 tbsp RAISINS, chopped

15ml | 1 tbsp finely chopped GLACÉ (CANDIED) GINGER

90g | 3½oz PLAIN (SEMISWEET) CHOCOLATE, broken into pieces

about 750ml | 1¼ pints | 3 cups DARK (BITTERSWEET) CHOCOLATE ICE CREAM

**1** Preheat the oven to 190°C | 375°F | Gas 5. Line two baking sheets with greased baking parchment. In a pan, heat the butter until it has melted and add the sugar and golden syrup. Off the heat, stir in the flour, almonds, cherries, raisins and ginger.

**2** Place a tablespoonful of the mixture at either end of one baking sheet, then spread each spoonful to a 13cm | 5in round.

**3** Bake for about 5 minutes until each round has spread even more and looks lacy and deep golden. Meanwhile spread more circles on the second baking sheet ready to put in the oven. Have ready several metal dariole moulds for shaping the baskets.

**4** Leave the biscuits on the baking sheet for about 2 minutes to firm up slightly. Working quickly, lift one biscuit on a fish slice and lay it over an upturned dariole mould. Gently shape the biscuit into flutes around the sides of the mould. Shape the other biscuit around a mould in the same way.

**5** Leave the biscuits in place for about 2 minutes until cool, then carefully lift the baskets away from the dariole moulds. Cook and shape the remaining biscuit mixture in the same way until you have eight baskets in total.

**6** Melt the chocolate in a heatproof bowl over a pan of gently simmering water. Carefully dip the edges of the baskets in the melted chocolate and place on individual dessert plates. Scoop the chocolate ice cream into the baskets to serve.

**COOK'S TIP** *If the biscuits feel as though they are going to fall apart when you lift them from the baking sheet, leave them a little longer to firm up slightly. If they become brittle before you've had a chance to shape them, pop them back in the oven for a few moments to soften.*

# Blackcurrant and Meringue Trifles

*These quick and easy desserts, made using crushed meringues, cream and sorbet, are suitable for every day or special occasions. Leave out the mint if you prefer.*

**SERVES SIX**

**INGREDIENTS**

350ml | 12fl oz | 1½ cups
BLACKCURRANT SORBET

3 bought MERINGUES

several sprigs of FRESH MINT

30ml | 2 tbsp ICING
(CONFECTIONERS') SUGAR

20ml | 4 tsp LEMON JUICE

300ml | ½ pint | 1¼ cups
DOUBLE (HEAVY) CREAM

90ml | 6 tbsp GREEK (US
STRAINED PLAIN) YOGURT

**2** Add the icing sugar, lemon juice and cream. Whip until the mixture just holds its shape. Stir in the Greek yogurt, then fold in the crushed meringues.

**3** Spoon a little of the cream mixture into small, deep dishes or glasses. Add layers of sorbet and cream mixture, ending with cream mixture. Decorate with mint sprigs.

**COOK'S TIP** *The amount this will serve will depend on the size of the dishes used. If you opt for large bowl-shaped glasses, the mixture will probably serve four.*

**1** Remove the blackcurrant sorbet from the freezer for 20 minutes to soften. Break the meringues into pieces. Chop the mint finely and put it into a bowl.

# Fig, Port and Clementine Sundaes

**SERVES SIX**

**INGREDIENTS**

6 CLEMENTINES

30ml | 2 tbsp CLEAR HONEY

1 CINNAMON STICK, halved

15ml | 1 tbsp
LIGHT MUSCOVADO
(BROWN) SUGAR

60ml | 4 tbsp PORT

6 FRESH FIGS

approx 500ml | 17fl oz | 2¼ cups
ORANGE SORBET

*The flavours of figs, cinnamon, clementines and port conjure up images of winter and hearty meals.*

**1** Finely grate the rind from two clementines and put it in a small, heavy pan. Using a small, sharp knife cut the peel away from all the clementines, then slice the flesh thinly. Add the honey, cinnamon, sugar and port to the clementine rind. Heat gently until the sugar has dissolved, to make a syrup.

**2** Put the clementine slices in a heatproof bowl and pour over the syrup. Cool completely, then chill.

**3** Slice the figs thinly and add to the clementines and syrup, tossing the ingredients together gently. Leave for 10 minutes, then discard the cinnamon stick.

**4** Arrange half the fig and clementine slices around the sides of six serving glasses. Half fill the glasses with scoops of sorbet. Arrange the remaining fruit slices around the sides of the glasses, then pile more sorbet into the middle. Pour over the port syrup and serve.

# Iced Raspberry and Almond Trifle

*This delicious combination of almondy sponge, sherried fruit, ice cream and mascarpone topping is sheer indulgence for trifle lovers. The sponge and topping can be made a day in advance and the assembled trifle will sit happily in the refrigerator for an hour before serving.*

**SERVES EIGHT TO TEN**

**INGREDIENTS**

**For the sponge**

115g | 4oz | ½ cup UNSALTED (SWEET) BUTTER, softened

115g | 4oz | ½ cup LIGHT MUSCOVADO (BROWN) SUGAR

2 EGGS

75g | 3oz | ⅔ cup SELF-RAISING (SELF-RISING) FLOUR

2.5ml | ½ tsp BAKING POWDER

115g | 4oz | 1 cup GROUND ALMONDS

5ml | 1 tsp ALMOND EXTRACT

15ml | 1 tbsp MILK

**To finish**

300g | 11oz | scant 2 cups RASPBERRIES

50g | 2oz | ½ cup FLAKED (SLICED) ALMONDS, toasted

90ml | 6 tbsp FRESH ORANGE JUICE

200ml | 7fl oz | scant 1 cup MEDIUM SHERRY

500g | 1¼lb | 2½ cups MASCARPONE CHEESE

150g | 5oz | ⅔ cup GREEK (US STRAINED PLAIN) YOGURT

30ml | 2 tbsp ICING (CONFECTIONERS') SUGAR

about 250ml | 8fl oz | 1 cup VANILLA ICE CREAM

about 250ml | 8fl oz | 1 cup RASPBERRY ICE CREAM or SORBET

**1** Preheat the oven to 180°C | 350°F | Gas 4. Grease and line a 20cm | 8in round cake tin (pan). Put the butter, sugar, eggs, flour, baking powder, almonds and almond extract in a large bowl and beat with an electric whisk for 2 minutes until creamy. Stir in the milk.

**2** Spoon the mixture into the prepared tin, level the surface and bake for about 30 minutes or until just firm in the middle. Transfer to a wire rack and leave to cool.

**3** Cut the sponge into chunky pieces and place these in the base of a 1.75 litre | 3 pint | 7½ cup glass serving dish. Scatter with half the raspberries and almonds. Mix the orange juice with 90ml | 6 tbsp of the sherry.

**4** Spoon over the orange and sherry mixture. Beat the mascarpone in a bowl with the yogurt, icing sugar and remaining sherry. Put the trifle dish and the mascarpone in the refrigerator until you are ready to assemble.

**5** To serve, scoop the ice cream and sorbet into the trifle dish. Reserve a few of the remaining raspberries and almonds for the decoration, then scatter the rest over the ice cream. Spoon over the mascarpone mixture and scatter with the reserved raspberries and almonds. Chill the trifle for up to 1 hour before serving.

**COOK'S TIP** *The trifle will set better if all the ingredients are thoroughly chilled in the refrigerator before assembling. Chill again before serving.*

**VARIATION** *There are many variations on this recipe that work equally well. Try any other soft summer fruits or tropical fruits and complementary ice creams or sorbets.*

# Pear and Gingerbread Sundaes

*The best sundaes do not consist solely of ice cream, but are a feast of flavours that melt into each other, rather like a trifle. Poach the pears and chill them well in advance, so that the dessert can be assembled in minutes.*

**SERVES FOUR**

**INGREDIENTS**

65g | 2½oz | ⅓ cup LIGHT MUSCOVADO (BROWN) SUGAR

90ml | 6 tbsp WATER

30ml | 2 tbsp LEMON JUICE

40g | 1½oz | ⅓ cup SULTANAS (GOLDEN RAISINS) or RAISINS

1.5ml | ¼ tsp MIXED SPICE

4 SMALL PEARS

150g | 5oz MOIST GINGERBREAD or GINGER CAKE

250ml | 8fl oz | 1 cup CLASSIC VANILLA ICE CREAM

**1** Heat the sugar and water in a heavy pan until the sugar has dissolved. Add the lemon juice, sultanas or raisins and spice. Peel, quarter and core the pears and add them to the pan.

**2** Cover and simmer very gently for 5–10 minutes until just tender. Cool the pears in the syrup. Lift them out of the syrup and put them in a bowl. Pour the syrup into a jug (pitcher). Chill both.

**3** Cut the gingerbread or ginger cake into four pieces and arrange in four serving glasses. Divide the pears among the glasses, then pile ice cream in the middle of each portion. Pour a little of the syrup over each sundae and serve.

**VARIATION** *This quick and easy dessert can be made just as successfully with tart dessert apples.*

# Coconut Ice Cream with Mango Sauce

*Halved coconut shells make impressive serving containers for this rich and delicious*
*ice cream. You'll need to crack open three coconuts to get six serving cups,*
*plus enough trimmings to use in the ice cream.*

**SERVES SIX**

**INGREDIENTS**

4 EGG YOLKS

115g | 4oz | ½ cup CASTER
(SUPERFINE) SUGAR

15ml | 1 tbsp CORNFLOUR
(CORNSTARCH)

5ml | 1 tsp ALMOND EXTRACT

600ml | 1 pint | 2½ cups MILK

150g | 5oz | 1½ cups FRESHLY
GRATED COCONUT, or GRATED
CREAMED COCONUT

300ml | ½ pint | 1¼ cups
WHIPPING CREAM

**For the sauce**

1 LARGE RIPE MANGO

30ml | 2 tbsp CASTER
(SUPERFINE) SUGAR

15ml | 1 tbsp LEMON JUICE

60ml | 4 tbsp FRESH ORANGE JUICE

**1** Beat the egg yolks, sugar,
cornflour, almond extract and a
little of the milk until combined.
If using freshly grated coconut, tip
it into a food processor and process
with 300ml | ½ pint | 1¼ cups of the
remaining milk until fairly smooth.

**2** Pour the fresh coconut milk into
a pan and stir in the rest of the
milk. If using creamed coconut,
heat it with the milk, stirring.
Bring the milk almost to the boil.

**3** Gradually pour the milk over
the egg yolks whisking constantly.
Return the mixture to the pan and
cook very gently, stirring until
thickened. Pour the custard into a
bowl, cover it with a circle of
baking parchment and leave to cool.

**4** **BY HAND:** Whip the cream and
fold into the custard. Transfer to a
freezer container and freeze for
3–4 hours, beating twice as it
thickens. Freeze again overnight.

**USING AN ICE CREAM MAKER:** Stir
in the cream and churn until it
holds its shape. Spoon into a
freezer container and freeze for
several hours or overnight.

**5** To make the sauce, slice the
mango flesh off the stone and put
it into a food processor. Add the
sugar, lemon juice and orange juice
and process until smooth. Pour
into a small jug (pitcher) and chill.

**6** To serve, scoop the prepared ice
cream into the halved coconut
shells, or into tall serving glasses.
Add the mango sauce and serve
immediately.

# ice creams

# with fruit

Whether served as an accompaniment or churned into ice cream or sorbet, an abundance of tangy fruit gives a light, fresh taste. For an invigorating summer cooler or finale to a rich meal, fruit ices make a vibrant marriage of colour and flavour.

# Passion Fruit Mousses

*Passion fruit has an exotic, tangy flavour that works wonderfully well in a creamy mousse. The raised paper collar is one of the tricks of the trade — peel it away and the texture and sophisticated shape of the mousse are revealed.*

**SERVES SIX**

**INGREDIENTS**

9 ripe PASSION FRUIT

10ml | 2 tsp POWDERED GELATINE

45ml | 3 tbsp WATER

3 EGGS, separated

75g | 3oz | 6 tbsp CASTER (SUPERFINE) SUGAR

30ml | 2 tbsp LEMON JUICE

250ml | 8fl oz | 1 cup DOUBLE (HEAVY) or WHIPPING CREAM

**1** Cut out six 30 x 7.5cm | 12 x 3in strips of baking parchment. Wrap each strip around a 150ml | ¼ pint | ⅔ cup ramekin, holding it in place with a paper clip. Secure with string under the rim of each paper collar.

**2** Cut the passion fruit in half and use a teaspoon to scoop the pulp and strain over a bowl. Press the pulp with the back of a large spoon to extract as much juice as possible.

**3** Sprinkle the gelatine over the water in a small, heatproof bowl and leave to soak for 5 minutes or until spongy. Whisk the egg yolks and sugar in a bowl until the mixture is pale and creamy.

**4** Stand the bowl of gelatine in a pan containing a little gently simmering water and leave until dissolved. Beat the passion fruit juice and lemon juice into the whisked mixture, then add the liquid. Mix well. Leave to stand until thickened but not set. Whisk the egg whites until stiff. Whip the cream until it forms soft peaks.

**5** Using a large metal spoon, fold the cream into the yolk mixture. Stir in a quarter of the egg whites to loosen the mixture, then fold in the remainder. Spoon into the prepared dishes so that the mixture comes well above the rim of each dish. Freeze the mousses for at least 4 hours.

**6** About 30 minutes before you intend to serve them, gently peel away the paper collars from the mousses and transfer them to the refrigerator to soften slightly.

**COOK'S TIP** *Before filling the ramekins, stand them on a small baking sheet. That way, you can transfer them all to the freezer in one go.*

# Iced Summer Pudding

**SERVES SIX TO EIGHT**

*This is a frozen version of the classic and ever-popular soft-fruit dessert. Made using good-quality fruit sorbet and strawberry or raspberry ice cream, the result is just as delicious and looks very impressive.*

### INGREDIENTS

25g | 1 oz | 2 tbsp
CASTER (SUPERFINE) SUGAR

60ml | 4 tbsp WATER

75ml | 5 tbsp
STRAWBERRY JAM

60ml | 4 tbsp
CRÈME DE CASSIS

225g | 8oz | 2 cups
SMALL STRAWBERRIES,
thinly sliced

250g | 9oz GOOD QUALITY
MADEIRA CAKE

250ml | 8fl oz | 1 cup
SOFT FRUIT SORBET

500ml | 17fl oz | 2¼ cups
STRAWBERRY
or RASPBERRY
ICE CREAM

**1** Line a 1.5 litre | 2½ pint | 6¼ cup pudding or dessert basin with clear film (plastic wrap). Heat the sugar and water in a small pan until the sugar has dissolved.

**2** Meanwhile, strain 30ml | 2 tbsp of the strawberry jam into a small bowl. Stir in 15ml | 1 tbsp of the syrup and brush the mixture up the sides of the lined pudding basin. Strain the remaining jam into the pan of syrup and stir in the crème de cassis until the mixture is smooth.

**3** Press the strawberry slices in a single layer over the base and sides of the basin, fitting them as tightly together as possible. Chill. Cut the cake into 1cm | ½in slices.

**4** Dip the cake slices in the remaining syrup and arrange in a single layer over the strawberries, cutting the sponge to fit and trimming off the excess around the edges. Freeze for 30 minutes.

**5** Remove the sorbet from the freezer to soften for about 15 minutes. Using a large metal spoon, pack the sorbet into the basin – it will fill it about three-quarters full – and level the surface. Return the basin to the freezer for 30 minutes. Remove the ice cream from the freezer for about 15 minutes to soften.

**6** Pack the ice cream over the sorbet, filling the basin. Level the surface and freeze for at least 4 hours or overnight.

**7** To serve, dip the bowl in very hot water for 2 seconds then invert the iced pudding on to a serving plate. Peel away the clear film and serve the pudding in wedges.

**COOK'S TIP** *Any soft fruit sorbet can be used. Raspberry sorbet has a wonderfully intense colour; blackcurrant or redcurrant sorbet would also be excellent choices.*

# Peach Mousse Cakes

*These light and airy frozen mousses, sandwiched between layers of whisked sponge, can be made ahead for a dinner party dessert or thawed and served for a special tea. You will need a couple of sheets of flexible Perspex for shaping the moulds.*

**MAKES EIGHT**

**INGREDIENTS**

**For the sponge**

3 EGGS

75g | 3oz | 6 tbsp CASTER (SUPERFINE) SUGAR

75g | 3oz | ⅔ cup PLAIN (ALL-PURPOSE) FLOUR

ICING (CONFECTIONERS') SUGAR, for dusting

**For the mousse**

10ml | 2 tsp POWDERED GELATINE

45ml | 3 tbsp WATER

6 RIPE PEACHES

finely grated rind of 1 ORANGE

75g | 3oz | 6 tbsp CASTER (SUPERFINE) SUGAR

2 EGG WHITES

150ml | ¼ pint | ⅔ cup DOUBLE (HEAVY) CREAM

45ml | 3 tbsp COINTREAU or other ORANGE-FLAVOURED LIQUEUR

**COOK'S TIP** *There are two main types of peaches: "freestone" and "clingstone". As the name suggests, the stone (pit) of the "freestone" type separates more easily from the flesh and is therefore better for this dish.*

**1** Preheat the oven to 180°C | 350°F | Gas 4. Grease a 33 x 23cm | 13 x 9in Swiss roll tin (jelly roll pan) and line with greased baking parchment. Put the eggs and sugar in a heatproof bowl, place over a pan of gently simmering water and whisk until the mixture forms a trail when the whisk is lifted from the bowl. Remove from the heat and whisk for 2 minutes until cool.

**2** Sift the flour into the bowl and fold in, using a large metal spoon. Scrape into the prepared tin, gently spreading the mixture into the corners. Bake for about 15 minutes until just firm. Leave to cool. Cut out eight 25 x 5cm | 10 x 2in strips of Perspex.

**3** Using a 7.5cm | 3in biscuit (pastry) cutter, cut out eight circles from the sponge. Carefully slice each round horizontally in half. Roll a piece of Perspex into a round and fit it around one of the pieces of sponge so that the sponge fits snugly in its Perspex collar.

**4** Secure the Perspex with tape. Make sure the cut side of the sponge is uppermost. Make seven more sponge-based cases in the same way and place them on a small tray.

**5** Make the mousse. Sprinkle the gelatine over the water in a small heatproof bowl. Leave for about 5 minutes or until spongy. Peel the peaches if you like, then cut them in half, remove the stones and chop the flesh roughly. Put it in a food processor, add the orange rind and process to a purée.

**6** Put about a quarter of the purée in a small pan with the sugar and soaked gelatine; heat until both sugar and gelatine have dissolved. Beat the mixture into the remaining purée. Leave until thickened but not set.

**7** Whisk the egg whites in a clean, grease-free bowl until stiff. Whip the cream with the liqueur until soft peaks start to form. Using a large metal spoon, carefully fold the cream into the purée, followed by the egg whites.

**8** Divide the mousse mixture evenly among the sponge-filled cases and gently level the tops.

**9** Position the remaining sponge rounds over the filling, making sure the uncut sides of the sponges are uppermost. Press down gently. Freeze for at least 3 hours.

**10** To serve, dust the tops of the cakes with icing sugar, then gently peel away the Perspex.

# Lemon Sorbet Cups with Summer Fruits

*In this stunning dessert, lemon sorbet is moulded into cup shapes to make pretty containers for a selection of*

*summer fruits. Other combinations, such as mango sorbet with tropical fruits, or*

*orange sorbet with blueberries, also work well.*

**SERVES SIX**

**INGREDIENTS**

500ml | 17fl oz | 2¼ cups
LEMON SORBET

225g | 8oz | 2 cups SMALL
STRAWBERRIES

150g | 5oz | scant 1 cup
RASPBERRIES

75g | 3oz | ¼ cup REDCURRANTS,
BLACKCURRANTS or
WHITECURRANTS

15ml | 1 tbsp CASTER
(SUPERFINE) SUGAR

45ml | 3 tbsp COINTREAU or other
ORANGE-FLAVOURED LIQUEUR

**1** Put six 150ml | ¼ pint | ⅔ cup metal moulds in the freezer for 15 minutes to chill. At the same time, remove the sorbet from the freezer to soften slightly.

**2** Using a teaspoon, pack the sorbet into the moulds, building up a layer about 1cm | ½in thick around the base and sides, and leaving a deep cavity in the middle. Hold each mould in a dish towel as you work (see Cook's Tip). Return each mould to the freezer when it is lined.

**3** Cut the strawberries in half and place in a bowl with the raspberries and red, black or whitecurrants. Add the sugar and liqueur and toss the ingredients together lightly. Cover and chill for at least 2 hours.

**4** Once the sorbet in the moulds has frozen completely, loosen the edges with a knife, then dip in a bowl of very hot water for 2 seconds. Invert the sorbet cups on a small tray, using a fork to twist and loosen the cups if necessary.

**5** If you need to, dip the moulds very briefly in the hot water again. Turn the cups over so they are ready to fill and return to the freezer until required.

**6** To serve, place the cups on serving plates and fill with the fruits, spooning over any juices.

**COOK'S TIP** *When lining a metal mould with the lemon sorbet it is a good idea to wrap your hand in a dish towel. This not only prevents your fingers from sticking to the metal, but also stops the heat from your hands from warming the mould.*

# Spiced Sorbet Pears

*Pears poached in wine make an elegant dessert at any time of the year. In this recipe the pears are hollowed out and filled with a wine-and-pear flavoured sorbet.*

**5** Cut a deep 2.5cm | 1in slice off the top of each pear and reserve. Use an apple corer to remove the cores.

**6** Using a teaspoon, scoop out the middle of each pear, leaving a thick shell. Put the scooped-out flesh in a food processor or blender and the hollowed pears and their lids in the freezer. Strain the juices. Set 75ml | 5 tbsp aside for serving and add the rest to the food processor. Blend until smooth.

**7 BY HAND:** Pour the mixture into a container and freeze for 3-4 hours, beating twice as it thickens.

**USING AN ICE CREAM MAKER:**
Churn the mixture in an ice cream maker until it holds its shape.

Using a teaspoon, pack the sorbet into the frozen pears, piling it up high. Position the lids and return to the freezer overnight.

**8** Remove the pears from the freezer and let them stand at room temperature about 30 minutes before serving. The pears should have softened but the sorbet remains icy. Transfer to serving plates and spoon a little of the reserved syrup around each one.

**SERVES SIX**

**INGREDIENTS**

600ml | 1 pint | 2½ cups
RED WINE

2 CINNAMON STICKS,
halved

115g | 4oz | generous ½ cup
CASTER (SUPERFINE) SUGAR

6 PLUMP PEARS

**1** Put the wine, cinnamon sticks and sugar in a heavy-based pan, that is big enough for the pears. Heat gently to dissolve the sugar.

**2** Peel the pears, leaving the stalks attached. Stand them upright in the syrup in the pan, taking care not to pack them too tightly.

**3** Cover and simmer very gently for 10–20 minutes until just tender, turning so they colour evenly. (The cooking time varies depending on the softness of the pears.)

**4** Lift out the pears with a slotted spoon and set them aside to cool. Boil the juices briefly until reduced to 350ml | 12fl oz | 1½ cups. Set aside and leave to cool.

# Marinated Fruits with Sorbet Sauce

*Whizzed briefly in the food processor with fruit juice and liqueur, sorbet makes a wonderful sauce for spooning over fruit. A refreshing treat on a hot summer's afternoon.*

**SERVES FOUR**

**INGREDIENTS**

12 LYCHEES, peeled

1 MANGO, peeled

1 PAPAYA, peeled

1 KIWI FRUIT, peeled

juice of 1 LIME

15ml | 1 tbsp CASTER (SUPERFINE) SUGAR

60ml | 4 tbsp VODKA

300ml | ½ pint | 1¼ cups MANGO or other TROPICAL FRUIT SORBET

30ml | 2 tbsp MANGO or ORANGE JUICE

**1** Halve the lychees and remove the stones (pits). Stone (pit) and slice the mango. Halve the papaya, remove the seeds and slice or chop the flesh. Slice the kiwi fruit.

**2** Put the fruits in a bowl. Add the lime juice, sugar and 15ml | 1 tbsp of the vodka and toss together lightly with a spoon. Cover and chill for at least 1 hour.

**3** Stir the fruits together lightly and divide among four tall, narrow glasses. Chill until ready to serve.

**4** Scoop the sorbet into a food processor, add the mango or orange juice and remaining vodka and blend very briefly until smooth and foamy. Immediately pour over the fruits and serve.

**COOK'S TIP** *Although the sorbet mixture has to be blended at the last minute, you can arrange the fruits in the glasses well in advance.*

# Mascarpone and Raspberry Ripple

*Mascarpone makes a perfectly smooth, refreshing base for ice cream, particularly when mixed with a tangy lemon syrup and streaked with raspberry purée.*

**SERVES EIGHT**

**INGREDIENTS**

250g | 9oz | 1¼ cups CASTER (SUPERFINE) SUGAR

450ml | ¾ pint | scant 2 cups WATER

finely grated rind and juice of 1 LEMON

350g | 12oz | 2 cups RASPBERRIES, plus extra, to decorate

500g | 1¼lb | 2½ cups MASCARPONE

**1** Put 225g | 8oz | 1 cup of the sugar in a heavy pan. Pour in the water and heat gently until the sugar dissolves. Bring to the boil, add the lemon rind and juice and boil for 3 minutes, without stirring, to make a syrup. Leave to cool.

**2** Crush the raspberries lightly with a fork until broken up but not completely puréed, then stir in the remaining sugar.

**3** Beat the mascarpone in a large bowl until smooth, gradually adding the lemon syrup.

**4 BY HAND:** Pour the mascarpone mixture into a freezer container and freeze for 3-4 hours, beating twice as it thickens.

**USING AN ICE CREAM MAKER:** Churn the mixture until thick, then transfer to a freezer container.

**5** Spoon the crushed raspberries over the ice cream. Using a metal spoon fold into the ice cream until rippled, making sure you reach the corners. Freeze for several hours or overnight until firm.

**6** To serve, scoop the ice cream into glasses and decorate with the extra raspberries.

# Iced Melon with Pimm's

*Freezing sorbet in hollowed out fruit, which is then cut into icy wedges, is an excellent idea. The novel presentation and refreshing flavour make this dessert irresistible on a hot summer's afternoon. The idea works particularly well with melon wedges, laced with chilled Pimm's.*

**SERVES SIX**

**INGREDIENTS**

50g | 2oz | ¼ cup CASTER (SUPERFINE) SUGAR

30ml | 2 tbsp CLEAR HONEY

15ml | 1 tbsp LEMON JUICE

60ml | 4 tbsp WATER

1 medium CANTALOUPE MELON or CHARENTAIS MELON, about 1 kg | 2¼lb

CRUSHED ICE, CUCUMBER SLICES and BORAGE LEAVES, to decorate

PIMM'S NO. 1, to serve

**1** Put the sugar, honey, lemon juice and water in a small heavy pan and heat gently until the sugar dissolves. Bring to the boil and boil for 1 minute, without stirring, to make a syrup. Leave to cool.

**2** Cut the melon in half and discard the seeds. Carefully scoop out the flesh and place into a food processor, taking care to keep the shells intact.

**3** Blend the melon flesh until smooth. Then transfer to a bowl, stir in the cooled syrup and chill in the refrigerator until very cold. Invert the melon shells and leave them to drain on kitchen paper, then transfer to the freezer while making the sorbet.

**4 BY HAND:** Pour the mixture into a container and freeze for 3-4 hours, beating twice with a fork, a whisk or in a food processor, to break up the ice crystals.

**USING AN ICE CREAM MAKER:** Churn the melon mixture in an ice cream maker until the sorbet holds its shape.

**5** Pack the sorbet into the melon shells and level the surface with a knife. Then use a teaspoon to scoop out the middle of each filled melon shell to simulate the seed cavity. Freeze overnight until firm.

**6** To serve, use a large knife to cut each half into three wedges. Serve on a bed of ice on a large platter or individual serving plates, and decorate with the cucumber slices and borage. Drizzle lightly with Pimm's to serve.

**COOK'S TIP** *If the melon sorbet is too firm to cut when taken straight from the freezer, let it soften in the refrigerator slightly. Take care when slicing the frozen melon shell into wedges. A serrated kitchen knife is easier to work with.*

# Iced Clementines

*These pretty, sorbet-filled fruits store well in the freezer, and will
prove perfect for an impromptu summer party, a picnic or simply a
refreshing treat on a hot summer's afternoon.*

**3** Finely grate the rind from the remaining clementines. Squeeze the fruits and add the juice and rind to the syrup.

**4** Process the clementine flesh in a food processor or blender, then strain over a bowl to extract as much juice as possible. Add this to the syrup. You need about 900ml | 1½ pints | 3¾ cups of liquid. Make up with fresh orange juice if necessary.

**5 BY HAND:** Pour the mixture into a shallow container and freeze for 3-4 hours, beating twice as the sorbet thickens.

**USING AN ICE CREAM MAKER:** Churn the mixture until it holds its shape.

Pack the sorbet into the clementine shells, mounding them up slightly in the middle. Position the lids and return to the freezer for several hours or overnight.

**6** Transfer the clementines to the refrigerator about 30 minutes before serving, to soften. Serve on individual plates and decorate.

**MAKES 12**

**INGREDIENTS**

16 LARGE CLEMENTINES

175g | 6oz | scant 1 cup CASTER
(SUPERFINE) SUGAR

105ml | 7 tbsp WATER

juice of 2 LEMONS

a little FRESH ORANGE JUICE
(if necessary)

FRESH MINT or LEMON
BALM LEAVES,
to decorate

**1** Slice the tops off 12 of the clementines to make lids. Set aside on a baking sheet. Loosen the clementine flesh with a sharp knife then carefully scoop it out into a bowl, keeping the shells intact. Scrape out as much of the membrane from the shells as possible. Add the shells to the lids and put them in the freezer.

**2** Put the sugar and water in a heavy pan and heat gently, stirring until the sugar dissolves. Boil for 3 minutes without stirring, then leave the syrup to cool. Stir in the lemon juice.

# Peach and Almond Granita

*Infused almonds make a richly flavoured "milk" that forms the basis of this light, tangy dessert, which would be the ideal choice to follow a rich main course.*

**3** Add the caster sugar and almond extract to the pan, with half the lemon juice and the remaining water. Heat gently until the sugar dissolves, then bring to the boil. Lower the heat and simmer gently for 3 minutes without stirring, taking care that the almond syrup does not boil over. Leave to cool completely.

**4** Cut the peaches in half and remove the stones (pits). Using a small knife, scoop out about half the flesh to enlarge the cavities. Put the flesh in a food processor. Brush the exposed flesh with the remaining lemon juice and chill the peaches until required.

**5** Add the almond syrup to the peach flesh and process until smooth. Pour into a shallow freezer container and freeze until ice crystals have formed around the edges. Stir with a fork, then freeze again until more crystals have formed around the edges. Repeat until the mixture has the consistency of crushed ice.

**6** Lightly break up the granita with a fork to loosen the mixture. Spoon into the peach halves and serve two on each plate. Drizzle a little Amaretto liqueur over the top, if you like.

**COOK'S TIP** *The scooped peach shells will keep overnight in the refrigerator if you brush them with lemon juice and wrap them in clear film (plastic wrap). If you want to make the granita further ahead, simply use the flesh of two peaches and serve the granita in glasses, instead of peach shells.*

**SERVES SIX**

**INGREDIENTS**

115g|4oz|1 cup GROUND ALMONDS

900ml|1½ pints|3¾ cups WATER

150g|5oz|¼ cup CASTER (SUPERFINE) SUGAR

5ml|1 tsp ALMOND EXTRACT

juice of 2 LEMONS

6 PEACHES

DISARONNO AMARETTO LIQUEUR,
to serve (optional)

**1** Put the ground almonds in a pan and pour in 600ml|1 pint|2½ cups of the water. Bring just to the boil then lower the heat and simmer gently for 2 minutes. Remove from the heat and leave to stand for 30 minutes.

**2** Strain the mixture over a bowl, and press lightly, with the back of a spoon, to extract as much liquid as possible. Pour the liquid into a clean, heavy pan.

# Strawberry Semi-freddo

*Serve this quick strawberry and ricotta dessert semi-frozen to enjoy the flavour at its best. The contrasting texture of crisp dessert biscuits makes them the perfect accompaniment.*

**SERVES FOUR TO SIX**

**INGREDIENTS**

250g | 9oz | generous 2 cups
STRAWBERRIES

115g | 4oz | scant ½ cup
STRAWBERRY JAM

250g | 9oz | generous 1 cup
RICOTTA CHEESE

200g | 7oz | scant 1 cup
GREEK (US STRAINED PLAIN)
YOGURT

5ml | 1 tsp VANILLA EXTRACT

40g | 1½oz | 3 tbsp CASTER
(SUPERFINE) SUGAR

EXTRA STRAWBERRIES and MINT
or LEMON BALM, to decorate

**1** Put the strawberries in a bowl and mash them with a fork until broken into small pieces but not completely puréed. Stir in the strawberry jam. Drain off any whey from the ricotta.

**2** Tip the ricotta into a bowl and stir in the Greek yogurt, natural vanilla extract and sugar. Using a teaspoon, gently fold the mashed strawberries into the ricotta mixture until rippled.

**3** Spoon into individual freezerproof dishes and freeze for at least 2 hours until almost solid. Alternatively freeze until completely solid, then transfer the ice cream to the refrigerator for about 45 minutes to soften before serving. Serve in small bowls with extra strawberries and decorated with mint or lemon balm.

**COOK'S TIP** *Don't mash the strawberries too much or they'll become too liquid. Freeze in a large freezer container if you don't have suitable small dishes. Transfer to the refrigerator to thaw slightly, then scoop into glasses.*

# Sorbets on Sticks

*Almost any firm-textured sorbet can be frozen in ice lolly moulds, making a convenient and "fun" presentation.*

*For summer entertaining, a splash of alcohol in the sorbet gives added appeal for adults,*

*but this can easily be omitted if an alcohol-free version is preferred.*

**MAKES ABOUT 24**
depending on the size
of the moulds

**INGREDIENTS**

**For the pineapple and
kirsch lollies**

1 medium PINEAPPLE,
about 1.2kg | 2½lb

115g | 4oz | ½ cup CASTER
(SUPERFINE) SUGAR

300ml | ½ pint | 1¼ cups WATER

30ml | 2 tbsp LIME JUICE

60ml | 4 tbsp KIRSCH

**For the pink grapefruit
and Campari lollies**

3 PINK GRAPEFRUIT, plus a little
extra GRAPEFRUIT or
ORANGE JUICE

115g | 4oz | ½ cup CASTER
(SUPERFINE) SUGAR

150ml | ¼ pint | ⅔ cup WATER

75ml | 5 tbsp CAMPARI

**VARIATION** *Yellow-fleshed grapefruit can be used instead of ruby grapefruit.*

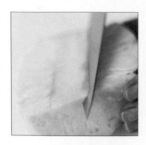

**1** For the pineapple lollies, slice the pineapple top and base, then cut away the skin. Cut the pineapple in half lengthways and cut away the core. Roughly chop the flesh and blend it in a food processor until smooth. Strain the pulp over a bowl to extract as much juice as possible.

**2** Heat the sugar and water in a heavy pan until the sugar dissolves. Bring to the boil and boil for 3 minutes, without stirring, to make a syrup. Remove from the heat and leave to cool. Stir in the lime juice and kirsch.

**3** Stir the pineapple juice into the syrup, then chill until very cold.
**BY HAND:** Pour the mixture into a container and and freeze for 3–4 hours, beating twice as it thickens.

**USING AN ICE CREAM MAKER:** Churn the sorbet until the mixture just holds its own shape but is not firm.

**4** Spoon into 12 ice lolly moulds. Press a wooden lolly stick into the middle of each sorbet. Freeze overnight until firm.

**5** To make the pink grapefruit and Campari lollies, cut away the skins from the grapefruit using a sharp knife. Slice the flesh, discarding any pips, and blend in a food processor until smooth, then strain over a bowl to extract as much juice as possible.

**6** Measure the juice. You will need 450ml | ¾ pint | scant 2 cups for the sorbet. If there is not enough, make it up with a little grapefruit or orange juice.

**7** Heat the sugar and water in a heavy pan until the sugar has dissolved. Bring to the boil and boil for 3 minutes, without stirring, to make a syrup. Leave to cool completely, then stir in the grapefruit juice and Campari. Chill until very cold.

**8 BY HAND:** Pour the mixture into a container and freeze for 3–4 hours, beating twice as it thickens.

**USING AN ICE CREAM MAKER:** Churn the mixture in an ice cream maker until the sorbet just holds its shape but is not firm. Spoon into 12 ice lolly moulds, position the sticks as in Step 4, and freeze overnight until firm.

**9** To serve the lollies, dip the moulds in very hot water for 1–2 seconds, then carefully pull each lolly from the mould.

**COOK'S TIP** *Don't let the fact that you haven't any ice lolly moulds deter you from making this delicious dessert. Use wooden lolly sticks and make use of small plastic cups or even ice cube trays for miniature ice lollies.*

**VARIATION** *Other variations that are just as delicious include orange sorbet with a dash of Cointreau, or lemon sorbet with gin. But don't be tempted to add too much alcohol or the sorbet will not freeze.*

# herb, spice & flower ices

For those with an adventurous taste in ice cream, here is an intriguing repertoire of less predictable flavours such as Turkish delight, lavender and even chilli. The ices in the following collection are quick and easy to make, and will have everyone guessing the intrinsic flavours.

# Rosemary Ice Cream

*Fresh rosemary has a lovely fragrance that works as well in sweet dishes as it does in savoury. Serve this ice cream as an accompaniment to soft fruit or plum compote, or on its own, with amaretti or ratafia biscuits.*

**SERVES SIX**

**INGREDIENTS**

300ml | ½ pint | 1¼ cups MILK

4 large FRESH ROSEMARY SPRIGS

3 EGG YOLKS

75g | 3oz | 6 tbsp CASTER (SUPERFINE) SUGAR

10ml | 2 tsp CORNFLOUR (CORNSTARCH)

400ml | 14fl oz | 1⅔ cups CRÈME FRAÎCHE

about 15ml | 1 tbsp DEMERARA (RAW) SUGAR

FRESH ROSEMARY SPRIGS and HERB FLOWERS, to decorate

RATAFIA BISCUITS (COOKIES), to serve

**1** Put the milk and rosemary sprigs in a heavy pan. Bring almost to the boil, remove from the heat and leave to infuse for about 20 minutes. Place the egg yolks in a bowl and whisk in the sugar and the cornflour.

**2** Return the pan to the heat and bring almost to the boil. Gradually pour over the yolk mixture and stir it in well. Return to the pan and cook over a very gentle heat, stirring constantly until it thickens. Do not let it boil or it may curdle.

**3** Strain the custard into a bowl. Cover the surface closely with baking parchment and leave to cool. Chill the custard until it is very cold, then stir in the crème fraîche.

**4 BY HAND:** Pour the mixture into a container and freeze for 3–4 hours, beating twice as it thickens. Return to the freezer until ready to serve.

**USING AN ICE CREAM MAKER:** Churn the mixture until it is thick, then scrape it into a tub or similar freezerproof container. Freeze until ready to serve.

**5** Transfer the ice cream to the refrigerator 30 minutes before serving to soften slightly. Scoop into dessert dishes, sprinkle lightly with demerara sugar and decorate with fresh rosemary sprigs and herb flowers. Serve with ratafia biscuits.

**COOK'S TIP** *For a very attractive effect use herb flowers that complement the colour of your dessert dishes.*

# Lavender and Honey Ice Cream

*Lavender and honey make a memorable partnership in this old-fashioned and elegant ice cream.*

*Serve scooped into glasses or set in little moulds and top with lightly whipped cream.*

*Pretty lavender flowers add the finishing touch.*

**SERVES SIX TO EIGHT**

**INGREDIENTS**

90ml | 6 tbsp CLEAR HONEY

4 EGG YOLKS

10ml | 2 tsp CORNFLOUR
(CORNSTARCH)

8 LAVENDER SPRIGS,
plus extra, to decorate

450ml | ¾ pint | scant 2 cups MILK

450ml | ¾ pint | scant 2 cups
WHIPPING CREAM

DESSERT BISCUITS (COOKIES),
to serve

**1** Put the honey, egg yolk, and cornflour in a bowl. Separate the lavender flowers and add them plus a little milk. Whisk lightly. In a heavy pan bring the remaining milk to the boil. Add to the egg yolk mixture, stirring well.

**2** Return the mixture to the pan and cook very gently, stirring until the mixture thickens. Pour the custard into a bowl, cover the surface closely with a circle of baking parchment and leave to cool, then chill until very cold.

**3 BY HAND:** Whip the cream and fold into the custard. Pour into a container and freeze for 3–4 hours, beating twice as it thickens. Return to the freezer until ready to serve.

**USING AN ICE CREAM MAKER:** Stir the cream into the custard, then churn the mixture until it holds its shape. Transfer to a tub or similar freezerproof container and freeze until ready to serve.

**4** Transfer the ice cream to the refrigerator 30 minutes before serving, so that it softens slightly. Scoop into small dishes, decorate with lavender flowers and serve with dessert biscuits.

# Bay and Ratafia Slice

*Bay leaves give a warm but delicate flavour to ices and combine particularly well with almond flavours. Serve with fresh apricots, plums, peaches or soft fruits.*

**SERVES SIX**

**INGREDIENTS**

300ml | ½ pint | 1¼ cups MILK

4 FRESH BAY LEAVES

4 EGG YOLKS

75g | 3oz | 6 tbsp CASTER (SUPERFINE) SUGAR

10ml | 2 tsp CORNFLOUR (CORNSTARCH)

150g | 5oz RATAFIA or MACAROON BISCUITS (COOKIES)

300ml | ½ pint | 1¼ cups WHIPPING CREAM

**1** Put the milk in a pan, add the fresh bay leaves and bring slowly to the boil. Remove from the heat and leave for 30 minutes to infuse. Whisk the egg yolks in a bowl with the sugar and cornflour.

**2** Strain the milk over the egg yolk mixture and stir well. Return to the pan and cook over a gentle heat, stirring constantly until the custard thickens. Do not let it boil or it may curdle. Transfer the custard to a bowl, cover the surface closely with baking parchment and leave to cool completely. Chill until very cold.

**3** Place the biscuits in a plastic bag and crush them using a rolling pin.

**BY HAND:** In a separate bowl lightly whip the cream and fold into the custard, then stir in 50g | 2oz of the crushed biscuits.

**USING AN ICE CREAM MAKER:** Add the cream and churn the mixture until thick, then scrape into a bowl. Add 50g | 2oz of crushed biscuits.

**4** Working quickly, spoon the ice cream on to a sheet of baking parchment, packing it into a log shape, about 6cm | 2½in thick and 25cm | 10in long.

**5** Bring the baking parchment up around the ice cream to pack it together tightly and give it a good shape. Support the ice cream log on a baking sheet and freeze for at least 3 hours or overnight.

**6** Spread the remaining crushed biscuits on a sheet of baking parchment. Unwrap the ice cream log and roll it quickly in the crumbs to coat. Return to the freezer until needed. Serve in slices.

**COOK'S TIP** *If the ice cream is too soft to successfully shape into a log, freeze it for a couple of hours first.*

# Peppermint Swirl

*This ice cream looks most sophisticated, with its delicate colours and marbled appearance. The refreshing taste of peppermint makes it ideal for serving after a rich main course.*

**SERVES SIX**

**INGREDIENTS**

75g | 3oz | 6 tbsp CASTER (SUPERFINE) SUGAR

60ml | 4 tbsp WATER

10 large FRESH PEPPERMINT SPRIGS

2.5ml | ½ tsp PEPPERMINT EXTRACT

450ml | ¾ pint | scant 2 cups DOUBLE (HEAVY) CREAM

a few drops of GREEN FOOD COLOURING

200g | 7oz | scant 1 cup GREEK (US STRAINED PLAIN) YOGURT

**1** Put the sugar, water and fresh peppermint in a small, heavy pan and heat gently, stirring occasionally, until the sugar has dissolved. Bring to the boil and cook without stirring for about 3 minutes to make a syrup.

**2** Strain the syrup into a medium bowl and stir in the peppermint extract. Transfer 60ml | 4 tbsp of the mixture to a large bowl.

**3** Remove from the heat and leave to cool. Dampen a 450g | 1lb loaf tin (pan) with a little water, then line with clear film (plastic wrap).

**4** Add 45ml | 3 tbsp of the cream and a few drops of food colouring to the medium bowl and stir until smooth. Add the remaining cream to the mixture in the large bowl, then stir in the Greek yogurt. Whisk the mixture until it starts to hold its shape.

**5** Place alternate spoonfuls of the two mixtures in the prepared tin. When the tin is full, swirl the two mixtures together, using a teaspoon. Cover and freeze for at least 4 hours or overnight.

**6** To serve, dip the tin in very hot water for 1–2 seconds, then invert the frozen swirl on to a serving plate. Serve in slices.

# Basil and Orange Granita

*More often associated with savoury dishes, basil has a sweet, aromatic flavour that complements tangy oranges beautifully. This classic combination makes a perfect refresher between courses.*

**SERVES SIX**

**INGREDIENTS**

5 LARGE ORANGES

175g | 6oz | scant 1 cup CASTER (SUPERFINE) SUGAR

450ml | ¾ pint | scant 2 cups WATER

ORANGE JUICE (if necessary)

15g | ½oz | ½ cup FRESH BASIL LEAVES

TINY FRESH BASIL LEAVES, to decorate

**1** Pare the rind thinly from three oranges and place in a pan. Add the sugar and water. Heat gently until the sugar has dissolved. Cool, pour into a bowl and chill.

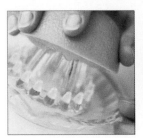

**2** Squeeze the juice from all the oranges and pour it into a large measuring jug (pitcher). You should have about 500ml | 17fl oz | 2¼ cups. Make it up to the required quantity with fresh orange juice if necessary.

**3** Pour the juice into a food processor or blender and add the basil leaves. Process the mixture in short bursts until the basil has been chopped into small pieces.

**4** Using a slotted spoon, remove the orange rind from the chilled syrup. Stir in the orange juice and basil mixture, then pour into a large plastic tub or similar freezerproof container. Cover and freeze for about 2 hours or until the mixture around the edges is mushy. Break up the ice crystals with a fork and stir well.

**5** Freeze for 30 minutes more until once again frozen around the edges. Mash with a fork and return to the freezer. Repeat the process until the ice forms fine crystals.

**6** To serve, spoon the granita into tall glasses and decorate with the tiny basil leaves.

# Star Anise and Grapefruit Granita

*With its aniseed flavour, star anise makes an interesting addition to many fruit desserts and its dramatic appearance makes it the ideal decoration. This refreshing granita will stand out as it is both tangy and sweet.*

**SERVES SIX**

**INGREDIENTS**

200g | 7oz | 1 cup CASTER (SUPERFINE) SUGAR

450ml | ¾ pint | scant 2 cups WATER

6 WHOLE STAR ANISE

4 GRAPEFRUIT

**1** Put the sugar and water in a pan and heat gently, stirring occasionally, until the sugar has completely dissolved. Stir in the star anise and heat the syrup gently for 2 minutes, without stirring. Remove from the heat and leave to cool.

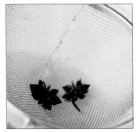

**2** Take a slice off the top and bottom of each grapefruit, then slice off the skin and pith. Chop the flesh roughly and put it in a food processor. Process until almost smooth, then strain the pulp into a bowl.

**3** Strain the syrup into the bowl, reserving the star anise. Mix well, then pour the mixture into a shallow freezerproof container. Cover and freeze for about 2 hours until the mixture starts to freeze and form ice crystals around the edges of the container.

**4** Using a fork, break up the ice crystals, then return the mixture to the freezer. Freeze for 30 minutes more, mash with a fork again, then return to the freezer. Repeat the process until the mixture forms fine ice crystals.

**5** To serve, spoon the granita into glasses and decorate with the reserved star anise.

**COOK'S TIP** *Buy whole star anise from a shop or market that sells spices loose or packaged in clear cellophane. When the spice is packed in boxes, it is often broken into sections and the quality and flavour has deteriorated.*

# Lemon and Cardamom Ice Cream

*The classic partnership of lemon and cardamom gives this rich ice cream a lovely "clean" tang. It is the perfect choice for serving after a spicy main course.*

### SERVES SIX

### INGREDIENTS

15ml | 1 tbsp CARDAMOM PODS

4 EGG YOLKS

115g | 4oz CASTER (SUPERFINE) SUGAR

10ml | 2 tsp CORNFLOUR (CORNSTARCH)

grated rind and juice of 3 LEMONS

300ml | ½ pint | 1¼ cups MILK

300ml | ½ pint | 1¼ cups WHIPPING CREAM

FRESH LEMON BALM SPRIGS and ICING (CONFECTIONERS') SUGAR, to decorate

**1** Put the cardamom pods in a mortar and crush them with a pestle to release the seeds. Pick out and discard the shells, then grind the seeds to break them up slightly.

**2** Put the egg yolks, sugar, cornflour, lemon rind and juice in a bowl. Add the cardamom seeds and whisk well.

**3** Bring the milk to the boil in a heavy pan, then pour it over the egg yolk mixture, stirring well. Return the mixture to the pan and cook over a very gentle heat, stirring constantly until the custard thickens.

**4** Pour the custard into a bowl, cover the surface closely with a circle of baking parchment and leave to cool. Chill until very cold.

**5 BY HAND:** Whip the cream lightly and fold into the custard. Pour into a container and freeze for 3–4 hours, beating twice as it thickens. Return to the freezer until required.

**USING AN ICE CREAM MAKER:** Whisk the cream lightly into custard and churn the mixture until it holds its shape. Transfer to a container and freeze until needed.

**6** Transfer to the refrigerator 30 minutes before serving. Scoop into glasses and decorate with the lemon balm and sugar.

**COOK'S TIP** *Lemon balm is an easy herb to grow. The leaves are best picked before the flowering period, when they are at their most fragrant.*

# Saffron, Apricot and Almond Cream

**SERVES SIX TO EIGHT**

*This vibrant, chunky ice cream has a slightly Middle-Eastern flavour. Although saffron is expensive, its intense colour and distinctive flavour are well worth it, and you only need a small amount.*

**INGREDIENTS**

150g | 5oz | ⅔ cup DRIED APRICOTS

60ml | 4 tbsp COINTREAU or other ORANGE-FLAVOURED LIQUEUR

2.5ml | ½ tsp SAFFRON THREADS, lightly crushed

15ml | 1 tbsp BOILING WATER

3 EGG YOLKS

75g | 3oz | 6 tbsp CASTER (SUPERFINE) SUGAR

10ml | 2 tsp CORNFLOUR (CORNSTARCH)

300ml | ½ pint | 1¼ cups MILK

300ml | ½ pint | 1¼ cups SINGLE (LIGHT) CREAM

75g | 3oz | ¾ cup UNBLANCHED ALMONDS, lightly toasted

AMARETTI BISCUITS (COOKIES), to serve (optional)

**1** Chop the apricots into small pieces and put them in a bowl. Add the liqueur and leave for about 1 hour or until absorbed. Put the saffron in a cup with the boiling water and leave to stand while you make the custard.

**2** Whisk the egg yolks, sugar and cornflour with a little of the milk in a bowl. Pour the milk into a pan, bring it almost to the boil, then pour it over the yolk mixture, stirring. Return the mixture to the pan and cook it over a very gentle heat, stirring until the custard thickens. Do not let it boil or it may curdle.

**3** Stir in the saffron, with its liquid, then cover the surface of the custard with baking parchment and leave it to cool. Chill until it is very cold.

**4 BY HAND:** Whip the cream and fold into the custard. Add the apricots and nuts and pour the mixture into a container. Freeze for 3–4 hours, beating twice as it thickens and return to the freezer.

**USING AN ICE CREAM MAKER:** Stir in the cream and churn until thick. Add the apricots and nuts and churn for 5 minutes more until well mixed. Spoon into a plastic tub or similar freezerproof container and freeze overnight.

**5** Transfer to the refrigerator 30 minutes before serving, to soften. Scoop into glasses and serve with amaretti biscuits.

**COOK'S TIP** *This ice cream looks most attractive served in small glasses or little glass cups with handles.*

# Ginger and Kiwi Sorbet

*Freshly grated root ginger gives a lively, aromatic flavour to sorbets and ice creams. Here, it is combined with kiwi fruit to make a refreshing sorbet.*

**SERVES SIX**

**INGREDIENTS**

150g | 2oz FRESH ROOT GINGER

115g | 4oz | ½ cup CASTER (SUPERFINE) SUGAR

300ml | ½ pint | 1¼ cups WATER

5 KIWI FRUIT

FRESH MINT SPRIGS or CHOPPED KIWI FRUIT, to decorate

**1** Peel the ginger and finely grate. Put the sugar and water in a pan and heat gently until the sugar has dissolved. Add the ginger and cook for 1 minute, then leave to cool. Strain into a bowl and chill until very cold.

**2** Peel the kiwi fruit and blend until smooth. Add the puree to the chilled syrup and mix well.

**3 BY HAND:** Pour the mixture into a container and freeze for 3–4 hours, beating twice as it thickens. Return to the freezer until ready to serve.

**USING AN ICE CREAM MAKER:** Churn the mixture until it thickens. Transfer to a plastic tub or similar freezerproof container and freeze until ready to serve.

**4** Spoon into glasses, decorate with mint sprigs or chopped kiwi fruit, and serve.

# Chilli Sorbet

*Served during or after dinner this unusual but refreshing sorbet is sure to become a talking point.*

**SERVES SIX**

**INGREDIENTS**

1 FRESH RED CHILLI

finely grated rind and juice of 2 LEMONS

finely grated rind and juice of 2 LIMES

225g | 8oz | 1 cup CASTER (SUPERFINE) SUGAR

750ml | 1¼ pints | 3 cups WATER

PARED LEMON or LIME RIND, to decorate

**1** Cut the chilli in half, removing all the seeds and any pith with a small sharp knife, and then chop the flesh very finely.

**2** Put the chilli, lemon and lime rind, sugar and water in a heavy pan. Heat gently and stir while the sugar dissolves. Bring to the boil, then simmer for 2 minutes without stirring. Let cool.

**3** Add lemon and lime juice to the chilli syrup and chill until very cold.

**4 BY HAND:** Pour the mixture into a container and freeze for 3–4 hours, beating twice as it thickens. Return to the freezer until ready to serve.

**USING AN ICE CREAM MAKER:** Churn the mixture until it holds its shape. Scrape into a container and freeze until ready to serve. Spoon into glasses and decorate with the thinly pared lemon or lime rind.

**COOK'S TIP** *Use a medium-hot chilli rather than any of the fiery varieties. For an added kick, drizzle with tequila or vodka before serving. To avoid getting chilli juice on your skin wash your hands after dealing with them.*

# Turkish Delight Sorbet

*Anyone who likes Turkish delight will adore the taste and aroma of this intriguing dessert. Because of its sweetness, it is best served in small portions and is delicious with after-dinner coffee.*

**4** Spoon the sorbet into the cups and tap them lightly on the surface to compact the mixture. Cover with the overlapping film and freeze for at least 3 hours or overnight.

**5** Make a paper piping (icing) bag. Put the chocolate in a heatproof bowl and melt it over a pan of gently simmering water.

**6** Meanwhile, remove the sorbets from the freezer, let them stand at room temperature for 5 minutes, then pull them out of the cups. Transfer to serving plates and peel away the film. Spoon the melted chocolate into the piping bag, snip off the tip and scribble a design on the sorbet and the plate. Scatter the sugared almonds over and serve.

**SERVES EIGHT**

**INGREDIENTS**

250g | 9oz ROSEWATER-FLAVOURED TURKISH DELIGHT

25g | 1oz | 2 tbsp CASTER (SUPERFINE) SUGAR

750ml | 1¼ pints | 3 cups WATER

30ml | 2 tbsp LEMON JUICE

50g | 2oz WHITE CHOCOLATE, broken into pieces

roughly chopped SUGARED ALMONDS, to decorate

**1** Cut the cubes of Turkish delight into small pieces. Put half the pieces in a heavy pan with the sugar. Pour in half the water. Heat gently until the Turkish delight has dissolved.

**2** Cool, then stir in the lemon juice with the remaining water and Turkish delight. Chill well.

**3 BY HAND:** Pour the mixture into a container and freeze for 3–4 hours, beating twice as it thickens. Return to the freezer until ready to serve.

**USING AN ICE CREAM MAKER:** Churn the mixture until it holds its shape.

While the sorbet is freezing, dampen eight very small plastic cups or glasses, then line them with clear film (plastic wrap).

**COOK'S TIP** *You will probably find it easiest to use scissors to cut the cubes of Turkish delight into smaller pieces, rather than a knife.*

# Mulled Wine Sorbet

*This dramatic-looking sorbet provides a brief and welcome respite from the general overindulgence that takes place during the festive season, or any other celebration. It is spicy and flavoursome, with quite a powerful kick to revive you from any seasonal sluggishness!*

**SERVES SIX**

**INGREDIENTS**

1 bottle MEDIUM RED WINE

2 CLEMENTINES or
1 LARGE ORANGE

16 WHOLE CLOVES

2 CINNAMON STICKS, HALVED

1 APPLE, roughly chopped

5ml | 1 tsp MIXED SPICE

75g | 3oz | scant ½ cup LIGHT
MUSCOVADO (BROWN) SUGAR

150ml | ¼ pint | ⅔ cup WATER

200ml | 7fl oz | scant 1 cup
FRESHLY SQUEEZED
ORANGE JUICE

45ml | 3 tbsp BRANDY

strips of pared ORANGE RIND,
to decorate

**1** Pour the bottle of wine into a pan. Stud the clementines or orange with the cloves, then cut them in half. Add to the wine, with the cinnamon sticks, apple, mixed spice, sugar and water. Heat gently, stirring occasionally, until the sugar has dissolved.

**2** Cover the pan and cook the mixture gently for 15 minutes. Remove from the heat and leave to cool.

**3** Strain the mixture into a large bowl, then stir in the orange juice and brandy. Chill until very cold.

**4 BY HAND:** Pour the mixture into a container and freeze for 3–4 hours, beating twice as it thickens. Return to the freezer until ready to serve.

**USING AN ICE CREAM MAKER:** Churn the mixture until it thickens. Transfer to a plastic tub or similar freezerproof container and freeze until ready to serve.

**5** To serve, spoon or scoop into small glasses and decorate with the strips of pared orange rind.

# Rose Geranium Marquise

*Rose geranium leaves give this ice cream a delicate, scented flavour. If you can't find savoiardi biscuits, ordinary sponge finger biscuits can be used instead. As they tend to be smaller, you may need to adjust the size of the marquise accordingly.*

**SERVES EIGHT**

**INGREDIENTS**

225g | 8oz | generous 1 cup
CASTER (SUPERFINE) SUGAR

400ml | 14fl oz | 1⅔ cups WATER

24 FRESH ROSE
GERANIUM LEAVES

45ml | 3 tbsp LEMON JUICE

250g | 9oz | generous 1 cup
MASCARPONE

300ml | ½ pint | 1¼ cups
DOUBLE (HEAVY) or
WHIPPING CREAM

200g | 7oz SAVOIARDI or
SPONGE FINGER
BISCUITS (COOKIES)

90g | 3½oz | scant 1 cup
ALMONDS, finely chopped
and toasted

GERANIUM FLOWERS
and ICING (CONFECTIONERS')
SUGAR, to decorate

**1** Put the sugar and water in a heavy pan and heat gently, stirring occasionally, until the sugar has dissolved. Add the geranium leaves and cook gently for 2 minutes. Leave to cool.

**2** Strain the geranium syrup into a measuring jug (pitcher) and add the lemon juice. Put the mascarpone in a bowl and beat it until softened. Gradually beat in 150ml | ¼ pint | ⅔ cup of the syrup mixture. Whip the cream until it forms peaks, then fold it into the mascarpone mixture. At this stage the mixture should hold its shape. If necessary, whip the mixture a little more.

**3** Spoon a little of the mixture on to a flat, freezerproof serving plate and spread it out to form a 21 x 12cm | 8½ x 4½in rectangle. Pour the remaining syrup into a shallow bowl. Arrange a third of the biscuits over the rectangle, having first dipped them in the syrup until they are very moist but not actually disintegrating.

**4** Spread another thin layer of the cream mixture over the biscuits. Set aside 15ml | 1 tbsp of the nuts for the topping. Scatter half the remainder over the cream. Make a further two layers of syrup-steeped biscuits, sandwiching them with more cream and the remaining nuts, but leaving enough cream mixture to coat the dessert completely.

**5** Spread the remaining cream mixture over the top and sides of the cake until it is evenly coated. Sprinkle with the reserved nuts. Freeze the marquise for at least 4 hours or overnight.

**6** Transfer the marquise to the refrigerator for 30 minutes before serving, so that it softens slightly. Scatter with geranium flowers, dust with icing sugar, and serve in slices.

**COOK'S TIP** *Lemon geranium leaves can also be used for this recipe, but other varieties of geranium are not suitable.*

# Elderflower and Lime Yogurt Ice

*These fragrant flowerheads have a wonderful flavour, but they are only in season for a very short time.*
*Fortunately, good quality bought or home-made elderflower cordial is readily available and combines*
*beautifully with limes to make a very refreshing iced dessert.*

### SERVES SIX

### INGREDIENTS

4 EGG YOLKS

50g | 2oz | ¼ cup CASTER
(SUPERFINE) SUGAR

10ml | 2 tsp CORNFLOUR
(CORNSTARCH)

300ml | ½ pint | 1¼ cups MILK

finely grated rind and juice of
2 LIMES

150ml | ¼ pint | ⅔ cup
ELDERFLOWER CORDIAL

200ml | 7fl oz | scant 1 cup
GREEK (US STRAINED PLAIN)
YOGURT

150ml | ¼ pint | ⅔ cup
DOUBLE (HEAVY) CREAM

GRATED LIME, to decorate

**1** Whisk the egg yolks in a bowl
with the sugar, cornflour and a
little of the milk. Pour the
remaining milk into a heavy pan,
bring it to the boil, then pour it
over the yolk mixture, whisking
constantly. Return the mixture to
the pan and cook over a very
gentle heat, stirring constantly
until the custard thickens. Do not
let it boil or it may curdle.

**2** Pour the custard into a bowl and
add the lime rind and juice. Pour
in the elderflower cordial and mix
lightly. Cover the surface of the
mixture closely with baking
parchment. Leave to cool, then
chill until very cold.

**3 BY HAND:** Whip the yogurt and
cream and fold into the custard
Pour the mixture into a container
and freeze for 3–4 hours, beating
twice as it thickens. Scoop into
individual dishes and return to the
freezer until ready to serve.

**USING AN ICE CREAM MAKER:** Stir the
yogurt and cream into the chilled
mixture and churn until it thickens.
Transfer the yogurt ice into
individual dishes or a plastic
container and freeze until required.

**4** Transfer the yogurt ice to the
refrigerator 30 minutes before
serving. Decorate with the grated
lime rind and serve.

**COOK'S TIP** *Yogurt gives this ice a
slightly tangier flavour than cream, but
use all cream if you prefer.*

# Pomegranate and Orange Flower Water Creams

*Take advantage of the availability of fresh pomegranates when in season to make this wonderfully coloured dessert. The colour will range from pastel pink to vibrant cerise, depending on the type of pomegranates used but whatever shade you achieve the finished result will be very impressive.*

**SERVES SIX**

**INGREDIENTS**

10ml | 2 tsp CORNFLOUR (CORNSTARCH)

300ml | ½ pint | 1¼ cups MILK

25g | 1oz | 2 tbsp CASTER (SUPERFINE) SUGAR

2 LARGE POMEGRANATES

30ml | 2 tbsp ORANGE FLOWER WATER

75ml | 5 tbsp GRENADINE

300ml | ½ pint | 1¼ cups WHIPPING CREAM

extra POMEGRANATE SEEDS and ORANGE FLOWER WATER, to serve

**1** Put the cornflour in a pan and blend to a paste with a little of the milk. Stir in the remaining milk and the sugar and cook, stirring constantly, until the mixture thickens. Pour it into a bowl, cover the surface closely with baking parchment and leave to cool.

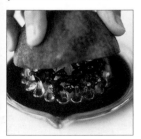

**2** Cut the pomegranates in half and squeeze out the juice, using a lemon squeezer. Add the juice to the cornflour mixture, with the orange flower water, grenadine and cream. Stir lightly to mix.

**3 BY HAND:** Stir to mix, then pour into a container and freeze for 3–4 hours, beating twice as it thickens.

**USING AN ICE CREAM MAKER:** Churn the mixture until it is thick enough to hold its shape.

**4** Spoon the ice cream into one large, or six individual freezerproof serving dishes and freeze for at least 2 hours, or overnight.

**5** Transfer the creams to the refrigerator 30 minutes before serving, to allow them to soften. Top each of them with pomegranate seeds tossed in the extra orange flower water.

**VARIATION** *To accentuate the Middle-Eastern flavour of this dessert, the seeds from 12 cardamom pods can be added with the orange flower water.*

# iced drinks

Keep a supply of classic ice creams
and sorbets for making a whole
range of exciting drinks. Blend with
a splash of liqueur for a cooler
drink with a kick, scoop into
glasses and top up with fizz,
or mix with fruit for a
wonderful drink and
dessert in one.

# Iced Margaritas

*This smooth, cooling sorbet drink has all the punch of Mexico's renowned cocktail! Serve it in tall, slim glasses with a capacity of about 200ml/7fl oz/scant 1 cup.*

**SERVES TWO**

**INGREDIENTS**

35ml | 7 tsp FRESHLY SQUEEZED LIME JUICE

a little CASTER (SUPERFINE) SUGAR, for frosting

4 LIME and 4 LEMON SLICES

60ml | 4 tbsp TEQUILA

30ml | 2 tbsp COINTREAU

6–8 small scoops of ORANGE or LIME SORBET

150ml | ¼ pint | ⅔ cup CHILLED LEMONADE

sprigs of LEMON BALM, to decorate

**1** Brush the rims of two tall glasses with 5ml | 1 tsp of the lime juice. Spread out the sugar on a plate. Dip the rims of the glasses in the sugar to give a frosted edge.

**2** Carefully add two lime and two lemon slices to each glass, standing them on end, so they will be fully visible through the glass.

**3** Mix the tequila, Cointreau and remaining lime juice in a bowl. Scoop the sorbet into the glasses.

**4** Spoon an equal quantity of the tequila mixture into each glass. Top up with the lemonade and serve immediately, decorated with lemon balm.

**VARIATION** *For a "shorter" version of this drink, use cocktail glasses and just one scoop of sorbet. The rims of the glasses can be frosted with salt instead of sugar, as for traditional Margaritas.*

# Gin and Lemon Fizz

*If gin and tonic is your tipple, try this chilled alternative. The fruit and flower ice cubes make a lively decoration for any iced drink.*

**SERVES TWO**

**INGREDIENTS**

mixture of small EDIBLE BERRIES or CURRANTS

pieces of thinly pared LEMON or ORANGE RIND

tiny edible FLOWERS

4 scoops of LEMON SORBET

30ml | 2 tbsp GIN

about 120ml | 4fl oz | ½ cup CHILLED TONIC WATER

**1** To make the decorated ice cubes, place each fruit, piece of rind or flower in a section of an ice cube tray. Carefully fill with water and freeze for several hours until the cubes are solid.

**2** Divide the sorbet among two cocktail glasses or use small tumblers, with a capacity of about 150ml | ¼ pint | ⅔ cup.

**3** Spoon over the gin and add a couple of the ornamental ice cubes to each glass. Top up with tonic water and serve immediately.

**COOK'S TIP** *When making the ice cubes, choose small herb flowers such as borage or mint, or edible flowers such as rose geraniums, primulas or rose buds.*

# Lemonade on Ice

*Home-made lemonade may not be fizzy, but it has a fresh, tangy flavour, unmatched by bought drinks.*
*The basic lemonade will keep well in the refrigerator for up to two weeks and makes a*
*thirst-quenching drink at any time of day.*

**SERVES SIX**

**INGREDIENTS**

6 LEMONS

225g | 8oz | 1 cup CASTER
(SUPERFINE) SUGAR

1.75 litres | 3 pints | 7½ cups
BOILING WATER

**For each iced drink**

4 scoops of LEMON SORBET

THIN LEMON and LIME SLICES

3 ICE CUBES, crushed

MINT SPRIGS and halved LEMON
and LIME SLICES, to decorate

**VARIATION** *Use freshly squeezed lime*
*juice instead of lemon juice or bruise*
*some mint leaves and add them to the*
*syrup for a subtle mint flavour. For pink*
*lemonade add a few drops of grenadine*
*to each glass when serving.*

**1** Start by making the lemonade.
Wash the lemons and dry them
thoroughly. Pare all the lemons
thinly, avoiding the bitter white
pith, and put the rind in a large
heatproof bowl. Add the sugar.
Squeeze the lemons and set the
juice aside.

**2** Pour the measured boiling water
over the lemon rinds and sugar.
Stir until the sugar dissolves. Leave
to cool, then stir in the lemon
juice. Strain the lemonade into a
large jug (pitcher) and chill.

**3** For each glass of iced lemonade,
place four scoops of sorbet in a
tall glass and tuck some lemon and
lime slices down the sides. Add the
crushed ice. Top up each glass
with about 200ml | 7fl oz | scant
1 cup of the lemonade. Decorate
with mint and halved lemon and
lime slices.

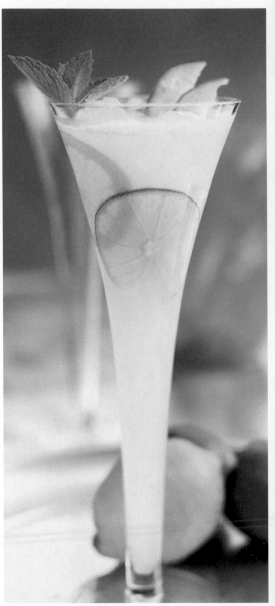

# Cranberry, Cinnamon and Ginger Spritzer

*Partially freezing fruit juice gives it a wonderfully slushy texture that is very refreshing. The combination of cranberry and apple juice contributes a tart, clean flavour that's not too sweet.*

**SERVES FOUR**

**INGREDIENTS**

600ml | 1 pint | 2½ cups
CHILLED CRANBERRY JUICE

150ml | ¼ pint | ⅔ cup
CLEAR APPLE JUICE

4 CINNAMON STICKS

about 400ml | 14fl oz | 1⅔ cups
CHILLED GINGER ALE

a few FRESH or FROZEN
CRANBERRIES,
to decorate

**1** Pour the cranberry juice into a shallow freezerproof container and freeze for about 2 hours or until a thick layer of ice crystals has formed around the edges.

**2** Mash with a fork to break up the ice, then return the mixture to the freezer for a further 2–3 hours until almost solid.

**3** Pour the apple juice into a small pan, add 2 cinnamon sticks and bring to just below boiling point. Pour into a jug (pitcher) and leave to cool, then remove the cinnamon sticks and set them aside with the other cinnamon sticks. Chill the juice until it is very cold.

**4** Spoon the cranberry ice into a food processor. Add the apple juice and blend very briefly until slushy.

**5** Pile into cocktail glasses or flutes, top up with chilled ginger ale and decorate with the fresh or frozen cranberries. Pop a long cinnamon stick into each glass, to use as a swizzle stick.

**VARIATION** *As an alternative decoration, thread cranberries on four cocktail sticks and add one to each glass instead of a cinnamon stick.*

# Soft Fruit and Ginger Cup

*A refreshing medley of soft fruits steeped in vodka and served with an icy blend of sorbet and ginger ale. You will definitely need spoons for this one.*

**SERVES FOUR**

**INGREDIENTS**

115g | 4oz | 1 cup STRAWBERRIES, hulled
115g | 4oz | ⅔ cup RASPBERRIES, hulled
50g | 2oz | ½ cup BLUEBERRIES
15ml | 1 tbsp CASTER (SUPERFINE) SUGAR
90ml | 6 tbsp VODKA
600ml | 1 pint | 2½ cups GINGER ALE
4 large scoops of ORANGE SORBET
about 8 ICE CUBES
20ml | 4 tsp GRENADINE
4 PHYSALIS FLOWERS, to decorate

**1** Cut the strawberries in half and put them in a bowl with the raspberries, blueberries and sugar. Pour over the vodka and toss lightly. Cover and chill for at least 30 minutes.

**2** Put the ginger ale and sorbet in a blender or food processor and process until smooth. Pour into four bowl-shaped glasses and add a couple of ice cubes to each glass of sorbet mixture.

**3** Spoon a teaspoon of grenadine over the ice cubes in each glass, then spoon the vodka-steeped fruits on top of the sorbet mixture and ice cubes. Decorate each glass with a physalis and serve the drinks immediately.

**VARIATION** *Any combination of soft fruit can be used for this iced drink. Blackberries, for example, would also work well.*

---

# Sparkling Peach Melba

*This fruit fizz is an excellent choice for summer celebrations. As with most soft fruit recipes, its success depends on using the ripest, tastiest peaches and raspberries available.*

**SERVES FOUR**

**INGREDIENTS**

3 RIPE PEACHES
90ml | 6 tbsp ORANGE JUICE
75g | 3oz | ½ cup RASPBERRIES
10ml | 2 tsp ICING (CONFECTIONERS') SUGAR
about 500ml | 17fl oz | 2¼ cups RASPBERRY SORBET
about 400ml | 14fl oz | 1⅔ cups MEDIUM SPARKLING CHILLED WHITE WINE
FRESH MINT SPRIGS, to decorate

**1** Put the peaches in a heatproof bowl and pour over boiling water to cover. Leave for 60 seconds, then drain the peaches and peel off the skins.

**2** Cut the fruit in half and remove the stones. Chop the peach halves roughly and purée them with the orange juice in a food processor or blender until smooth. Scrape the purée into a bowl.

**3** Put the raspberries in the food processor or blender. Add the icing sugar and process until smooth. Press the raspberry purée through a sieve (strainer) into a bowl. Chill both purées for at least 1 hour.

**4** Spoon the chilled peach purée into four tall glasses.

**5** Add scoops of sorbet to come to the top of the glasses. Spoon the raspberry purée around the sorbet.

**6** Top up each glass with sparkling wine. Decorate with the mint sprigs and serve.

**VARIATION** *When fresh ripe peaches are unavailable, use canned peach halves in juice or light syrup.*

# Iced Mango Lassi

*Based on a traditional Indian drink, this is excellent with spicy food, or as a welcome cooler at any time of day.*

*The yogurt ice that forms the basis of this drink is a useful recipe to add to your repertoire –*

*it is lighter and fresher than cream-based ices.*

**SERVES THREE TO FOUR**

**INGREDIENTS**

**For the yogurt ice**

175g | 6oz | ¾ cup CASTER (SUPERFINE) SUGAR

150ml | ¼ pint | ⅔ cup WATER

2 LEMONS

500ml | 17fl oz | generous 2 cups GREEK (US STRAINED PLAIN) YOGURT

**For each drink**

120ml | 4fl oz | ½ cup MANGO JUICE

2–3 ICE CUBES (optional)

FRESH MINT SPRIGS and WEDGES of MANGO, to serve

**1** To make the yogurt ice, put the sugar and water in a pan and heat gently, stirring occasionally, until the sugar has dissolved. Pour the syrup into a jug (pitcher). Leave to cool, then chill until very cold.

**2** Grate the lemons and then squeeze them. Add the rind and juice to the chilled syrup and stir well to mix.

**3** **BY HAND:** Pour the syrup mixture into a container and freeze until thickened. Beat in the yogurt and return to the freezer until thick enough to scoop.

**USING AN ICE CREAM MAKER:** Churn the mixture until it thickens. Stir in the yogurt and churn for 2 minutes more until well mixed. Transfer to a plastic tub or similar freezerproof container and freeze.

**4** To make each lassi, briefly blend the mango juice with three small scoops of the yogurt ice in a food processor or blender until just smooth. Pour the mixture into a tall glass or tumbler and add the ice cubes, if using.

**5** Top each drink with another scoop of the yogurt ice and decorate. Serve at once.

**VARIATION** *Add one small chopped banana when blending the ingredients together for a substantial summer smoothie.*

**COOK'S TIP** *Make sure you buy Greek (US strained plain) yogurt for this drink as it adds a lovely, sharp tang.*

# Tropical Fruit Sodas

*For many children, scoops of vanilla ice cream served*

*in a froth of lemonade, would make the perfect treat.*

*This more elaborate version will appeal to adults too.*

**SERVES FOUR**

**INGREDIENTS**

10ml | 2 tsp GRANULATED
(WHITE) SUGAR

1 PAPAYA

1 SMALL RIPE MANGO

2 PASSION FRUIT

8 large scoops of
CLASSIC VANILLA ICE CREAM

8 large scoops of CARAMEL or
TOFFEE ICE CREAM

about 400ml | 14fl oz | 1⅔ cups
CHILLED LEMONADE or
SODA WATER

**1** Line a baking sheet with foil.
Make four small mounds of sugar
on the foil, using about 2.5ml |
½ tsp each time and spacing them
well apart. Place under a moderate
grill (broiler) for about 2 minutes
until the sugar mounds have
turned to a pale golden caramel.

**2** Immediately swirl each pool of
caramel with the tip of a cocktail
stick or skewer to give a slightly
feathery finish. Leave to cool.

**3** Cut the papaya in half. Scoop
out and discard the seeds, then
remove the skin and chop the flesh.
Skin the mango, cut the flesh off
the stone and chop it into bitesize
chunks. Mix the papaya and mango
in a bowl.

**4** Cut each passion fruit in half
and scoop the pulp into the bowl
of fruit. Mix well, cover and chill
until ready to serve.

**5** Divide the chilled fruit mixture
among four large tumblers, each
with a capacity of about 300ml |
½ pint | 1¼ cups.

**6** Add one scoop of each type of
ice cream to each glass. Peel the
caramel decorations carefully away
from the foil and press gently into
the ice cream. Top up with
lemonade or soda and serve.

**VARIATIONS** *Use a mixture of
strawberries and raspberries or other
more familiar fruits for children. For
adults, a splash of vodka or kirsch can
be added to the fruits.*

# Snowball

*For many of us, a "snowball" is a drink we indulge in once or twice at Christmas time. This iced version,*

*enhanced with melting vanilla ice cream, lime and nutmeg, may provide the motivation*

*for drinking advocaat on other occasions too.*

**SERVES FOUR**

**INGREDIENTS**

8 scoops of
CLASSIC VANILLA ICE CREAM

120ml | 4fl oz | ½ cup ADVOCAAT

60ml | 4 tbsp FRESHLY SQUEEZED
LIME JUICE

FRESHLY GRATED NUTMEG

about 300ml | ½ pint | 1¼ cups
CHILLED LEMONADE

**1** Put half the vanilla ice cream in a food processor or blender and add the advocaat and the lime juice, with plenty of freshly grated nutmeg. Process the mixture briefly until well combined.

**2** Scoop the remaining ice cream into four medium tumblers. Spoon over the Advocaat mixture and top up the glasses with lemonade. Sprinkle with more nutmeg and serve immediately.

**COOK'S TIP** *Freshly grated nutmeg has a warm, nutty aroma and flavour that works as well in creamy drinks as it does in sweet and savoury dishes. A small nutmeg grater is a worthwhile investment if you don't have one.*

# Strawberry Daiquiri

*Based on the classic cocktail, this version is a wonderful drink which retains the essential ingredients*

*of rum and lime and combines them with fresh strawberries and strawberry ice cream*

*to create a thick iced fruit purée.*

**SERVES FOUR**

**INGREDIENTS**

225g | 8oz | 2 cups
STRAWBERRIES, hulled

5ml | 1 tsp CASTER
(SUPERFINE) SUGAR

120ml | 4fl oz | ½ cup
BACARDI RUM

30ml | 2 tbsp FRESHLY
SQUEEZED LIME JUICE

8 scoops of STRAWBERRY
ICE CREAM

about 150ml | ¼ pint | ⅔ cup
CHILLED LEMONADE

extra STRAWBERRIES
and LIME SLICES,
to decorate

**1** Blend the strawberries with the sugar in a food processor or blender, then press the purée through a sieve (strainer) into a bowl. Return the strawberry purée to the blender with the rum, lime juice and half the strawberry ice cream. Blend until smooth.

**2** Scoop the remaining strawberry ice cream into four cocktail glasses or small tumblers and pour over the blended mixture.

**3** Top up with lemonade, decorate with fresh strawberries and lime slices, and serve.

**VARIATION** *Orange-flavoured liqueur or vodka could be used instead of the rum, if you prefer.*

**COOK'S TIP** *For the best results use luxury ice cream, or preferably, home-made. This will avoid the risk of a synthetic flavour and garish colour.*

# Coffee Frappé

*This creamy, smooth creation, strictly for adults, makes a wonderful alternative to a dessert on a hot summer's evening. Use cappuccino cups or small glasses for serving and provide your guests with both straws and long-handled spoons.*

**SERVES FOUR**

**INGREDIENTS**

8 scoops of
CLASSIC COFFEE ICE CREAM

90ml | 6 tbsp KAHLÚA or TIA
MARIA LIQUEUR

150ml | ¼ pint | ⅔ cup
SINGLE (LIGHT) CREAM

1.5ml | ¼ tsp
GROUND CINNAMON
(optional)

CRUSHED ICE

CINNAMON, for sprinkling

**1** Put half the coffee ice cream in a food processor or blender. Add the liqueur, then pour in the cream, with a little cinnamon, if you like. Scoop the remaining ice cream into four cups or glasses.

**2** Spoon the coffee cream over the ice cream, then top with the crushed ice. Sprinkle with cinnamon and serve immediately.

**VARIATION** *For a non-alcoholic version, substitute strong black coffee for the liqueur.*

# Warm Chocolate Float

*Hot chocolate milkshake and scoops of chocolate and vanilla ice cream are combined here to make a meltingly delicious drink which will prove a big success with children and adults alike.*

**SERVES TWO**

**INGREDIENTS**

115g | 4oz PLAIN (SEMISWEET)
CHOCOLATE, broken into pieces

250ml | 8fl oz | 1 cup MILK

15ml | 1 tbsp CASTER
(SUPERFINE) SUGAR

4 large scoops of
CLASSIC VANILLA ICE CREAM

4 large scoops of
DARK (BITTERSWEET)
CHOCOLATE ICE CREAM

a little lightly WHIPPED CREAM

GRATED CHOCOLATE or
CHOCOLATE CURLS,
to decorate

**1** Put the chocolate in a pan and add the milk and sugar. Heat gently, stirring with a wooden spoon until the chocolate has melted and the mixture is smooth.

**2** Place two scoops of each type of ice cream alternately in two heatproof tumblers.

**3** Pour the chocolate milk over and around the ice cream. Top with lightly whipped cream and grated chocolate or chocolate curls.

**VARIATION** *Try substituting banana, coconut or toffee ice cream for the chocolate and vanilla.*

# Picture credits

The publishers would like to thank the following companies for their kind permission to reproduce their photographs: , p9 left and right, Charmet; p7 top right and centre, p11 top, p12 right, left, and bottom, p14 right and bottom, p15 top right, bottom right and centre, Hulton Getty; p7 top left, The Advertising Archives; p8 top and bottom, private collection, The Bridgeman Art Library; p10 left and right, p11 bottom, p13 top left, AKG Photographic Library.

All other photographs are by Gus Filgate and Craig Robertson

# Acknowledgements

The author and publishers would like to thank Magimix and Gaggia for their invaluable help. The recipe development and photography of this book would not have been possible without the kind loan of their ice cream machines.

The authors would like to extend their special thanks to Julie Beresford, Annabel Ford and Kate Jay for their enthusiasm and help throughout the busy days of photography and to their families for trying every ice cream that has appeared in this book.

# Suppliers

Worldwide, ice cream makers are generally available from electrical suppliers and also from department stores. Ice cream moulds and other equipment are usually available from specialist kitchenware shops and also by mail order.

**UNITED KINGDOM**

**ICE CREAM MACHINES**

**Cuisinart**
The Conair Group Ltd
Prospect Court
3 Waterfront Business Park
Fleet
Hampshire
GU51 3TW
Tel: 0370 2406902

**Magimix (U.K.) Ltd**
19 Bridge Street
Godalming
Surrey
GU7 1HY
Tel: 01483 427411 for your
nearest stockist of Magimix
ice cream machines.

**KitchenAid Division**
D R Kitchen Appliances Ltd
91 Goswell Road
London EC1V 7EX
Tel: 020 7336 8400
www.kitchenaid.co.uk

**ICE CREAM MOULDS**

**Divertimenti**
227-229 Brompton Road
London, SW3 2EP
Tel: 020 7823 8151 for details,
goods available by mail order.
www.divertimenti.co.uk

## PLASTIC KULFI MOULDS

**Popat Store**
138 Ealing Road
Wembley, Middlesex
HAO 4PY
Tel: 020 8902 2543
www.popatstores.co.uk

## GENERAL EQUIPMENT

Including plastic ice bowl kits,
ice cream machines, ice cream
scoops and containers.

**Lakeland Ltd**
Alexandra Buildings
Windermere, Cumbria
LA23 1BQ
Tel: 01539 488100 for details
of your nearest shop or to
obtain a mail-order catalogue,
or shop online.
www.lakeland.co.uk

## UNITED STATES

**New York Cake & Baking
Distributor**
56 West 22nd Street
New York, NY 10010
Tel: (212) 675-CAKE
www.nycake.com

**Chef's Catalog**
5070 Centennial Blvd.
Colorado Springs
CO 80919
Tel: (719) 272-2600
www.chefscatalog.com

**A Cook's Wares**
485 Third Street
Beaver
PA 15009
Tel: (800) 915-9788
www.cookswares.com

**Sur La Table**
PO Box 840
Brownsburg, IN 46112
Tel: (800) 243-0852
www.surlatable.com

**Bridge Kitchenware**
198-B Mount Pleasant Avenue,
East Hanover
NJ 07936
Tel: (973) 884-9000
www.bridgekitchenware.com

**Broadway Panhandler**
65 East 8th Street,
New York NY 10003
Tel: (212) 966-3434
www.broadwaypanhandler.com

**Bowery Kitchen Supply**
460 West 16th Street
New York, NY 10011
Tel: (212) 376-4982
www.bowerykitchens.com

**Williams-Sonoma, Inc.**
3250 Van Ness Ave.
San Francisco
CA 94109
Tel: (877) 812-6235
www.williams-sonoma.com

## AUSTRALIA

**all David Jones and
Myer Stores**
Stockist of Breville and Phillips
ice cream machines.
shop.davidjones.com.au
www.myer.com.au

SYDNEY
**Accoutrement**
611 Military Road
Mosman NSW 2088
Tel: (02) 9969 1031
www.accoutrement.com.au
Stockist of ice cream machines
and equipment.

**The Bay Tree**
40 Queen Street
Woollahra NSW 2025
Tel: (02) 9328 1101
www.thebaytree.com.au
Stockist of ice cream machines
and equipment.

**Peter's of Kensington**
57 Anzac Parade
Kensington NSW 2033
Tel: (02) 9662 1099
www.petersofkensington.com.au

MELBOURNE
**London & American Supply
Stores**
483 Elizabeth St
Melbourne VIC 3000
Tel: (03) 9329 1052
www.chefsales.com.au

**Minimax**
www.minimax.com.au
Tel: (03) 9826 0022

**Scullerymade**
The largest range of ice cream
moulds in Australia and distributed
nationally. (Does not supply
ice cream machines.)
www.scullerymade.com.au
Tel: (03) 9509 4003 for your
nearest stockist.

QUEENSLAND
**Robins Kitchen**
Over 150 stores, 13 in Queensland,
www.robinskitchen.com.au
Tel: (1300) 136 936 for details
of your nearest shop.

# Bibliography

*Mrs Mary Eales Receipts* (1718. Prospect Books, London, reproduced from the 1733 edition.)

Marshall, A.B. *The Book of Ices* (Marshall's, London 1885)

Paul, Charlie. *American and other Iced Drinks* (Farrow and Jackson, London 1909)

Herman Senn, C. *Luncheon and Dinner Sweets including the Art of Ice Making* (Ward Lock 1919)

*The History of Ice Cream* (International Association of Ice Cream Manufacturers, Washington DC 1978)

Extracts from Petits Propos Culinaires 3rd November 1979
Stallings, W.S. Jr. *Ice Cream and Water Ices in 17th- and 18th-century England*
David, Elizabeth. (articles in the same journal)

*The Great Ice Cream Book*, edited by Edwards, R. and Croft, J. (Absolute Press 1984)

Beamon, Sylvia P. and Roaf, Susan. *The Ice Houses of Britain* (Routledge 1990)

Copi, Terri. *The Italian Factor: The Italian Community in Great Britain* (Mainstream, Edinburgh 1991)

Buxham, Tim. *Icehouses* (Shire Publication 1992, reprinted 1998)

David, Elizabeth. *Harvest of the Cold Months: The Social History of Ice and Ices* (Michael Joseph 1994)

Weir, Robin and Liddell, Caroline. *Ices The Definitive Guide* (Grub Street, London 1995, reprinted 1996, 1998)

# Glossary

**Bleeding** The term used to describe the merging of flavours orsyrups when making a layered iced dessert. To prevent this, smooth each additional layer of ice cream or sorbet and freeze until firm before adding the next, so that the layers of the finished ice cream appear well defined.

**Cassata** This is the name given to an Italian ice cream dessert, which is made with three different ice creams, set in layers in a round, bombe-shaped mould. The mould is sometimes lined with thinly sliced Madeira or Genoese sponge cake, or ready-made trifle sponges.

**Dasher** A plastic-coated paddle used in ice cream machines.

**Float** This American-style drink is made with cream soda or fizzy lemonade, fruit syrup and a scoop of vanilla ice cream.

**Frappé** Similar in texture to a granita, this snow-like iced drink can be made with fruit purée, fruit syrup or liqueur mixed with lots of crushed ice. The best remembered is the vibrant, green crème-de-menthe frappé.

**Gelato** This is the Italian word for ice cream. The style for a true Italian ice cream is lighter, with less cream and sugar, than American, English or French ice creams.

**Granita** An Italian water-based iced dessert that is beaten frequently during freezing to form grainy snow-like flakes of ice. Coffee granita is the classic version, but fruit flavours are also popular.

**Knickerbocker glory** This technicolour American sundae was quickly popularized in Britain and is made with scoops of vanilla ice cream and spoonfuls of different coloured jelly layered in tall sundae glasses, topped with whipped cream, strawberry sauce and sweets, then decorated with a wafer biscuit.

**Kulfi** This rich Indian ice cream is made by slowly boiling milk over several hours before flavouring with cardamom. It is traditionally frozen in small, conical-shaped moulds.

**Neapolitan ice cream** First sold in ice cream parlours and tea rooms in the 1850s, this ice cream is made of three contrasting colours of ice cream. It is set in a rectangular mould and served sliced. The most famous combination is chocolate, strawberry and vanilla ice creams.

**Parfait** This rich, creamy ice cream does not need to be beaten during freezing. It is made by whisking a hot sugar syrup into beaten egg yolks and, because the syrup is heated to the soft-ball stage, the finished ice cream has a wonderful texture even when served straight from the freezer. Parfait is usually set in individual serving dishes or moulds.

**Popsicle** The American name for an ice lolly, the very first of which was patented in America in 1923 as the Epsicle by Frank Epperson. The original Epsicle was flavoured with lemon.

**Saccharometer** This glass measuring device is used to check the sugar density of sorbet and ice cream mixtures. If there is too much sugar, the sorbet or ice cream will be too soft; too little and the sorbet or ice cream will have a hard, icy texture. It is used by professionals and enthusiastic amateurs, but it is not essential unless you intend creating your own recipes or variations.

**Semi-freddo** This term is used for a semi-frozen Italian ice cream. The ice cream is mixed with crumbled biscuits (cookies), sponge cake or chopped candied fruit and set in containers or moulds. Semi-freddo is never beaten during freezing and is served when only just firm enough to scoop or slice.

**Sherbet** This is made in the same way as a sorbet, but with the addition of milk or cream. The term is most probably derived from the Arabic "Sharab", an early semi-frozen, sweet, milk-based drink.

**Sorbet** Classically made with sugar syrup and puréed fruit, this French water ice can also be made using wine or liqueurs. Sorbets are usually mixed with a little egg white to lighten the mixture.

**Sorbetti** This is the Italian word for sorbet.

**Sundae** This American iced dessert is served in rounded glass dishes generously filled with scoops of different coloured ice creams, then topped with fruit syrups or sauces, spoonfuls of cream and tiny sweets (candies), grated chocolate or wafers.

**Syrup** All water-ice desserts are based on a simple sugar syrup, which is usually made with caster (superfine) or granulated (white) sugar. If making a large quantity of sorbet, prepare a large batch of syrup. It can be stored in the refrigerator in a covered container for 2–3 days or until required.

**Water ice** This is made like a sorbet but usually without the addition of eggs, although egg whites are sometimes added to improve the texture. Water ices were very popular in England during the Georgian and Victorian eras and were often flavoured with flowers, spices, fruits, wine and liqueurs.

**Zester** This useful, hand-held gadget is used to pare fine curls of rind from citrus fruits. It has four or five tiny metal holes that slice narrow strips of rind. Quick and easy to use, the citrus curls make a pretty finishing touch to even the most simple ice cream desserts and sorbets.

# Index